Global Ecopolitics

Global Ecopolitics

Crisis, Governance, and Justice

Peter J. Stoett

UNIVERSITY OF TORONTO PRESS

Library and Archives Canada Cataloguing in Publication

Stoett, Peter John, 1965–
Global ecopolitics : crisis, governance, and justice / Peter J. Stoett.

Includes bibliographical references and index.
Issued also in electronic formats.
ISBN 978-1-4426-0193-2

1. Environmental policy—Political aspects. 2. Environmental policy—International cooperation.
3. Environmental justice—International cooperation. 4. Political ecology. I. Title.

JA75.8.S76 2012   304.2   C2012-901763-9

We welcome comments and suggestions regarding any aspect of our publications—please
feel free to contact us at news@utphighereducation.com or visit our Internet site at
www.utppublishing.com.

NORTH AMERICA
5201 Dufferin Street
North York, Ontario, Canada,
M3H 5T8

2250 Military Road
Tonawanda, New York, USA, 14150

Orders
PHONE: 1–800–565–9523
FAX: 1–800–221–9985
E-MAIL: utpbooks@utpress.utoronto.ca

UK, IRELAND, AND CONTINENTAL EUROPE
NBN International
Estover Road, Plymouth, PL6 7PY, UK

Orders
PHONE: 44 (0) 1752 202301
FAX: 44 (0) 1752 202333
E-MAIL: enquiries@nbninternational.com

This book is printed on paper containing 100% post-consumer fibre.

The University of Toronto Press acknowledges the financial support for its publishing activities
of the Government of Canada through the Canada Book Fund.

Printed in Canada

This book is dedicated to my three wonderful
children, who will face and meet the challenges of
future ecopolitics: Alexandra, Giuliana, and Gianluca.

Contents

List of Acronyms

CBD	Convention on Biological Diversity
CEC	Commission on Environmental Cooperation
CFCs	chlorofluorocarbons
CITES	Convention on International Trade in Endangered Species of Wild Flora and Fauna
CLRTAP	Convention on Long-Range Transboundary Air Pollution
CMS	Convention on the Conservation of Migratory Species of Wild Animals
COPs	conference of the parties (various conventions)
CSD	Commission on Sustainable Development
CTBT	Comprehensive Test Ban Treaty
ECOSOC	Economic and Social Council (UN)
EEZ	exclusive economic zone (UNCLOS)
ENMOD	The Convention on the Prohibition of Military or Any Other Hostile Use of Environmental Modification Techniques
EU	European Union
FAO	Food and Agriculture Organization
GEF	Global Environment Facility
GHGEs	greenhouse gas emissions
GMOs	genetically modified organisms
IAS	invasive alien species
ICC	International Criminal Court
ICJ	International Court of Justice
IEA	International Energy Agency
IFIs	international financial institutions
IJC	International Joint Commission (Canada–United States)
IMF	International Monetary Fund
IMO	International Maritime Organization
IPBES	Intergovernmental Platform on Biodiversity and Ecosystem Services
IPCC	Intergovernmental Panel on Climate Change
IPPC	International Plant Protection Convention
ITTO	International Tropical Timber Organization

IUCN   International Union for the Conservation of Nature
IWC   International Whaling Commission
LTBT   Limited Test Ban Treaty
MNCS   multinational corporations
NAFTA   North American Free Trade Agreement
NBSAPS National Biodiversity Strategies and Action Plans
NGOS   non-governmental organizations
NPT   Nuclear Non-Proliferation Treaty
OECD   Organization for Economic Cooperation and Development
OPEC   Organization of Petroleum Exporting Countries
REDD   Reducing Emissions from Deforestation and Forest Degradation
SPS   sanitary and phytosanitary
UN   United Nations
UNCCD   UN Convention to Combat Desertification
UNCED   UN Conference on the Environment and Development
        (Rio de Janeiro, 1992)
UNCHE   UN Conference on the Human Environment (Stockholm, 1972)
UNCLOS UN Convention on the Law of the Sea
UNDP   UN Development Programme
UNEP   UN Environment Programme
UNFCCC UN Framework Convention on Climate Change
UNWTO   UN World Tourism Organization
WCED   World Commission on Environment and Development
WHO   World Health Organization
WTO   World Trade Organization

Preface

FORTY YEARS AFTER THE UNITED NATIONS CONFERENCE ON THE HUMAN Environment in Stockholm, twenty years after the United Nations Conference on the Environment and Development in Rio de Janeiro, ten years after the World Summit on Sustainable Development in Johannesburg, and on the eve of the United Nations Conference on Sustainable Development, commonly known as Rio +20, it is high time to take stock of the evolution of global ecopolitics.

The idea of writing a short, concise treatment of global environmental governance was first broached by the University of Toronto Press, which was looking into a longer term project involving a series of short texts. Faithfully, I began working with the intention of creating just such a brief text. But I soon abandoned this idea as I realized that there was simply too much to say about too many complex issue-areas. I did strive to keep this text as short as humanly possible, however, and have presented but a fraction of the material, including historical analysis and policy option debates, that a reader should have access to if he or she wants a sound education in global ecopolitics. I enthusiastically refer the reader, therefore, to competing texts (Bodansky, 2010; Clapp and Dauvergne, 2008; DeSombre, 2006; Pirages and DeGeest, 2004), as well as to the Earth System Governance Project of the International Human Dimensions Programme on Global Environmental Change (Biermann et al., 2009), though I also hope this book will serve to both enlighten and encourage further reading, reflection, action, and resolve on our collective environmental dilemmas.

I focus on several themes in this book, and one of them is that of anxious uncertainty, which seems to animate much of the public discussion on planetary futures today; and the theme of justice looms large because a humane and fair response to the anxiety that accompanies crisis is what defines the best of the human spirit. Fears of cataclysmic events—ones related both to climate change and to more "natural" disasters—are certainly ripe. They may almost be compared to the fear of nuclear annihilation that marked the cold war period (a fear I recall quite clearly as a young scholar of international relations at the time). But I would suggest we suffer our primary angst due to the gnawing knowledge that we are slowly, by a billion cuts, diminishing the future opportunities of the next generation. We realize that some of the more pressing environmental problems, on a local and global scale, are literally out of control. We realize that the incessant belief in unrestricted economic growth is as passé as the blind faith in technology that once reassured the mildly concerned. It is commonly understood that species are nearing extinction on a daily basis; that air, water and soil pollution is increasing dramatically in some regions; and that the oceans are in ecological turmoil. Yet there is little corresponding sense of a plan to escape these predicaments.

This book does not provide this plan, to be clear. But it does suggest that we are working toward one, that we can succeed, and that we must succeed. The sheer volume of work being done by diplomats, scientists, activists, bureaucrats, and others is, in itself, a sign of hope: never before our time has so much activity been concentrated on efforts to solve the pressing problems of environmental decay and ecological injury. Contrary to popular opinion, there is much being done at both the international and local levels, even though ameliorative actions may be uneven and often uncoordinated. I have covered only a fraction of this work in this book. Though I suggest it is vital to use a critical eye when viewing global ecopolitics, I do not ascribe to the notion that we are helplessly watching the advent of a disaster. We can take positive steps, rooted in a nuanced understanding of green politics and international relations, to make things better.

We need to replace relentless uncertainty and helplessness with firm, educated resolve. Given the foundational efforts at global governance described in this book, there is even cause for restrained optimism. I loosely utilize a parsimonious framework to analyze the collective governance that has emerged from global ecopolitics, observing legal and historical depth, environmental impact, cognitive evolution, and democratic legitimacy. In most of the cases I examine, there has been some measure of success in all of these categories. Of course, this does not diminish the reality of the ecological crisis we face, or diminish the size of the challenges ahead. But we can move on from here, even if we are also aware that there will always be drawbacks and limitations given the gloriously competitive but all too often unfair structure of the world economy. This book is intended as an analytic introduction to the dazzling promises, as well as the inherent weaknesses, of the international institutions and arrangements that color the fascinating landscape of global ecopolitics. But, above all, I hope it encourages readers to seek more knowledge—and take personal steps toward a greener lifestyle and a more humane world.

Acknowledgments

THIS BOOK WOULD NOT HAVE BEEN POSSIBLE WITHOUT THE SUPPORT OF an army of students who have taken classes with me and worked as research assistants over the preceding three years. I will mention only a few names here, with apologies for those omitted: Leah Mohammed, Erle Lamothe, Mariel Angus, Shawn Katz, Ashvin Ramasamy, Randy Pinsky, Arsalan Ibnalnasir, Quynh Nhu Vu, Karim DeCoster, and Maryam Behrouzi. No doubt these students will recognize their own research results in various sections of the text, though, of course, I take full responsibility for any errors.

I am also grateful to the Social Sciences and Humanities Research Council of Canada for related funding. I would also like to thank the secretarial staff at the Department of Political Science at Concordia University; though I finished this project on a much-needed sabbatical year, much of it was written while I was chair of the department, and I could not have asked for a better administrative team to ease that burden. Special thanks are due to Jeannie Krummel, the department administrator. I am also grateful to all the faculty members in the department who made my chairship an enjoyable, collegial period of my career. The manuscript was completed as I moved to Washington, DC, to assume a Fulbright Research Chair in Canada–U.S. Relations at the Woodrow Wilson International Center for Scholars, and I am grateful to the wonderful staff at the center as well as to the director of the Canada Institute, David Biette, who encouraged me to pursue a broad research agenda while there.

At the University of Toronto Press, Tracey Arndt has been with this project from the beginning and must be thanked for her patience and willingness to part somewhat from the original conception in order for me to produce what I hope is a more satisfying version. Thanks also to Karen Taylor for fantastic copyediting and grace under pressure, and to Beate Schwirtlich and Ashley Rayner at UTP. There are too many colleagues, both academics and practitioners, to thank in the global ecopolitics field to begin to do justice here; as the saying goes, you know who you are, and we will meet again. Thanks to three anonymous reviewers for their extensive input on an earlier version of the manuscript.

For patience and inspiration I thank my beautiful and brilliant wife and "tulipano," Cristina Romanelli, who, by fortunate coincidence, worked at the Secretariat to the Convention on Biological Diversity here in Montreal during the closing months of this project, making possible a mutual learning experience. For unwavering support over the course of my career, I thank my parents, Fred and Irene. And, as always, I thank my three children—Ally, Giuliana, and Gianluca—who have shared many hours with me by various riversides and beaches in Canada, Europe, and Costa Rica, and with whom I hope I will share many, many more in a greener future.

CHAPTER ONE

Planetary Anxiety and Collective Dilemmas

"The whole point of being a doomsayer is to agitate the world into proving you wrong or into doing something about it if you are right."

LES KAUFMAN (1993:12)

CAN WE SAVE THIS WONDERFUL, GREEN AND BLUE, MOUNTAIN HIGH AND ocean deep planet from further human abuse? Will it save itself without us?

A sharper question: Can we overcome the political divisions (and attendant conflict) that have so far limited the probability of an effective, collective response? And, to borrow a tired but still useful cliché, if we are to make a commensurate investment, where do we need to put our money? Perhaps we are passively deluding ourselves, and the billions of people whose futures depend on it, to think such change is even possible, given the structural constraints imposed by competition, misunderstanding, greed, and fear. Can we arrive at arrangements designed to limit our destructive tendencies without provoking the classic "free rider," who carries on regardless at everyone else's expense?

Chances are you would not be reading this textbook if you were convinced the answers to the opening questions are negative; and I would certainly not have written these pages if I were convinced the challenges we face are insurmountable. But these questions are also difficult to answer, with any real confidence, in the affirmative. The challenges are so broad and steep that there is often an air of despair about future prognoses. Possible solutions are so encompassing in scope that we face an uphill struggle of mountainous proportions, even if "we" can agree on who "we" are, and even if we can generate a widespread consensus about what needs to be done. It should not surprise us that no such consensus exists; yet there are so many energized channels of communication and cooperation on environmental issues that we should be forgiven for holding out some hope that things are not only getting done but could get better in the near future.

Indeed, if there is a common cultural motif today, one that runs across national and ethnic differences and that has superseded the narrative of unstoppable human progress, it is that we are in collective trouble, and this theme is reflected in a postmodern planetary anxiety, which engulfs much of the public thinking about our collective future. This is not without good reason, as we helplessly watch oil spill into the Gulf of Mexico, the Aral Sea evaporate, the mountain gorilla approach extinction, politicians bicker endlessly as scientists warn of sea levels rising and extreme weather events proliferating, and human cancer rates soar even as the biodiverse forests and coral reefs that may offer medical relief are burned and bleached. We seem to be standing still, like frozen passive-aggressive witnesses to our own demise, even as well-known commentators suggest "we're on the cusp of a planetary emergency" (Homer-Dixon, 2006:308). In short, the post–cold war era has not been free from the existential fears of previous generations who were made to hide under school desks in futile nuclear attack drills. If anything, the angst is sharper today because of the gnawing feeling that we could, should, must, do more. Our children will know we should have acted, and theirs will certainly know it as well. In essence, the anxiety has amplified since the World Commission on Environment and Development (WCED) wrote these words in *Our Common Future*:

> When the [20th] century began, neither human numbers nor
> technology had the power to radically alter planetary systems.
> [Now]..., not only do vastly increased human numbers and
> their activities have that power, but major, unintended changes
> are occurring in the atmosphere, in soils, in waters, among plants
> and animals, and in the relationship among all of these. The rate
> of change is outstripping the ability of scientific disciplines and
> our current capabilities to assess and advise. It is frustrating the
> attempts of political and economic institutions, which evolved

in a different, more fragmented world, to adapt and cope. It deeply worries many people who are seeking ways to place those concerns on the political agenda. (Brundtland et al., 1987:343)

If this was true in the mid-1980s, it is certainly more urgently apparent today. I do not use the word "crisis" in the subtitle of this book lightly.

This text is intended to introduce readers, in as concise a fashion as possible, to the major *ecopolitical challenges* of our time. Ecopolitics takes place at the intersection of ecology and politics at various levels, but, in this book, we are primarily concerned with global governance, and the broad aim is to present a succinct examination of the effectiveness of multilateral arrangements designed to mitigate recognized anthropogenic environmental problems. These arrangements are made among states but involve many other actors as well. The book also asks whether international arrangements, involving not just governments but many others in civil society and in the private sector, are able to adapt to changing circumstances and to promote justice as part of collective responses to crisis. For, if there is a route away from overwhelming anxiety, it is a path toward multilayered, adaptive governance that is as socially legitimate as possible while capable of adjusting to shifting demands and imperatives.

Because the case studies presented in this book—biodiversity reduction, deforestation, desertification, atmospheric pollution, climate change, the oceans crisis, freshwater sharing, and other hallmarks of the carbon-dependent Anthropocene epoch—necessarily encompass an updated description of the state of earthly affairs, I will not devote much space to the task of convincing the reader that we are in fact in a rather dire one.[1] Again, it is unlikely you are reading this book if you feel that environmental problems are ephemeral or simply the result of opportunistic conjecture on the part of scheming environmental activists. Indeed, the empirical evidence that there are multiple and interconnected environmental crises and that human communities are threatened by their culminated impact is rather incontrovertible to this author.[2] There are, however, significant differences in how the environmental crises we face are understood, both in terms of their immediate and long-term impact and in terms of their sociopolitical and policy implications. Later in this chapter, I will expand on these "green debates," with an eye open principally toward the latter issue. While some observers feel it is time to change everything, from our habits to our institutions to our deep-seated social constructions and mental maps of the natural and human worlds, others believe the market economy will eventually induce the technological and habitual changes we need to keep us from the brink. Others are prepared to embrace authoritarianism or anarchism or antiglobalization or even some form of world government: the list of options is a long one. I argue that, in today's interconnected but still bifurcated world, whatever forms of governance follow the recognition of crisis, justice must be a primal animating factor in our collective response if we expect adaptive institutions to carry any legitimacy and prove sustainable.

Chapter 2 will describe the main actors and institutions involved in global ecopolitics, from forestry workers to Greenpeace activists to CEOs of major corporations to state leaders. We will discuss the international institutions developed over the preceding decades and their interaction with each other, as well as the many points of political authority—from national governments down to municipal committees—involved in multilevel (or, preferably, "multi-scaled") adaptive governance. The chapter will also present an analytic framework that we can use to evaluate the international arrangements and commitments that have been made in the name of environmental protection. We will also consider alternative explanations as to why such institutions have been constructed, since they are often as related to preserving the legitimacy or profitability of certain types of economic or state strategic behavior as they are designed to preserve aspects of the environment. This critical viewpoint informs the work of international relations (IR) specialists who see global governance as a deceptively benign front for either traditional geopolitics or globalization-as-usual. I am not convinced, but I would suggest that this critical view often offers a very plausible explanation, and one to consider before jumping on any institutional bandwagons. Again, keeping the themes of justice and democratic legitimacy in mind can serve as a needed tonic if the prospects of quick fixes get too sweet.

The framework emerging from Chapter 2 will serve as a loose guide to discussions of several issue areas where we have seen considerable action, as well as lamentable inaction, in global ecopolitics, including biodiversity, wildlife conservation, deforestation and desertification, air pollution and climate change, oceans and freshwater, trade, and military conflict. In none of these cases has an effective, permanent, consensual solution been found. But in some there has been more progress than in others, in terms of advancing concrete solutions that have reduced the rate of ecological degradation or in terms of advancing a progressive conception of human rights tied to environmental health. In each case, the sheer breadth of environmental diplomacy today is impressive; the extent to which substate and non-state actors are involved is analytically daunting; and the potential for more progress is promising. It is, of course, a difficult task to delineate these issues because they are so intertwined. And there are crosscutting themes, such as population growth, density, and movement; energy provision; climate change; and many others. These topics will make appearances in each chapter, and I discuss them as this chapter closes.

The last chapters examine linked threats to and future paths toward various forms of global sustainability, beginning with a chapter highlighting the links between trade, investment, and ecology and continuing with a chapter on the links between war, environmental change, and human security. These chapters will, in effect, tie together many of the common threads mentioned previously and return us to the normative theme of environmental justice. I've taken the unusual step of devoting an entire chapter to a major global governance gap, the prevention of invasive alien species, because it permits a brief foray into a detailed examination of the challenges we face in the broader effort to preserve biodiversity and economic security. Finally, in Chapter 10, I present several other governance gaps, including nanotechnology, global tourism, energy provision, and food security, before returning to our central question: Can we turn the decline around, despite ourselves?

I think we can; I think we will. But I also think we need to dedicate ourselves to living collective lives in which this project is central, indeed, fundamental to our plans and purposes; and international environmental diplomacy must be stepped up several notches to reflect the magnitude of the challenges and the inherent dilemmas in the international context. Anyone who has enjoyed a brilliant sunset, heard birds greet morning sun, or smiled back at a child's happy eyes knows it is worth trying.

Sovereignty, Global Governance, and Public Goods

"In the last analysis, decision-making can grow to the international dimension if, and only if, the sacrosanct nature of national sovereignty is surrendered. A full recognition of the historical obsolescence of that principle is the single greatest precondition for recovering the governability of contemporary societies in regard of two of the most pressing issues of our times: world security, and biospheric sustainability."

ERVIN LASZLO (1991:221)

I still have vivid memories of the first time I entered the General Assembly of the United Nations in New York City, nestled along the shore of the dirty Hudson River in the midst of bustling Manhattan. I was an undergraduate student researching a thesis on nuclear weapons proliferation in Asia, and I wanted to hear the delegates from India and Pakistan lie to the world about their nuclear programs. (I was not disappointed in that regard.) The UN General Assembly can be a breathtaking sight for a young student, with row after row of alphabetically arranged states and little flags and microphones and an imposing podium on which people as varied as Fidel Castro and Ronald Reagan could make pronouncements to the world. The place was soaked in dramatic importance, even if its significance was exaggerated by my enthusiasm. The sovereign states represented here had formal autonomy, legal recognition, and the opportunity to pursue solutions to collective action problems. Of course, that same distinction—the formal sovereignty of states—is often viewed as the biggest single obstacle to those solutions. Just how jealously it is guarded is evident by any serious observation of General Assembly speeches, as I was to learn over the next few days. Since then, of course, my expectations have been tempered and complicated by a broader understanding of international relations, but the residue of that early optimism infecting a small-town Canadian kid's first day in New York City, at the citadel of international diplomacy, near the end of the debilitating cold war, remains an animating factor in my thinking. Environmental problems had yet to become one of the General Assembly's more pressing preoccupations at that time, but would soon emerge as central.

The specific challenge posed by ecological awareness—that is, recognition of the fundamental interdependence of ecosystems and of the fragility of the ecosystems on which humanity relies—is to arrive at effective solutions to collective action problems within an unequal geopolitical and globalized economic context without provoking the so-called tragedy of the commons.[3] This question has, to some degree, shaped the project of modern international relations studies for quite some time, as inequality and interdependence are two ongoing themes in the study of power and relationships at any level.[4] Global ecopolitics, however, brings them out in sharp relief, raising questions about sacrifice, burden sharing, trust and distrust, the fear of "free riders" who take but do not give back, and other dilemmas.[5] It also throws into question the logic and legitimacy of the sovereign state itself, because it is utterly incapable of dealing with large-scale environmental problems on its own, and gives rise to predictions and calls for different mutations of sovereignty to emerge as states adjust to new imperatives (Eckersley, 2004; Litfin, 2003).

Much of the debate centers on our understanding of the propensity of human beings to manage the commons—areas where there is no authoritative sovereign jurisdiction or where sharing space, including air and water, is unavoidable. Nobel Prize winner Elinor Ostrom (1990) argued that the ethical compulsions needed to avoid the tragedy of the commons can spontaneously grow in small communities, which can control behavior due to group stability, the repetition of interactions, the threat of exclusion through ostracism, and reputational concerns. Milgrom, North, and Weingast (1990) demonstrate that larger groups need more formalized institutional coercion mechanisms, but that does not mean we cannot deal with collective action problems if given the chance. Because we have so many actors at play, from nearly 200 national governments to thousands of private multinational corporations (MNCs), international organizations, and nongovernmental organizations (NGOs) and billions of individuals who make important daily decisions, and because no one can dictate the behavior of everyone else, anytime we are faced with a collective action problem—a problem that cannot be solved without widespread agreement and mutual trust—we hit a philosophical and practical wall we need to at least see over, if not overcome. Inequality and interdependence are two of the main characteristics of that wall. Eric Laferrière and I have argued elsewhere that conceptions of humanity's relationship to nature, both in the ontological and the epistemological sense, are also an integral aspect of how we understand international relations, and I will return to this theme shortly (Laferrière and Stoett, 1999).

Global environmental governance is tied inextricably to the collective action problems and efforts at solutions presented by the challenges of sovereignty, globalization, and ecological interdependence, or what Oran Young calls the "environmental experience" (Young, 1997). The term *global governance* itself is admittedly broad (too wide to be meaningful for many observers), and it encompasses any process of decision and rule making and policy implementation at local, national, regional, and global levels that addresses issues of international or transnational concern (see Diehl and Frederking, 2010). Importantly, it does not suggest that a world government or even strong supranational regional governance will form any time soon, or at all. A school of thought broadly labeled *international society* (often referred to as the "English School") has long held that, while anarchy (the absence of a central source of authority) characterizes the global system, its members (sovereign states) are still bound by social constraints on their behavior, which, taken as a whole, construct a system resembling a society; thus the importance of international law, for example (Bull, 1977). One can also take a critical perspective on such institutions and on global governance in general, arguing not only that they reflect present inequalities of wealth and power but that they will exacerbate them in the future, even as they are designed to present the image of efforts to mitigate environmental harm.

The provision of global public goods is often viewed as a solution to collective action problems (Kaul, Grunberg, and Stern, 1999; Sandler, 2004). Collective goods are typically defined by the absence of rivalry (otherwise known as "non-rivalry"): their use by one individual does not diminish the possibility of their use by another. They are further defined by non-excludability: excluding a user is very costly if not impossible. Common-pool resources (such as non-privately owned water, trees, or fish stocks) are partially rivalrous and non-excludable, while "club goods" (such as intellectual property rights or IPRs) are non-rivalrous but are excludable. The provision of global public goods is the central goal of global governance, but this is easier said than done, especially when it must take place within the context of a highly divided and competitive world economy and political system. We forge multilateral arrangements in our efforts to curtail environmental harm, as discussed in our case studies, but we do so in the absence of a reliable mechanism by which global public goods can be delivered to all participants. Since no centralized mechanism exists, this process will remain a decentralized application of multilevel governance. The hope is that the sum of all these efforts will somehow eclipse their parts, and a new era will emerge whereby we overcome our planetary anxiety by establishing newfound security and purpose in a reliable, if still competitive and invariably unequal, global context. Global environmental governance, then, may seem a rather optimistic, ambitious term to employ in this discussion; others may find it a threatening or even counterproductive goal and conceptual mantle. The phrase *global ecopolitics*, first introduced by visionary academic Dennis Pirages (1978), better conveys the inherent complexity of the task: the centrality of collective action problems, the wide range of actors, the technological and scientific challenges and opportunities, and the need for both leadership and widespread legitimacy. Moving toward reliable, adaptive, just governance remains the goal; ecopolitics reflects the structures and processes that hinder or help us on that path.

Shades of Green

Several perspectives have emerged as mainstays in thinking about the collective action problem of global environmental degradation, and there are a variety of ways to organize them (see Clapp and Dauvergne, 2008; Laferrière and Stoett, 1999). Of course, there are those who, either through an elaborate prism of self-deception or genuine belief, do not think such problems exist, or at least doubt their long-term significance. I won't bother intellectualizing this perspective, at the risk of offending any reader of this rather foolish and, given the empirical evidence, incomprehensible persuasion.

Many would argue that the dominant approach to the environment has been *utilitarian*: the natural world exists for humankind's consumption; it is to be used to further the end of human needs. The fruits of nature are commodities waiting to be picked and sold for profit. This utilitarian perspective does not mean disregarding efforts to conserve the fruit, however, even at the international scale. Clearly, the future existence of fruit is desirable. However, there are large differences in terms of the prescribed role of governmental regulation among utilitarians of different stripes. Some, more commonly labeled neoconservative liberals, argue the state should play a minimal role, and the real business of allocating society's wealth is better left to the market; the state should simply ensure the market survives (in other words, it should protect private property and investment but not redistribute wealth in any form). Others hold that it is essential that an intervening state can participate in, and often lead, the development of society and international affairs; "administrative rationalism" (Dryzek, 1997) suggests the state is most capable of managing the ecological risks associated with modern society. This "welfare state liberalism" is commonly associated with the growth of international organizations such as the various subunits of the United Nations system.

Ecological modernization is often offered as the commensurate paradigm. It does not demand radical change but argues that technological changes can save us; strategies such as eco-efficiency—cleaner, more efficient, less resource-intensive technologies—can help us achieve the "organizational internalization of ecological responsibility" (Cohen, 1997:109; Dryzek, 1997). Economic growth can continue, but we need to change the way we think about the inherent value of utilitarianism and make wiser technological choices. Indeed, many observers feel that cooperating on international issues can have a neofunctionalist or eco-functionalist impact, improving overall relations between states and protecting scarce resources such as water supplies (Wolf et al., 2005), though scholars from the "realist" IR tradition (Morgenthau, 1948) would warn us these are but ephemeral arrangements that do not change the fundamental problem of assuring sovereign states permanent security. Others worry that ecological modernization has led to a "post-sacrifice environmentalism" that misleads people into thinking there is no real need for real changes on the path to sustainability (Wapner, 2010).

Utilitarianism and ecological modernization inform the mainstream perspectives on global environmental governance. The ontology is fairly simple: the world is composed of atomistic centers of power that often collide and cooperate, whether it is in the ongoing capitalist world economic system, in the world of sovereign competing states, or in the relationship between humans and nature. Critical theorists generally reject this viewpoint and tend to see the conflict inherent in the world system as a consequence of historically rooted forms of injustice, not as a natural development. But this is, admittedly, a gross oversimplification. In fact, there are many critical perspectives, and some of them have greener "credentials" than others. For example, green socialists tend to see the environmental crises as a result of the historic rise of capitalism and believe only class struggle can actually save us from the ecological impacts of modern commerce. Ecofeminists view violence against nature as part of the same historical pattern of epistemic violence, which justifies violence against women as well. A feminist-oriented critical reading of mainstream IR theory (Tickner, 2002) would thus be instrumental to their conception of international change and progress. Deep ecologists reject the utilitarian viewpoint altogether, arguing we need a totally new paradigm— an ecocentric or biocentric one; some go much further, suggesting we need an authoritarian superstate that can tame our passion for ecological destruction with the necessary coercive implements. Most of these positions reject the idea, still held dearly by liberals, that economic growth can continue unabated, regardless of peak oil, peak soil, ocean degradation, and other contemporary near crises. A concern with justice is front and center, though there are differences about who (or what) deserves the most attention; this concern has become especially pronounced as calls for "climate justice" take center stage on the global left's agenda (Angus, 2010). The related normative questions that climate justice raise about north-south relations, management of the commons, intra- and intergenerational responsibility, interspecies ethics, the precautionary principle, and other themes are certainly not systematically avoided by mainstream thinking, but they tend to be viewed more as variables that threaten to complicate or compromise true progress rather than as issues in their own right.

Indeed, I suggest that the theme of justice is in fact central to any discussion of global ecopolitics because, without it, we respond to crisis in an ethical void that can render our work illegitimate in too many eyes to have any serious long-term impact. For example, many authors are treating the ecopolitics of climate change as an aspect of environmental justice, at the local to global levels (Athanasiou and Baer, 2002; Boyle and Anderson, 1998; Roberts and Parks, 2007). This emerges in the context of a much broader ongoing discourse on global environmental justice (Ehresman and Stevis, 2011; Hossay, 2006) and global equality among earth's citizens defined in terms of their life chances and material capability to choose life paths (Sen, 1999). In this context, the question of *adaptation* to climate change is emerging as a dominant human rights issue because there is ample opportunity to ensure some measure of fairness exists as people strive to adapt to changes over which they have little or no control.

There are at least three obvious reasons that climate change is an ethical, justice-oriented issue, and they generally apply to all the cases covered in this book. First, its effects were not caused in equal fashion; this is a classic case of differentiated responsibility. Just who is responsible is difficult to gauge in anything approaching exact terms, but it is clear that most of the fossil fuels that have been released throughout history originated from northern industrialization and transportation. The contemporary balance of responsibility is not dissimilar, and the inequality here is startling. According to Roberts and Parks (2007), "the average U.S. citizen dumps as much greenhouse gas into the atmosphere as nine Chinese ... eighty Bangladeshis ... [and] over five hundred citizens of Ethiopia, Chad, Zaire, Afghanistan, Mali, Cambodia, and Burundi" (p. 146). Of course, China, India, Brazil, Indonesia, and other large economies with significant industry, transportation, or forestry sectors have increased aggregate emissions in recent decades, though these still pale in comparison to the per capita emissions of the West. There may well come a day when rational analysis suggests that these countries or others have actually overcome the historical deficit, but it is years away. I tend to agree with Paul Harris (2011), however, who suggests that, although it "may be too soon to demand that Brazil or India agree to binding limitations on their own emissions … it may also be past time to demand that wealthy Brazilians and Indians do so" (p. 116).

Just as important, if not more so, the deleterious impact of climate change will also have a disproportionate effect on those who contributed the least to its cause. This is the fundamental claim made by those advocating climate justice, who largely equate it with redistributive policies compensating the least advantaged, especially in Africa. Indeed, the UN Convention to Combat Desertification (UNCCD; see Chapter 4) has become a conduit for the argument that drought and land degradation related to climate change justifies northern investment in sustainable development initiatives in the south, particularly in Africa.[6] Much of this justification is based on plausible conjecture. A recent report from Climate Change, Agriculture and Food Security (CCAFS) estimates that, due to the impact of climate change, "at least $7 billion per year in extra funding will be needed for irrigation investments, agricultural research and rural infrastructure."[7] Already, the line between life and mass starvation is a very thin one, especially in the drought and conflict-prone horn of Africa. But regardless of the continent, the disadvantaged will suffer disproportionately when society faces ecological crises: despite their widely demonstrated ingenuity, they do not have access to the legal and material resources to adapt to new situations. In the case of inhabitants of small island states and heavily populated coastal zones facing rising sea levels, they may not even have a place to call home.

Third, future generations will bear a disproportionate impact as well. This intergenerational aspect has been well covered by Edith Brown Weiss (1989; 1992) and others (Agius, 2006; Page, 2006; Vanderheiden, 2008:111–142).[8] The idea of intergenerational climate justice goes beyond mitigating climate change and must also embrace the question of how future generations will adapt to this change. The latter is, perhaps, even more important for future generations if we accept the premise that we should strive as cosmopolitan citizens to afford equal opportunities at life chances to all. To deepen the hole from which future Africans and Asians begin their life journeys seems not only unjust but, put bluntly, downright cruel. This is not to suggest that something as superficial as climate change adaptation funding will equalize life opportunities. Women's rights, debt relief, nutrition, education: all of these are much more important pursuits. But the innocence of future generations is a fair presumption and, in many worldviews, entails an obligation to dedicate present activities to ensuring they have as good a chance at survival as we enjoy. Indeed the classic definition of sustainable development, adopted by the Brundtland Commission and many others, is "development that meets the needs of the present without compromising the ability of future generations to meet their own needs" (Brundtland et al., 1987). We can view (and evaluate) all of the arrangements described in this book as efforts to achieve this difficult and often intangible balance.

Beyond questions of intra- and intergenerational justice, much of the debate among green thinkers of various shades hinges on the proper definition of democracy: how much citizen involvement, beyond elections and public debate, is necessary to achieve a sustainable society? As mentioned previously, some observers feel that the strong role played by civil society members has cumulated in the development of a new international system. This has especially been the case with students of environmental activism (Wapner, 1995). Yet environmental questions are but one aspect of most people's daily lives; and many live in fundamentally undemocratic polities, such as North Korea or Burma. And a long line of political thought suggests that the only way we will cope with future ecological crises will be with the establishment of authoritarian governments that put democracy aside in favor of local and global survival.[9] Such a stark choice is perhaps unrealistic today, but there will always be trade-offs between freedom of choice and movement and the need for tight regulation. I tend to view environmental justice as a two-pronged ideal: it entails the protection of nature from overexploitation but also that specific social groups do not bear the brunt of the physical risks associated with development or even with pro-environment efforts. Legitimacy demands both these conditions, but I realize how difficult they are to implement at the local level when we retain structural inequalities from the past. And, even if this transition makes sense on the local level, how can it be transposed onto the international stage? Do international organizations such as the World Trade Organization (WTO) have any real legitimacy outside of the world of trade and commerce? Even the United Nations Environmental Program (UNEP) has contested legitimacy as a leader in global environmental governance, though it is located in an African country (Kenya) and its agenda is often sympathetic to southern causes. One of the questions we will raise in the analytic framework constructed in the next chapter is that of the democratic legitimacy of various efforts toward global environmental governance.[10] Do international arrangements promote environmental justice as well as national security?

Beyond these perennial concerns lie burning questions about the need for radical change in our present lifestyles, especially if we are to take the welfare of future generations seriously and seek a more equitable distribution of risks in present society. Proponents of ecological modernization suggest that serious changes are indeed necessary, but not necessarily changes that will reshape the international or domestic political order. More radical thinkers insist we need to rethink fundamentally the way we produce goods, the way we relate to each other, the way we walk on the earth. Beyond the usual platitudes, however, the green agenda is a surprisingly pragmatic one, with calls for increased investment in alternative energy research and development, eco-efficient homes, and cuts to greenhouse gas emissions. These and other policy options have been expounded for many decades now, and they have inspired many positive developments in

Europe and elsewhere. The question remains: How much more needs to be done, and is there a cohesive political philosophy that captures the extent of the crisis in terms of both causes and solutions?

My own impression is that there is not; while the demands placed on ecology by the modern state, military industrial complex, commercial agriculture, pharmaceutical and chemical industries, and other structures are tremendous, there is a dire need for short-term solutions, and this need makes calls for a global green socialist revolution (or, worse, a green Leviathan that can control everything everywhere and will do it in some vaguely defined benevolent green manner only) too long term for my liking, even on those days when I am more prepared than usual to tilt at the windmill of global capitalism. On the other hand, ecological modernization in itself is not enough; we need to think in terms of legitimacy, of acquiring the important "buy-in" of the billions of participants in global ecopolitics. Environmental justice must be at the table, for it is patently unfair to expect the poor to make sacrifices based on unsustainable consumption and pollution levels from which they barely benefit. We need diplomats infused with purpose, driven by the secure knowledge that they are making a difference and have support back home for their efforts; but as analysts and students, we need to keep a critical eye open when evaluating the work of governments, MNCs, NGOs, and other actors with authority and influence.

The Crosscutting Dilemma: Our Growing Numbers

Without apologies for dramatic effect, the main issue we are concerned with is nothing less than the survival of a biosphere safe for human life. Our life support systems are under dire threat, and the interdependent character of nature will not permit any easy escape.[11] This problem reflects a crisis in governance as much as it does biological and climatic unbalance, and it is, arguably, the task of global ecopolitics to fix it. And we are not just talking about a problem limited to our use of the commons or of shared resources but one that stretches across the planet's atmosphere, biosphere, sea, and tundra. No small task!

We will cover a variety of case studies in this text, from biodiversity protection to hazardous waste disposal to tropical warfare, and there are many crosscutting themes that infuse each of these discussions. The provision of energy, including food for the human race and the animals we raise for slaughter, is one of those issues, and though I return to the twin themes of energy and food security in Chapter 10, we should note that they are always with us. Similarly, though I treat it explicitly in Chapter 5, climate change has become a permeating topic, touching international diplomacy across the bargaining tables, igniting a range of activists, and capturing unparalleled media attention.

Overpopulation is another crosscutting issue that often overshadows discussions of more specific problems. There is an ongoing debate about whether the reproduction of people in the south or overconsumption by people in the north is the greater threat to planetary survival, but most of us have moved along and realize these are both serious problems. Indeed, as the consumer base in countries such as China and India increases in size and appetite, the consumption versus overpopulation debate becomes less of a debate, and both are seen as more of a threat to collective survival. Karen Litfin (2010), for example, refers to the environmental crisis as "really a creeping megacrisis, in which the exponential expansion of human populations is coupled with even greater increases in consumption" (p. 117). Regardless of the topic under discussion, population density will be a major factor. For example, much of the deforestation that contributes to global warming and reduces biodiversity in places such as the Amazon Basin is related to population pressure, but it is also the result of commercial greed, public debt, and regulatory failure. Although fertility rates vary remarkably across the globe, with some countries experiencing population decline, I tend to agree with Thomas Homer-Dixon's warning that "the claim we don't have to worry about any more population growth is entirely premature ... greater than replacement birthrates, declining death rates, and demographic momentum" will ensure that "the population of most poor countries will continue to grow for many decades, even as their birthrates fall" (Homer-Dixon, 2006:62–63). This puts them at a distinct disadvantage in the absence of commensurate national wealth. It also adds to migratory pressures, which, in turn, strain relations between states and raise various human rights concerns. Whether we are discussing deforestation or overfishing, population pressure is a constant factor.

But, of course, not all people have the same demands, and, arguably, affluence is as big a threat to ecosystems as dense human populations. Viewed globally, the United States has a very large population accustomed to absurd habits of consumption (and on a per capita basis Canadians like me have a similarly oversized ecological footprint). Indeed, national identity has been consciously tied to this voracious appetite, which is even viewed as a character strength. As the economy slides or the country suffers major terrorist attacks, Americans are exhorted to "go shopping." The destructive brutalization of temperate forests to extract oil from tar sands is justified with reference to maintaining the Canadian standard of living—this in a country with a population density most urban planners can only dream about. If the real agenda of global ecopolitics is to protect this lifestyle-oriented pragmatism, we are not on the path to creating a more sustainable world economy, nor a more just world order. Thus, the discussion of overpopulation, to me, must morph into a deeper discussion of international environmental and ecological justice.[12] International arrangements should reflect, and not deflect, these concerns if we want global institutions to have global legitimacy in the long run. But we are perhaps getting ahead of ourselves.

Delving Deeper into Global Ecopolitics

"… if we are already socialized into taking for granted the notion
that a child's vulnerability must be protected for the sake of
sustaining societies beyond one generation, even if it means
having to engage in routine acts of self-sacrifice, then it is not
inconceivable that we make the collective leap into believing
in the need for other forms of sacrifice for the longer term. The
tragedy, though, is that we may run out of time before we fully
develop our mythical and ritual apparatuses to embed the
requisite forms of sacrifice to avert global climate catastrophe."

SUDHIR CHELLA RAJAN (2010:182)

The quotation above, with its poignant imagery of vulnerable children and parental responsibility, ends on the note of planetary anxiety that forms the core of our concern. The hope embedded in these words is also infectious, however: we have an opportunity here, and though it is daunting to think of global environmental governance as a collective project, as global citizens we have a responsibility to be aware of recent developments and to think about how we can make our own singular and community contributions.

We will not settle the debates raised in this introductory chapter, and one might argue that they will never be settled, nor should they be; they are part of the fabric of deliberative democracy today and often serve to underpin international diplomacy and the evolution of international law. What we can say with surety is that no single approach captures the totality of the various responses needed to avert future ecological crises or deal with those we face presently, though the precautionary approach, suggesting we should avoid taking chances in the absence of relative scientific certainty about the consequences of our actions, is a fairly solid place to start (see Burns, 2006; Whiteside, 2006). We certainly need to rethink our infatuation with ceaseless economic growth, but we cannot afford to ignore the mass poverty afflicting so much of humanity. We need to modernize the technologies we employ to reduce the ecological harm they cause but also to consider alternatives to the industrialized agriculture and globalization that have come to define lifestyle for many in the West and East. Assuming a wide range of long-term conceptual options exist, we need to look closer at various modes of governance at the international level and ask how they can affect the effectiveness of the agreements and commitments made through environmental diplomacy.

The next chapter continues the journey: we will discuss the various actors in global ecopolitics, as well as the idea of adaptive multilevel governance, which—though not the focus of this book—is an important contextual factor in any successful effort to mitigate or adapt to serious environmental problems today. We will then construct an analytical framework we can use to evaluate the effectiveness of extant efforts toward global environmental governance, and thus gain insight into its process, structure, limitations, and possibilities.

Notes

1. The Anthropocene is regarded as a new geological era in which the impact of human activity has become one of the defining features of the physical/natural world. For an engaging discussion on how the advent of this new epoch intersects with contemporary notions of security, see Dalby (2006).

2. A quick scan of the online pages of the United Nations Environmental Programme (UNEP.org) will provide the reader with ample evidence of this threat, as would daily newspaper reading.

3. Collective action problems cannot be solved unilaterally or by any one actor involved no matter how powerful that actor may be. Of course, some actors (sometimes referred to as "hegemons" in the literature) may have more influence and play leading or debilitating roles. The crux of the tragedy of the commons is that one individual will benefit from pursuing self-interest, but we will all suffer from taking a similar path at the aggregate level. Ostrom (1990) and others have demonstrated this idea is fallacious in many contexts, but the term sticks, especially as Hardin (1968) employed it to refer to the need to overcome the sanctity of the right to procreate.

4. There is no single discipline of IR but rather a loose network of scholars dedicated to understanding how global politics take shape. There are also serious divisions between the theories involved; I will trust the interested reader to pursue other readings that cover international relations theory (e.g., Boucher, 1998; Bull, 1977; Carr, 1939; Cox, 2008; Der Derian, 1995; Dougherty and Pfaltzgraff, 2000; Jackson and Sorensen, 2007; Morgenthau, 1948; Sens and Stoett, 2010; Singer, 1961; Sterling-Folker, 2005; Waltz, 1959; Weber, 2005).

5. There is a long pedigree of famous work on this topic. See Wapner (2010:40–41) for a succinct discussion, Hardin's famous essay on the "tragedy of the commons" (1968), and Mancur Olsen's work (1971).

6. Paul Harris summarizes the Intergovernmental Panel on Climate Change: "regional affects will vary, ranging from up to hundreds of millions of people exposed to water

stress in Africa, increased flooding in the coastal and delta regions of Asia, significant loss of biodiversity in Australia, the retreat of glaciers in the mountains of Europe and water shortages in southern Europe, the loss of tropical forests and biodiversity in Latin America, water shortages and heat waves in North America, detrimental changes to natural ecosystems in polar regions, and inundations and storm surges in small islands…" (Harris, 2011:109).

7. "Act Now to Diversify Crops: Experts," *Montreal Gazette*, Oct. 3, 2011, p. A3.

8. This is referred to as "inter-generational ethics," as opposed to "intra-generational ethics" which is more concerned with the discrepancy in wealth and access to basic services among those presently alive (see Weiss, 1992). The utilitarian position is especially criticized for failing to take inter-generational ethics into account.

9. Most famously, perhaps, William Ophuls asserted in the 1970s that once our "relative abundance and wealth of opportunity are no longer available to mitigate the harsh dynamics of scarcity, the pressures favoring greater inequality, oppression, and conflict will build up … the return of scarcity portends the revival of age-old political evils … the golden age of individualism, liberty and democracy is all but over" (Ophuls, 1977:145). See Paehlke (2005) for a concise and Dobson (2003) for a broader discussion.

10. See the Dryzek and Schlosberg text (2005) for some key writings on the theme of democracy and environmentalism. Nor should we forget the key role played by large corporations, and how this can compromise or support democratic decision making. As Schreuder (2009) writes in relation to climate change policy, the "ability of these economic actors to dictate national economic and environmental policies to the detriment of democratic civic society … is also a factor to consider as we move towards a more sustainable and equitable emissions-reduction scheme" (p. 101–02).

11. This line of reasoning applies whether or not we accept the Gaia hypothesis put forward by James Lovelock and others, which suggests the earth can be conceived as a single organism and actively responds to threats to its welfare. See Lovelock (2006). DeGeest and Pirages (2004) offer an interesting discussion of the implications of globalization and ecological interdependency.

12. See Ehresman and Stevis (2011) for a recent survey. They use the terms "environmental justice" and "international equity" interchangeably.

CHAPTER TWO

International Arrangements: Actors and Effectiveness

"A belief in the accountability and legitimacy of a governance system on the part of subjects ... may play a significant role in enhancing compliance on the part of a variety of actors. But it is clear that this is an area calling for much more analytic rigor. As the interest in good governance rises, the need to develop suitable tools for evaluating specific governance systems in these terms becomes a higher priority."

ORAN YOUNG (2010:33)

ALL OF THE ARGUMENTS, DISCUSSIONS, DELIBERATIONS, CONCLUSIONS, illusions, and disillusions that result from environmental diplomacy and activism at a variety of levels will be colored by the green debates explicated in the previous chapter. But, to better understand how global ecopolitics work (or don't work), we need to know more about who the main actors are at each level. We need to know how they interact and produce tangible and intangible results and what conflicts result from this interaction. We need to know who is making decisions and not only what their primary motivations are (insofar as it is possible for an observer to gleam such things) but also what resources they have at their disposal. They, in turn, form the ongoing human element of the institutions they help create and that, for better or worse, contribute to the evolution of global ecopolitics.

We also need a framework we can employ to gauge the effectiveness of the formal arrangements shaping the context of global ecopolitics today. Although it would be trite to reduce this framework to a single question (such as "are these arrangements actually achieving anything tangible?"), we can with some degree of confidence assert that several factors have emerged from the vast literature on international regimes and institutions so as to form a basis for evaluation. We will be interested in the environmental impact, obviously, though it is often a chronological challenge to assess the impact of any long-running international arrangement; but we also need to look at the legal, social-cognitive, and democratic impact as well. Although this menu for evaluation offers a partial picture, it will provide a framework we can employ in subsequent chapters to examine in more detail extant efforts to solve the major collective action problems of our time. I do not apply the framework with religious vigor, but encourage the reader to refer to it when making her or his own assessment of how much progress we are making toward effective global governance.

Multi-scaled Adaptive Governance

Obviously, there are many opinions on how and even whether collective action problems should be dealt with by actors on the international stage as well as by private corporations and individuals. But it has become increasingly obvious to those of us who study this stuff for a living that making the majestic assumption that there is any singular solution for all collective action problems is a dead end, as is thinking we can apply some magical blueprint that will produce invariable results. So many idiosyncratic factors come into play; the proverbial roll of the dice has almost as good a chance of predicting results as theories of public administration. What we can say, however, is that the successful management of collective ecopolitical dilemmas will not result from reliance on any one level of governance. Indeed, this point may be one of the few on which all analysts of global ecopolitics can agree. Although it was previously normal to argue reflexively that we needed either top-down or bottom-up solutions, it is now quite common to realize either are futile on their own, hierarchical thinking is limiting, no form of authority has pure sovereignty over others, and sophisticated policies will emerge only when various scales of governance (not limited to governments) are taken into account. The term *governance* refers to efforts to assert authority, but it also connotes the quest for legitimacy in that process, and it should not be confused with the simple administration of government. The ultimate form of governance is self-control or, viewed from a darker perspective on the assertion of power, self-censorship. This view is more in line with the work of Michel Foucault and others, and it suggests that we are really looking at the transmission of political power into the realm of knowledge and vice versa. I try to keep both aspects of governance in mind at all times: the formal structure and process of organized authority and legitimacy and the more ideational or constructivist approach to understanding the spread and strength of that authority and legitimacy and the counter-hegemonic challenges to both.

Arguably, observers have adapted a newfound emphasis on multilevel environmental governance, stemming from the partial failure of over 20 years of high-level international diplomacy to deal effectively with collective action problems. There have certainly been successes; many would argue that the *Vienna Convention on the Ozone Layer*, for example, has proven instrumental in precluding further damage to the stratospheric ozone layer, which protects us and other creatures from excessive ultraviolet radiation. But, generally speaking, we would not need books like the one you are now reading if the hundreds of agreements—or what I simply enough term *arrangements*, implying that multi-scaled obligations and entitlements exist beyond the legality of a single agreement—had done the job. Rather, observers increasingly realize, we must conceptualize what is needed and measure progress along multiple lines of power, authority, and implementation, as well as from the heights of environmental, economic, and military diplomacy to the valleys of civil society, where those who must actually change their behavior actually tend to live.[1] And the importance of environmental impact assessment should not be overlooked either; it is carried out by government agencies, corporations, or experts hired by small communities to determine whether a proposed project will have a detrimental social or ecological impact. Social and physical scientists play an instrumental role by defining and analyzing the environmental problems of our day; engineers outline problems and design and construct solutions; educators and the media inform the public about environmental dilemmas.

The implications of a shift to multilevel governance are quite profound. The suggestion that no one level of authority can effectively administer the solution to a collective action problem flies in the face of conventional, Hobbesian theory, which suggests one sovereign or leviathan should dominate the affairs of otherwise divided and contentious people. The drafting and final negotiations of global environmental governance agreements should, though they rarely do, reflect this shift in thinking also. When the Canadian government signed and ratified the Kyoto Accord on climate change in 2002, it did so without the explicit consent of the Canadian provinces, and this oversight proved fatal to the subsequent implementation of the accord itself. Local communities, such as fishing villages and remote Inuit towns, must be consulted by officials and experts if we are not only to understand their viewpoint but also to ensure they are part of the process and thus inclined to participate. The criticism that this consultation would make international negotiations too cumbersome and unwieldy overlooks the fact that implementation is vital to the success of any plan. Indeed, many have argued that foreign policy negotiations proceed along a two- or three-level game matrix, at any rate, with negotiators playing to different audiences simultaneously (Putnam, 1988). The final form of an international arrangement is the result of interplays between various actors involved in the negotiation process, but the effectiveness of its implementation will be the result of actions taken by a much broader array of actors, who may or may not support its central demands and whose exposure to risk may decrease or increase as a result.

The increasingly significant role played by transnational advocacy networks has long been the stuff of formal IR studies (Keck and Sikkink, 1998). According to Joas, Kern, and Sandberg (2007), policy networks are best seen as "more or less institutionalized interaction[s] between autonomous and interdependent actors" (p. 237), including "hybrids" involving both governmental and nongovernmental actors (the latter include "civil society" groups and the private sector). Hybrid global public policy networks "give access to resources otherwise out of reach and also serve as arenas for actors who otherwise would not be able to influence policymaking"; however, hybrid networks "may challenge the democratic legitimacy of governmental actors, the efficiency of private sector actors, or the innovativeness and freedom of nongovernmental actors" (Joas, Kern, and Sandberg, 2007:238–9; see also Bache and Flinders, 2005; Delmas and Young, 2009; and Djelic and Sahlin-Andersson, 2006). Such networks also act as transnational advocates.

Finally, we are entering an era when many analysts are employing the concept of "adaptive governance" (see Webster, 2009) as a more focused approach to the coupled development of social and ecological systems, as well as to the coevolution of governmental and nongovernmental policy.[2] Adaptation is an effort to increase resilience in the face of change, prompting responsive modifications and alternative interactions among units in a system; and it takes place within a series of overlapping historical understandings and cultural contexts. Indeed adaptiveness, as "an umbrella term for a set of related concepts [including] vulnerability, resilience, adaptation, robustness, adaptive capacity, social learning" (Biermann et al., 2009:45) is one of the most important elements in collective action responses to environmental change (Smit and Wandel, 2006). While some might argue, from a systems perspective, that this adaptation takes place on its own, others would insist it takes individuals to achieve it (this disagreement echoes the agent-structure debate within political theory). Regardless, the emphasis is on information, flexibility, responsiveness, and legitimacy. Despite a long-term relationship with a major dispenser of commercial bottled water, my university in Montreal, after a concerted campaign by environmentalists, recently banned the sale of bottled water on campus, yet it maintained a strong relationship with the dispenser, which sells other products. This case could be viewed as an example of adaptive governance on a small scale.

Individuals and Communities

Late September, 2011: environmentalists and human rights advocates across the world are in mourning because a giant individual has been claimed by cancer—Kenyan scholar, activist, and Nobel Prize winner Wangari Muta Maathai. She was a leader in many ways: the first woman from central Eastern Africa to obtain a PhD; a traveling scholar who once gave a guest lecture to one of my classes in Canada, inspiring students to care about ecology and to believe they could make a difference; and, most important, the courageous leader of the Green Belt Movement, a self-organized community of African women who decided that planting trees was the best defense against desertification, even if it meant changing their daily activities, facing government oppression, and reconceptualizing their role as women in traditionally male-dominated societies. If anyone seriously doubts the importance of individuals in a world dominated by states and corporations, they need only think of one number: 45 million. This is the number of trees it is estimated that the Green Belt Movement has planted across Africa, and Dr. Maathai's role was central to this remarkable achievement. Her long-term goal of a billion may one day be realized, to the benefit of us all.

There are many ways to categorize the multitude of individual stakeholders involved in global environmental governance. In the general sense, we are, with too many unfortunately displaced exceptions, citizens of states and thus part of a political community, which must make decisions about its future. But we exist as members of multiple overlapping communities. One may be a Barcelonan, a Catalan, a Spaniard, and a citizen of the European Union all at once or a Montrealer, a Quebecois, and a Canadian. Further, people are members of communities not defined by geography, such as various ethnic and social groups. Also, organizing around the general theme of environmental protection is quite common today, across the globe. It is no longer a fringe issue, and it is often the most important issue among communities who feel that their ecological habitat is threatened by large-scale development projects, decrepit technology, shared and diminishing natural resources, unfair exposure to risk, and other challenges. People living on small islands do not need to be reminded that they are, as individuals and as members of a community, playing a key role in environmental politics as they respond to the threat of rising sea levels. Some NGOs, such as Greenpeace and Friends of the Earth, have widespread memberships, which are not dependent on any one issue or geographic focus; others are very local in nature, representing grassroots activism often based on what some refer to as NIMBY ("Not In My Backyard") politics. Some identify with broader causes on the left or right spectrum of politics and thus become environmentally active by default; others are driven primarily by concern for their children's health or because they are employed by industries that activate them as environmental impact specialists or, even, as counter-environmentalist agents. The list goes on and on.

Indeed, billions of people are certainly linked to global ecopolitics through their employment. Most obvious, perhaps, is the case of workers in the many extractive industries that have shaped the physical and political infrastructures of today's states, from coal mining to forestry to oil rigs. These workers certainly have a monetary stake in the sustainability of their work, as do the billions of people employed in agriculture across the planet. The oceans crisis described in Chapter 6 will ultimately affect every living thing on earth; but its most visible impact now is perhaps on those employed by the thousands in the fishing industries that are reaching their own extinction through a combination of overfishing and aquatic pollution. International regulations, though they are indeed often ignored, are often implemented as well and can have a serious impact on the daily lives of individuals, limiting their ability to build, hunt, burn forest, and even travel in certain "protected" areas. When they clamor for change, whether they are protesting damaging infrastructure projects such as large dams or calling for more protection from environmental hazards or opposing the regulations resulting from international agreements designed to mitigate environmental harm, they are ecopolitical actors, and they are often subjected to oppressive government actions, smear campaigns, and even outright violence. They can also be known as heroes to millions of people.

Other actors who wield unprecedented influence are scientists working for universities, international organizations, NGOs, MNCs, and, in some cases, in an independent capacity. The controversy over climate change exists because of what science has told us about increased carbon dioxide in the atmosphere and its long-term impact on temperature rise and, in turn, on the oceans, forests, semiarid land, weather, and other features of the geophysical landscape (see, for example, Bauer and Stringer, 2009). We learn from medical science about the impact on human health of deforestation, atmospheric particle pollution, biodiversity loss, and other facets of ecosystem decline. From social scientists and experts in the humanities, we learn about the effects of environmental degradation on social groups and human culture, as well as about potential policy options and shifts in societal values. More than ever, science helps set the agenda of global ecopolitics, and a lively debate flourishes over whether Western science is too dominant in the field, crowding out other epistemological avenues toward knowing. Of course, science is inherently politicized: it can be bought and sold, can be misconstrued and fabricated, can be suppressed and used to create weapons of mass destruction. But the importance of the pursuit of accurate information about the environmental crises we face and the significance of the ability to steer public discussions based on this information should not be overlooked. And some scientists openly adopt an advocacy role, convinced of the need to educate and inspire action; people such as David Suzuki, James Lovelock, and E.O. Wilson are well known inside and outside of environmentalist circles.

Given the existence of multiple community identities today and the visible political nature of ecopolitics, we should not be surprised that there is a great deal of collision and collusion between and among the actors described previously. Companies, lobby groups, political campaigns, scientific bodies: these are all social structures that unite people in common causes and promote alliance formation among like-thinking groups or individuals. These actors often engage in self-regulating activities designed to foster mutual trust and common goals (one of which might be greenwashing corporate activity, of course). Further, ecopolitics are often embedded in wider conflicts: clashes over land-use issues can reflect cultural and religious differences, racism, and ethnic cleansing campaigns; protests against corporate pollution rise from and contribute to antiglobalization or anti-Western sentiment; activists concerned with ecocide are primarily motivated by a peace-building or pacifist agenda; corporations pursuing "greener" national and international policies are certainly as concerned with improving their public image and increasing sales as they are with the intrinsic value of nature. All of these actors, with their radically differing agendas, strengths, weaknesses, visions for the future, community links, and public appeal, must operate in the global governance context with three main sources of authority in mind: states (more specifically, governments), international law, and the institutions created through international arrangements. However, it would be shortsighted to overlook the new social networks that can form around any issue area of such fundamental transnational significance to both environmental and human health as the air we breathe, the water we drink, or the other life-support systems of our distressed planet.

Governments and Governance

The state level of analysis is often assumed to be the most important when it comes to global ecopolitics because state governments must, ideally, enforce both international law and protect and preserve local democratic outcomes. There are several layers of government at work here, from local city, town, or rural community-based municipal governments and less formal structures to substate regional governments such as the provincial or state governments under Canadian and American federalism, respectively, to the nearly 200 internationally recognized national governments that are usually responsible for negotiating international treaties. Arguably, all three governments at these basic levels have a large role to play in actually implementing most country's international obligations, and though some governments are much more centralized and authoritarian than others, even countries such as China show remarkable variation across internal regions. Central to this discussion is the question of sovereignty and just how far governments will take the need for its partial violation. Although there is some optimism that—as influential private actors learn complying with regulations is good for them—state leaders will be pressured to accept the "new normal" of a more elastic understanding of sovereignty (Chayes and Chayes, 1995; DeSombre, 2005; Eckersley, 2004; Litfin, 2003), many observers cling to the notion that the protection of sovereignty is akin to the perpetuation of state survival itself. Beyond this is the question of internal legitimacy: some states, such as Mexico, Afghanistan, or Nigeria, have serious legitimacy problems and are arguably not in "control" of much of their territory. Indeed, it is a misnomer to think of absolute sovereign control in any state because informal economies, patronage relationships, and network activities outside the realm of the state will always exist, even in countries such as the United States and Germany.

Political decision making and action or inaction never take place in a context as simple as the spectrum of municipal-substate-state levels of government described here. For example, students interested in environmental issues and adaptive governance in Canada must take into consideration several layers of analytic space. On the one hand, most problems have local manifestations and affect the local politics of the area involved. Forestry, oil drilling, fishing, agriculture, and other extractive industries take place within a geographically identifiable place, and nearby communities are intrinsically involved. On the other hand, these processes are part of the global economy and contribute to the national wealth of Canada even as they threaten global biospheric health. In the Canadian case, we need to consider the continental dimension, including not only Canada's circumpolar circumstances but, most especially, the US-Canada relationship.[3] To take a dramatic but empirical example, there are over 4,500 known hazardous waste sites on both sides of the border in the Great Lakes Basin alone. Even pollution in Mexico affects Canada and vice versa, and there are migratory species such as the monarch butterfly that live in both countries. Despite intense and long-standing disputes, the continent has also been the theater of much cooperation and the birthplace of two major international institutional innovations: the International Joint Commission (IJC) and the Commission for Environmental Cooperation (CEC) of the North American Free Trade Agreement (NAFTA). Generally, cooperation first addressed commercial concerns or specific pollution problems and then expanded into a larger approach to environmental protection. Environment Canada (2010c) estimates that there are over 20 Canada–United States environmental agreements, and many more exist at the provincial and state levels, such as the New England Governors/ Eastern Canadian Premiers Climate Change Action Plan of 2001 or the Great Lakes Charter of 1985 arranged by the Council of Great Lakes Governors (which includes the Ontario and Quebec premiers) or more recent ones on the derivation of Great Lakes' waters.[4] Indeed, the substate level of cooperation appears to be on the rise as bilateral efforts are clogged by other foreign policy concerns. Transnational citizens' movements (such as Great Lakes United) are also increasingly important in the study of bilateral environmental diplomacy.

However, though we need to take into account governmental activity at a variety of levels if any claim to a comprehensive examination is to take place, our main focus will inevitably fall on national governments because they ultimately make the key decisions as to whether substate governing structures will be obliged to participate in international arrangements. Here we see remarkable diversity and, again, the embedding of environmental diplomacy within other foreign and domestic policy issues. For example, the United States has displayed a fairly consistent unilateral impulse since the year 1990, not just in environmental matters but in any foreign policy questions that involve multilateral institutions and especially the United Nations; many southern countries are adamant that environmental negotiations take place within the loaded context of north-south issues and the redressing of colonial wounds; and Japan's vocal pro-whaling policies have as much to do with asserting Japanese autonomy as with a particular fondness for cetacean dishes (Tanno and Hamazaki, 2000). Each of our case studies will tease out many collisions and collusions between state agents, which take place at the substate, transnational, intergovernmental, and international levels. The latter is especially pertinent to global ecopolitics, so we turn now to its brief introduction.

International Law and Institutions

Although the topic of international environmental law was once considered rather peripheral to international legal studies, it is now arguably a central branch and has been covered by many excellent texts. We can introduce only some of the basic factors here.[5] International law is often criticized as being illegitimate, unenforceable, and ineffective. All this may be true to some degree: such law is not formed as national representative legislatures form domestic law, nor is it necessarily reinforced by the threat of violent coercion or even of any dire consequences resulting from noncompliance. Yet it remains a pivotal aspect of international relations (or, according to some, of an evolving global society), as a peaceful means by which disputes can be resolved and future pathways toward greater state and individual accountability can be forged. Treaties and conventions are the breathing bodies of international law, and they form the basis of global governance efforts. However, they are often disconnected from local populations, who see them as impositions from afar; and, at worst, they are interpreted as legalistic efforts to maintain inequality or as outright oppression. Certainly, states have obtained obligations under international environmental law that should affect domestic policy making; for example, Birnie, Boyle, and Redgwell (2009) write that "we can take it for granted that states are responsible ('liable') in international law to make reparation for transboundary damage, or the risk of damage, resulting from their own failure to regulate and control potentially harmful activities to the standard of due diligence required by international law, or from their failure to cooperate" (p. 216). This statement is remarkable in itself given the history of IR.

Traditional sources of authority in international law include treaties and conventions (which may or may not be binding), customary law (identified norms of state behavior and the "soft law" of UN General Assembly resolutions), general principles derived from declarations and other treaties or conventions, judicial decisions taken by international and national courts, and the writings of experts in the field. Though the International Court of Justice (ICJ) deals with state governments only, the International Criminal Court (ICC), established by the Rome Statute of 1998, pertains to individuals charged with war crimes, crimes against humanity, genocide, and other violations of human rights. States sign international conventions, but must ratify them—convert them into actual domestic legislation—in order for them to be implemented. In many cases, therefore, democratically elected representatives do make the final decision regarding their constituents' obligation to adhere to international law.

And, of course, it is up to states to enforce international law. This situating of responsibility with individual nations is international law's strength, as only such a voluntary system would attract many participants in a world of legally sovereign states. It is also its weakness, as ensuring compliance with international law and regulations will always be a challenge. Generally, states do not resort to serious measures to enforce international environmental law. But, as Birnie, Boyle, and Redgwell (2009) inform us,

> [T]here are some situations for which states have agreed that conduct is sufficiently objectionable that criminal penalties are required. This is typically the case in treaties covering trade in hazardous wastes, marine pollution, and trade in or possession of endangered species. Criminal penalties are normally also employed to deal with illegal fishing. (P. 330)[6]

However, we should not exaggerate the extent to which these crimes are pursued. Article 8(2)(b)(iv) of the Rome Statute refers to environmental crimes, but it is unlikely we will see the ICC prosecute them in the near future, unless they are tied directly to war crimes (as was the case in the non-ICC trial of former Liberian dictator Charles Taylor, who traded in banned timber products for weapons). Simply put, if states do not enforce international environmental law, it will not get done; this creates a possible moral hazard (the ability of some to "free ride" on the backs of others, who are observing the law) with which we must live until the establishment of more coercive or persuasive global governance structures.

That said, the absence of international environmental law would make environmental diplomacy moot. The idea that behavior can become codified in formal legal code, signed by two or more states in the spirit of *pacta sunt servanda* (the willingness to respect the obligation), is central to the pursuit of sustainable development in a highly competitive and resource-hungry world economy. But most international legal obligations would be merely ornamental if not for the institutions they have facilitated. In itself, state responsibility has been very limited under international environmental law.[7] I will refer to the combination of legal and institutional action toward environmental protection as an *international arrangement for global environmental governance*.[8]

At a less abstract level, international institutions are often created for the express purpose of implementing conventions on shared resources and environmental problems. Others, such as the WTO, were created to help regulate the world economy and maintain "order" (though one person's order is often another's oppression). The United Nations established the UNEP after the 1972 Stockholm Conference on the Human Environment (UNCHE). Twenty years later, the United Nations Conference on the Environment and Development (UNCED) established several mechanisms of interest in Rio, including the Rio Declaration on Environment and Development (a weak version of a highly anticipated Earth Charter), Agenda 21 (a loose set of nonbinding objectives), the Framework Convention on Climate Change (UNFCCC), the Convention on Biological Diversity (CBD), and the somewhat hilariously named Non-legally Binding Authoritative Statement of Principles for a Global Consensus on the Management, Conservation and Sustainable Development of All Types of Forests. A Convention to Combat Desertification would follow in 1994. The 2002 World Summit on Sustainable Development in Johannesburg would produce little in terms of solid outcomes, though Steven Bernstein (2005) suggests that it marked a further innovation, "multi-stakeholder deliberation and public-private partnership agreements" (p. 149), which we would also see with the UN Global Compact signed by many MNCs. Many such arrangements have evolved in recent decades, adding to the plethora of examples of "governance without governments" (Rosenau and Czempiel, 1992).

Specialized agencies of the UN abound, and many of them, such as the International Maritime Organization (IMO), the Food and Agriculture Organization (FAO), and the World Health Organization (WHO), have obvious links with the UNEP's mandate. Still other UN bodies of relevance include the Security Council, which wields considerable power (including the ability to engage in collective security actions) and has discussed human security issues openly, and the Commission on Sustainable Development (CSD), established after the UNCED as part of the Economic and Social Council (ECOSOC). The CSD is supposed to oversee the implementation of Agenda 21, though it is at times difficult to see how this is possible given its weak legitimacy.[9] In 1991 the World Bank, the UNEP, and the UN Development Programme (UNDP) established the Global Environmental Facility (GEF), which provides funding to southern states for biodiversity protection, the elimination of ozone depleting substances, and other endeavors. Indeed, it is a task in itself to keep up with the establishment of new institutions related to sustainability issues; for example, the Statute of the International Renewable Energy Agency (IRENA) just went into effect after the 25th state ratified it in June of 2010. There are many regional organizations, most notably the European Union, which have developed their own environmental rules and regulations, and others, such as NAFTA, with side agreements and related institutions (in this case, the CEC) devoted to environmental issues (see Commission for Environmental Cooperation, 2008). We should bear in mind also that NGOs play an increasingly important role in the institutional setting of multilateral arrangements, especially in those, such as the Convention on International Trade in Endangered Species (CITES, 2011b), where they have both advocacy and scientific roles. And there are a plethora of global environmental problems, such as the spread of invasive alien species (IAS), for which no truly international agreement or commensurate organization exists but concerning which many and varied international experts, regulatory agencies, and regional organizations are highly involved (see Chapter 9).

International conventions themselves have complex governance structures, usually involving some sort of conference of the parties (COP), which meets on a biannual basis to make key collective decisions. However, the brunt of daily work falls to the people who staff the secretariat, which is usually created in tandem with the convention itself. The work of international secretariats should not be overlooked or exaggerated (see Bauer, 2006). Clearly, international bureaucrats are key to the organization of environmental diplomacy, as well as to information gathering and dissemination; they also play an open advocacy role. On the other hand, they have limited autonomy, rarely have a direct impact on policy formation at the country or regional level, and engage in limited consultation with the local populations affected by international agreements. In what is emerging as a landmark study on various international environmental secretariats, Bierman and Siebenhuner (2009) conclude that all the bureaucracies they analyzed "have autonomous cognitive, normative, and executive influence in their policy domain," but they are quick to concede large differences among them (p. 326).[10] Not all secretariats are created equal, nor are all bureaucrats equally competent. Nonetheless, they—and the overall structure of international arrangements—serve to enhance cooperation, define the roles of key players and bestow authority upon them, facilitate learning, and make other vital contributions as we move forward (Young, 1999). They are not our only hope, thankfully; but they are an important source of it.

Finally, I would be sorely remiss if I did not stress the importance of international financial institutions such as the World Bank and the various regional multilateral development banks, the GEF, the International Monetary Fund (IMF), and other funding clearinghouses and sources. They are important in at least three principal ways. First, they exhibit tangible power: they often make axiomatic decisions that affect millions of lives. Traditionally, most activists and many academic observers see the World Bank as a less-than-green institution, driven by a utilitarian view of nature. Critics point to its early penchant for investing in heavy, capital-intensive energy infrastructure projects, such as large dams and fossil fuel plants; its fondness for emphasizing transportation infrastructure, funding roads that split rainforests and other ecosystems; its habitual disrespect for indigenous peoples, gender issues, and animal welfare; and its involvement in the structural adjustment programs imposed by the IMF, which demand export-crop orientation and the lessening of regulations as countries struggle to repay international debts. The World Bank has, arguably, improved a great deal since the 1970s and 1980s, and it now devotes considerable attention to environmental impact assessment; one might even conclude it has largely embraced the green perspective of ecological modernization.[11] However, many critical observers insist that a fundamental change has not occurred, and even the GEF—developed specifically to promote sustainable development and to reduce key global problems—can barge ahead with projects that reinforce old colonial ties and produce dubious results (a new UN forestry funding mechanism, REDD+, has been similarly criticized). Another important aspect of IFIs is their cognitive power: to some extent, they are able to disseminate their own driving ideological perspectives (namely, a neoliberal, pro-globalization agenda based on a utilitarian perspective toward nature). Environmentalists can view this power as both a danger and an opportunity because, arguably, ideological fixations are not immutable. Finally, international financial institutions act as focal points for the media, activists, indigenous groups, corporations, and other lobbyists who want to influence decision making.

A Rudimentary Chronology of Selected International Arrangements, Events, Celebratory Dates, and the Establishment of Selected Environmental Nongovernmental Organizations (ENGOs)

1815	Legal framework for the Central Commission for Navigation on the Rhine River
1892	Formation of the ENGO Sierra Club in San Francisco, United States
1909	Boundary Waters Treaty between the United States and Great Britain (for Canada) establishes the International Joint Commission
1911	Great Britain (for Canada), Russia, Japan, and the United States reach agreement to limit pelagic sealing
1931	Formation of the ENGO International Council for Scientific Unions (ICSU)
1933	The Convention Relative to the Preservation of Fauna and Flora in their Natural State
1945	Food and Agriculture Organization (FAO) of the United Nations established
1946	The International Convention for the Protection of Whaling, establishing the International Whaling Commission
1948	International Maritime Organization (IMO), originally known as the Inter-Governmental Maritime Consultative Organization
1948	International Union for Conservation of Nature and Natural Resources (IUCN), later known as the World Conservation Union
1949	International Convention for the Northwest Atlantic Fisheries (now known as the North Atlantic Fisheries Commission or NAFO)
1951	The International Plant Protection Convention (IPPC)
1956	United Nations Educational, Scientific and Cultural Organization (UNESCO) Major Project on Scientific Research on Arid Lands
1957	International Geophysical Year
1958	The Convention on Fishing and Conservation of the Living Resources of the High Seas
1958	First UN Conference on the Law of the Sea

1961	Formation of ENGO World Wildlife Fund (WWF; now known outside of Canada and the United States as the World Wide Fund for Nature)
1961	Antarctic Treaty System enters into force
1963	Convention for the Protection of the Rhine River (European Community)
1964	International Biological Programme established by ICSU (ends 1974)
1966	Helsinki Rules on the Uses of the Waters of International Rivers
1966	International Convention for the Conservation of Atlantic Tunas
1969	Formation of ENGO Friends of the Earth
1971	Man and the Biosphere Programme (UNESCO) launched
1971	The Convention on Wetlands of International Importance Especially as Waterfowl Habitat (also known as the Ramsar Convention)
1971	Formation of ENGO Greenpeace in Vancouver, Canada
1972	UN Conference on the Human Environment (UNCHE) in Stockholm (also known as the Stockholm Conference)
1972	United Nations Environment Programme (UNEP)
1972	The Convention Concerning the Protection of the World Cultural and Natural Heritage, under UNESCO
1972	The Convention for the Conservation of Antarctic Seals
1972	Biological and Toxin Weapons Convention (in force 1975)
1973	CITES (the Convention on International Trade in Endangered Species of Wild Fauna and Flora)
1973	International Agreement on the Conservation of Polar Bears
1973	MARPOL Convention, officially called the International Convention for the Prevention of Pollution from Ships
1973	Formation of modern Chipko movement in Uttar Pradesh, India
1974	World Population Year
1974	Third World Population Conference (more significant than the first in 1954 or the second in 1965)
1975	UNESCO International Hydrological Programme (IHP) founded
1978	UNEP Principles of Conduct in the Field of the Environment for the Guidance of States in the Conservation and Harmonious Utilization of Natural Resources Shared by Two or More States

1977	UN Conference on Desertification
1977	Convention on the Prohibition of Military or Any Other Hostile Use of Environmental Modification Techniques (ENMOD)
1977	Formation of the ENGO Green Belt Movement in Kenya
1979	The Convention on the Conservation of Migratory Species of Wild Animals (also known as CMS or the Bonn Convention)
1979	First World Climate Conference takes place in Geneva
1979	Convention on Long-Range Transboundary Air Pollution (CLRTAP)
1981–90	International Drinking Water Supply and Sanitation Decade
1982	The United Nations Convention on the Law of the Sea (UNCLOS)
1982	Convention on the Conservation of European Wildlife and Natural Habitats (also known as the Bern Convention)
1983	World Commission on Environment and Development convened (also called the Brundtland Commission)
1983	International Tropical Timber Agreement (ITTA) signed
1985	Vienna Convention for the Protection of the Ozone Layer signed
1985	Canada–United States Pacific Salmon Treaty
1987	Report of the World Commission on Environment and Development (also known as *Our Common Future* or the Brundtland Report)
1987	Montreal Protocol on Substances that Deplete the Ozone Layer
1987	International Geosphere Biosphere Programme started
1988	Intergovernmental Panel on Climate Change (IPCC) established
1989	The Basel Convention on the Control of Transboundary Movements of Hazardous Wastes and Their Disposal
1990	Multilateral Fund for the Implementation of the Montreal Protocol
1991	Global Environment Facility (GEF) created
1991	Protocol on Environmental Protection to the Antarctic Treaty
1991	Arctic Environmental Protection Strategy (AEPS) adopted
1992	Commission on Sustainable Development established by the UN Economic and Social Council

1992	UN Conference on Environment and Development (UNCED) or the Rio Earth Summit, where the Rio Declaration and Agenda 21 were adopted
1992	UN global moratorium on large-scale pelagic driftnet fishing on the high seas, including enclosed and semi-enclosed seas, comes into effect
1992	Aarhus Convention on Access to Information, Public Participation in Decision-making and Access to Justice in Environmental Matters (UN Economic Commission for Europe)
1992	North Atlantic Marine Mammal Commission (NAMMCO) Agreement reached in Nuuk, Greenland
1992	Convention on the Prohibition of the Development, Production, Stockpiling and Use of Chemical Weapons and on Their Destruction (in force in 1997)
1993	UN International Year for World's Indigenous People
1993	UN Convention on Biological Diversity (CBD) comes into force
1994	UN Framework Convention on Climate Change (UNFCCC) comes into force
1994	UN International Conference on Population and Development
1995	The Agreement on the Application of Sanitary and Phytosanitary Measures (SPS) comes into force under the new World Trade Organization
1996	UN International Year for the Eradication of Poverty
1996	UN Convention to Combat Desertification
1996	International Seabed Authority becomes operative
1996	Ottawa Declaration establishes the Arctic Council
1996	The International Organization for Standardization (ISO) publishes the ISO 14000 for environmental management standards
1997	Kyoto Protocol of the UNFCCC signed
1998	UN International Year of the Ocean
1998	Rotterdam Convention on the Prior Informed Consent Procedure for Certain Hazardous Chemicals and Pesticides in International Trade (entered into force in 2004)
2000	Millennium Summit of the United Nations
2000	European Union Water Framework Directive
2001	Stockholm Convention on Persistent Organic Pollutants (entered into force in 2004)
2002	UN International Year of Mountains

2003	UN International Year of Freshwater
2003	Cartagena Protocol on Biosafety comes into force
2004	UN International Year of Rice
2004	The International Treaty on Plant Genetic Resources for Food and Agriculture (housed by the FAO of the United Nations)
2004	IMO adopts the International Convention for the Control and Management of Ships Ballast Water and Sediments
2005	Millennium Ecosystem Assessment series published
2005	UN General Assembly adopts the 2005 World Summit Outcome as a follow-up to the 2000 Millennium Summit
2005–15	International Decade for Action: "Water for Life"
2006	UN International Year of Deserts and Desertification
2007	Bali Road Map on climate change adopted
2008	UN International Year of Planet Earth *and* UN International Year of the Potato
2008	First commitment period of the Kyoto Protocol of the UNFCCC begins
2009	UN International Year of Natural Fibres
2009	Year of the Gorilla (UNEP and UNESCO)
2009	Copenhagen Accord on climate change drafted
2010	Cancun Agreements create a Green Climate Fund
2010	UN International Year of Biodiversity
2011–20	UN Decade on Biodiversity
2010	*Global Biodiversity Outlook 3* published by the CBD
2010–20	International Decade for Deserts and the Fight against Desertification
2011	UN International Year of Forests
2011	Nagoya Protocol of the CBD (on access and benefit sharing in the international governance of biodiversity)
2011	Durban Conference of UNFCCC produces an agreement to agree to emissions reductions for all countries by 2015
2012	International Year of Sustainable Energy for All
2012	"Rio+20" United Nations Conference on Sustainable Development in Rio de Janeiro, assessing 20 years of global environmental governance since the UNCED of 1992
2013	International Year of Water Cooperation

SOURCES: Adapted from Birnie, Boyle, and Redgwell (2009); Hutchinson and Herrmann (2008:133); United Nations (2011); United Nations Association in Canada (UNA-Canada, 2011); and including observations by the author.

Wicked Problems: Measuring Effectiveness
in International Arrangements

"Wicked problems" are especially difficult to solve because they "challenge established social values and institutional frameworks, defy [easy] analysis, and have no obvious solutions" (Jordan et al., 2010:4; Rittel and Webber, 1973). Keeping in mind the conceptual approaches and different actors we have introduced so far, we need an operational framework with which to analyze the effectiveness of efforts to reduce the deleterious impact of human activities on our fragile biosphere. The rest of this book will be devoted largely to analyzing efforts to achieve and implement international arrangements in a variety of "wicked" issue areas. We will, of necessity, deal primarily with multilateral arrangements because collective action problems of gravity demand a coordinated response among states, the participation of millions of people, and the work of dedicated institutions. However, we will also note the existence of regional and bilateral arrangements, and the importance of action at the national and substate levels, including civil society and private industry.

There are several ways to measure the effectiveness of multilateral environmental arrangements (see Victor, Raustiala, and Skolnikoff, 1998; Young, 1999). For example, we could ask whether the actual problem that stimulated the arrangement has been solved. This question demands a concrete and acceptable understanding of what, exactly, the problem is and a common understanding of how we can actually determine whether it is solved, or mitigated. More narrowly, perhaps, have the concrete goals set down on paper and signed for been reached (the goals of the "constitutive instrument")? Have the patterns of behavior that have led to the problem, or at least to widespread perceptions that there is a problem, been altered as a consequence of the arrangement? This behavioral shift is perhaps the most difficult thing to measure, in the sense that we cannot truly isolate the arrangement itself as a causal variable and must always be conscious of the "time horizon" involved (Barkin, 2004). Easier to ask is whether there has been, to date, widespread and demonstrably enriched compliance among national governments, which is not necessarily a good thing; as Birnie, Boyle, and Redgwell (2009) suggest, "the effectiveness of different regulatory and enforcement techniques is largely determined by the nature of the problem" they are designed to regulate (p. 12). In some cases, such as fisheries management or reforestation efforts, applying the same approach to widely divergent cultural contexts and geographical areas could be a great hazard in itself.[12]

I suggest there are four central important criteria for measuring the effectiveness of global environmental governance efforts, and each of them is as concerned with the impact on local people, communities, and institutions as it is with the broader international impact it has generated. Each demands a multi-governance approach to analyze these differentiated impacts and promises, though international arrangements are a good place to start.

First, we need to describe and evaluate the historical trajectory and scope of the arrangement: is it sufficiently widespread so as to include the various actors involved? How widely and deeply have related treaties, conventions, protocols, and memoranda spread into domestic legislatures and community regulations? Arguably, the IUCN's draft Covenant on Environment and Development (first completed in 1995 with the third revision appearing in 2004) provides the most comprehensive assessment and proposal for concretizing the huge body of extant international environmental law, but it has yet to gain formal acceptance.[13] So we need to look at individual issue areas and commensurate arrangements; generally, I will describe two in each of the subsequent chapters.

Second, we must also examine the question of whether there have been concrete environmental improvements since the creation and implementation of international arrangements. Again, it is generally too soon to say, but, in some cases, we have many decades of experience and can at least make educated guesses about whether efforts are paying off, both at the local and global levels. The importance of international agencies in taking stock of the ecological situation cannot be overstated here, though they are themselves usually highly dependent on government sources we may or may not wish to trust. Overall, it is self-evident that we are failing. Nevertheless, there are areas where success is quite breathtaking, and that is enough to encourage more effort. Ultimately, one might argue that a successful arrangement would, in effect, put itself out of business, but this would miss the broader point: even if the environmental "problem" is solved entirely—and we are far from this occurring—the arrangement will have become a part of the architecture of global environmental governance.[14] Of course, this may be a good or bad thing, depending on one's view of the value of global governance in the first place. Though individuals and specific mandates, collaborative efforts, and even side-agencies may come and go, I am convinced that the major international arrangements discussed in this book are here to stay, permanent if evolving fixtures.

Third, we can ask whether arrangements have met with any cognitive success: have they led to an increased awareness of and subsequent efforts to correct the environmental problem? Has there been a change in prevalent thinking about an issue? Again, it is impossible to isolate the international arrangement itself as the causal agent here, but we might be able to suggest that it played a role in publicizing issues and in framing the public perception of them. This category of evaluation (cognitive evolution and success) is, of course, very subjective, more attuned to the constructivist approaches discussed in Chapter 1. Public opinion surveys can be useful here, but they, too, are limited by their reliance on the self-evaluation of respondents. I will not hide this subjective aspect, to which you and

I are also susceptible: we often see things working because we so badly *want* to see them working. Indeed, we can be self-induced to seeing failure the same way. But the category of cognitive evolution and success remains, in my view, an important one for analysis because most action, arguably, begins with thought. Even if an arrangement does little else but stir public debate over controversial actions and principles, it has demonstrated some cognitive success: silence is deadly. If an environmental problem is not even on the public agenda—if scientists, NGO members, concerned individual citizens, and private investors do not manage to capture the public's attention—it is often ignored until the costs of response are prohibitive. On the other hand, international arrangements should and can play an instrumental role in publicizing an environmental cause, and, if they fail to do so, then surely something important is lacking.

Finally, I will explore the questions raised in Chapter 1 about democratic legitimacy and environmental justice, questions of participatory access, shared benefits, and accountable transparency. This exploration relates to a broader discussion about the *legitimacy* of both multilateral institutions and international arrangements (see Hurd, 2008). Do the arrangements protect or advance environmental justice as well as promote sustainable development, or are they simply efforts to assuage the guilt of Westerners or the rage of the affected? Birnie, Boyle, and Redgwell (2009) write that there "is now widespread provision for national and international NGOs qualified in relevant fields to be accorded observer status at meetings of treaty parties" (p. 90); but is this enough? The CBD (2002), for example, calls explicitly for the "fair and equitable sharing of benefits arising out of the utilization of genetic resources," and we have seen progress— at least rhetorical progress—in this direction (p. iv). But not all arrangements feature this aspect in any serious light, even if we can argue that the normative context in which they are evolving demands more than cursory attention to issues of democratic participation and social justice. We will return to this general theme in our conclusion, when we discuss environmental justice as a primary factor in moving ahead with reform. In my view, it should animate everything we do at the global level, and it demands that we take the connections discussed above seriously, even if it would be physically impossible to discuss them all in this text. There is a strong correlation between economic inequality and biodiversity loss (Holland, Peterson, and Gonzalez, 2009; Pogge and Schroeder, 2009), exposure to environmental risks, and compromised human health and future life chances. The United Nations, the principal umbrella international organization, does have a mandate to consider economic and social rights and to pursue greater equality. International multilateral arrangements to deal with environmental problems must inherit this mandate as well; at the very least, they should aim to help give voice to those often invisible at the international level of diplomatic interaction. Here, however, we can be forgiven if our expectations are generally low, given the elite nature of international law and diplomacy and the mismatch in financial power between poor citizens and wealthy corporations.

These four general categories (institutional and legal development, ecological improvement, cognitive impact, and democratic legitimacy and environmental justice) will inform brief discussions of the case studies presented in this text. Finally, in Chapters 9 and 10, we will look at some glaring "governance gaps," most notably the absence of an international convention on alien invasive species, the absence of strong regulations on tourism, the absence of regulation in the emerging nanotechnology field, the absence of a concerted food security policy network, and—perhaps most daunting—the absence of a global energy strategy. In addition to the issue areas covered in other chapters, these are where we will need to develop governance tools in the near future, though preliminary efforts have already been made.

Each of the subsequent chapters in this book will deal with an issue area of great concern for adaptive global environmental governance. They overlap and intersect in many interesting ways, yet what they all have in common is that they demand almost unparalleled cooperation among participants in the international arrangements that have been formed, and they all challenge us to think further about deeper changes that are necessary if we are to make serious progress. Since brevity is one of the main attributes of this text, our case studies will necessarily only scratch the surface of each issue's complexity, but it is my hope that they will encourage the reader to look further, perhaps with the analytic framework offered above in mind.

Notes

1. The mountain and valley imagery used here is for illustrative purposes only, though I suppose it does betray the underlying assumption by IR specialists that international diplomacy, with its stamp of state involvement, is where the real action is. Still, the history of global ecopolitics suggests that NGOs, MNCs, scientists, and others play as important a role.

2. "Adaptive governance is an evolving research framework for analyzing the social, institutional, economical and ecological foundations of multilevel governance modes that are successful in building resilience for the vast challenges posed by global change, and coupled complex adaptive SES [social-ecological systems]" (http://www.stockholmresilience.org/research/researchthemes/adaptivegovernance.4.aeea469 11a3127427980006994.html).

3. Historically, largely because of its economic and security dimensions, the environment has been central to Canadian-American relations. The two countries share a nearly 9,000 km border that cuts through a wide diversity of ecosystems, such as shared river

basins and the Great Lakes, mountain ranges, arctic wilderness, coastal zones, and old-growth forest. Prevailing winds push air pollution from the Midwest to New England and the Canadian east. Native Americans and First Nations Canadians are often more prone to recognize this ecosystemic continuity than they are any borders negotiated by Europeans (startling findings of PCBs and other toxic pollutants in the breast milk of Inuit mothers in the late 1980s offered evidence of this interdependence and of the unsymmetrical vulnerability it reflects). Moreover, the similarities between Canadian and American economic systems, with their intensive consumption of resources and disposal of waste, make the treatment of nature an even more obvious topic for sustained analysis. See LePrestre and Stoett (2006).

4. On transnational cooperation on North American climate change policy, see Chapter 6 and especially Selin and VanDeveer (2009).

5. See in particular Sand (1999) and Sands (2003); and for two recent, outstanding texts, see Birnie, Boyle, and Redgwell (2009) and Bodansky (2010).

6. In 1998, the Council of Europe adopted the Convention for the Protection of the Environment through Criminal Law, but it is not yet in force and holds little promise.

7. See Birnie, Boyle, and Ridgwell (2009): "The only precedent which holds a state unequivocally responsible for environmental damage in international law is UN Security Council Resolution 687, adopted following Iraq's invasion and occupation of Kuwait in 1991.... The main reason for discussing state responsibility at all ... is thus not its immediate practical utility but because an understanding of what it can and cannot offer is essential to an explanation of other developments in the international legal system that have largely taken its place" (p. 212).

8. IR specialists will note that I refrain from using the term "international regime" with great regularity, believing it implies too much and carries too much connotation. Rather, I will stick with the perhaps more mundane but more accurate term *international arrangements*; but this does not by any means imply we are not interested in a broader understanding of their cognitive impact on human thinking and action.

9. "In effect the CSD is a permanent diplomatic forum for continued negotiation on all matters concerned with sustainable development, but one with no powers, few resources, and limited influence" (Birnie, Boyle, and Redgwell, 2009:64).

10. Readers interested in the role of secretariats are strongly advised to consult this excellent text, which includes chapters on the OECD, the World Bank, the IMO, the UNEP, the GEF, the UNEP Ozone Secretariat, the UNFCC, the CBD, and the Secretariat of the UNCCD.

11. It has even withdrawn from controversial projects such as the Narmada Dam complex construction in India.

12. It is often suggested, for example, that applying the same theoretical constructs of economic development to different states and human populations has not led to development but to increased resentment of Westernization.

13. This is an extraordinary document, which should be consulted by anyone engaged in detailed studies of international environmental law today; it was composed by the IUCN Commission on Environmental Law, the International Council of Environmental Law, and the UNEP Environmental Law and Institutions Programme Activity Centre.

14. Of course, international arrangements can be disbanded for lack of funding or for other reasons; see Chapter 9, where I discuss the very unfortunate death of the Global Invasive Species Programme, for example. But the GISP was in effect a collaborative effort among several much firmer institutions, including the CBD and IUCN, neither of which is in immediate danger of peril.

CHAPTER THREE

Conserving Biodiversity and Wildlife

"I offer this as a formula of re-enchantment to invigorate poetry and myth: mysterious and little known organisms live within walking distance of where you sit. Splendor awaits in minute proportions."

EDWARD O. WILSON (1984:139)

IT'S NOT EVERY DAY ONE CAN SIT AND WRITE IN SEMI-URBAN SPACES where conservation efforts have had some impact, such as the waterfowl park near the mighty Lachine Rapids in Quebec. When you are this close to the sound of cascading water, late summer crickets, and an amusing assortment of birdcalls (though seagulls certainly dominate), when a short walk reveals hundreds of plant and insect species, with ample evidence of beavers and the occasional snake, it is easy to forget that we are in the middle of what may well be the greatest mass extinction in history. Yet a reality check indicates that we are not only in its midst, we are perpetrating it on a daily basis.

Some scientists estimate that extinction rates are 1,000 times higher than the "background" or naturally expected rate (Millennium Ecosystem Assessment [MEA], 2005a:3). Put bluntly, the richness of biodiversity that helped form the present biosphere has been vastly impoverished by human activity in the last century. Some of the cases of impoverishment have been high profile, galvanizing public outrage and Hollywood producers alike: the whales, buffalo, gorillas, pandas, and tigers. These "charismatic vertebrae" do receive a great deal of attention, which, in turn, sheds light on the overall issue of species impoverishment and the general decline of biodiversity. But most of the impoverishment we are witnessing takes place at a much less visible level, and it is more closely associated with habitat destruction, climate change, and invasive species than with mass slaughter or trophy hunting.

The Convention on Biological Diversity (CBD) and a plethora of other institutions are devoted to various aspects of biodiversity protection, but they face a steep uphill battle. Here is an understatement: the laudable, ambitious, yet vague goal to achieve a "significant reduction of the rate of biodiversity loss" by the year 2010 has not been met (CBD, 2006b:6). According to *Global Biodiversity Outlook 3*, the CBD's signature publication, there are "multiple indications of continuing decline" in all three of the main components of biodiversity: genes, species, and ecosystems.

- Amphibians face the greatest risk and coral species are deteriorating most rapidly in status. Nearly a quarter of plant species are estimated to be threatened with extinction.
- The abundance of vertebrate species, based on assessed populations, fell by nearly a third on average between 1970 and 2006, and continues to fall globally, with especially severe declines in the tropics and among freshwater species.
- Natural habitats in most parts of the world continue to decline ... although there has been significant progress in slowing the rate of loss for tropical forests and mangroves, in some regions. Freshwater wetlands, sea ice habitats, salt marshes, coral reefs, sea grass beds, and shellfish reefs are all showing serious declines.
- Extensive fragmentation and degradation of forests, rivers and other ecosystems have also led to loss of biodiversity and ecosystem services.
- Crop and livestock genetic diversity continues to decline in agricultural systems. (CBD, 2010a:9)

All this takes place within the context of rising concerns over climate change, fluctuating food and oil prices, and the further pollution of marine and land habitat. The uncertainty over total species populations makes long-term projections difficult, but there is no doubt about the central fact: we are witnessing, and indeed enabling, a catastrophe.

TABLE 3.1 Measuring and Estimating Biodiversity: More than Species Richness

LEVEL	BIODIVERSITY	IMPORTANCE OF VARIABILITY	IMPORTANCE OF QUANTITY AND DISTRIBUTION	EXAMPLE OF HUMAN USAGE
Genes	Variability among the building blocks of life that determine the uniqueness of individuals	Allows every individual the ability to adapt to variations in the environment and to other changes and challenges to different degrees	Provides "local resistance and resilience"	Bioengineering
Species	Variability among a unit of living organisms that can reproduce	Constitutes "the ultimate reservoir of adaptive variability, representing option values"	Enables "community and ecosystem interaction ... through the co-occurrence of species"	Food, clothing, shelter
Populations	Variability among populations that allows them to share environments	Different populations retain local adaptations, allowing them to interact and form dynamic communities	Enables "local provisioning and regulating services, food, fresh water"	Industrial fishing of schools of fish
Ecosystems	Variability among the dynamic complex of plant, animal, microbial, and other organism populations and communities that interact within their environment	Different ecosystems deliver diverse roles; for example, the plants and microorganism populations that form a wetland community purify and clean water	Delivers various ecological services: "the quality and quantity of service delivery depends on distribution and location"	Pollination, air and water purification: basically, ecosystem services

SOURCE: Modified from MEA, 2005a:81.

Biodiversity is the "term given to the variety of life on Earth, including plants, animals and micro-organisms, as well as the ecosystems of which they are a part ... including the genetic differences within species, the diversity of species and the variety of ecosystems" (CBD, 2005:iv). The greatest threat to biodiversity is habitat destruction, which has many linked causes: deforestation, desertification, intentional or natural flooding and fire, land conversion for agriculture or commercial development, the spread of pollution including oil and radiation, and the introduction (intended or not) of invasive alien species.

As many observers would suggest, however, it is perhaps best to view biodiversity as a quality-of-life issue. Ecosystems provide services that sustain the basic necessities of life: they offer food, shelter, and protection from natural disasters and diseases, and are the natural foundation of human cultures. The Millennium Ecosystem Assessment (MEA 2005a, 2005b, 2005c), a scientific global assessment carried out by over 1300 experts in 95 countries, summarizes the benefits of biodiversity, its losses, the drivers of change, and ways in which decision making needs to be ameliorated for the conservation and sustainable use of biodiversity. Specifically, the report (2005a: 1–2; known as the MEA for short) divides ecosystem services into four types: provision services (such as food, water, and timber), regulating services (such as wetland water filtration and forest air purification), cultural services (such as recreation and spiritual fulfillment), and supporting services (such as photosynthesis, nutrient cycling, and soil formation). Ecosystem services are constituents of human well-being and survival in numerous ways: they provide natural and personal security, the basic materials for a good life, healthy living, and good social relations.

The multi-scale assessment conducted for the MEA made these calculations:

> More land was converted to cropland in the 30 years after 1950
> than in the 150 years between 1700 and 1850. Between 1960
> and 2000, reservoir storage capacity quadrupled, and as a result
> the amount of water stored behind large dams is estimated
> to be three to six times the amount of water flowing through
> rivers at any one time. Some 35% of mangroves have been
> lost in the last two decades in countries where adequate data
> are available.... Already 20% of known coral reefs have been
> destroyed and another 20% degraded in the last several decades.
> (MEA, 2005c:2)

Of course, many would argue that this loss is what is often referred to as "the price of development" and not in itself a negative thing. But it is accompanied by the homogeneity associated with agricultural spread, whereby mono-cropping and poor livestock bioengineering diminishes biodiversity, increasing human dependence on reduced numbers of species for food security.[1] And if you are like me, you have genuine, if perhaps unanswered, questions about the ethical validity of our actions. Few would argue with our own right to survive as a species or even with the assertion that this struggle should take precedence over the survival of other species. But does our pursuit of wealth justify wiping out swaths of species that would otherwise continue along their own evolutionary paths? Most pointedly, perhaps, do we not have an obligation to future generations to leave them as rich a natural tapestry as possible, so they might both utilize it wisely and enjoy it profoundly? Though international arrangements are often cloaked in this type of language, I suspect most politicians and the vast majority of citizens would answer in the affirmative, regardless of their religious or political stripes, if they just gave this question some serious thought.

Rising Concerns: The Historical Context

"... the fundamental requirement for the conservation of biological diversity is the in-situ conservation of ecosystems and natural habitats and the maintenance and recovery of viable populations of species in their natural surroundings."

THE CONVENTION ON BIOLOGICAL DIVERSITY,
PREAMBLE (UNITED NATIONS, 1992)

The good news is that widespread recognition of these issues and the potent symbolism of species endangerment and extinction have galvanized significant political action and financial investment, including "a new suite of professional environmentalists and conservationists who venture to the ends of the earth in search of solutions" (Borgerhoff, Mulder, and Coppolillo, 2005:27). This is a relatively recent phenomenon; formal conservation efforts began slowly with the first generation (about 100 years ago) mainly concerned with the widespread disappearance of flora and fauna. Connecting it to human exploitation, these early conservationists sought to conserve nature through the creation of biotic reserves protected through legislation. Such reserves were treasured for the value of the species they contained, were often used as hunting grounds for the wealthy, and were arguably part of a broader colonial project that involved subjugating the locals or "natives" (Warner, 2006).

As discussed in Chapter 2, divergent approaches to protecting biodiversity emerged in the previous century, but the most lasting division is between the conservationist and preservationist. The former recognizes the value of conserving natural resources, provided they are ultimately serving the purpose of supplying humanity with sustenance; the latter would rather preserve natural space as is and declare certain species off limits (see Stoett, 2004):

> This tension between using and preserving natural resources is not novel; it reproduces a rift running deep throughout the history of environmental issues. For long before the degraded air, soils, seas or devastated forests attracted much more attention, extinguishing species had brought home the need for policies to protect the environment. It was also the issue that first brought states together to develop collective policies to protect rather than merely to exploit nature, modifying centuries of international relations driven by the appropriation of land and the exploitation of its resources. (Epstein, 2006:32)

Before the link between pollution and social justice was made a permanent concern, we began to worry over the fate of exhaustible mammal populations.

Growing recognition of the problem resulted in concrete action at the national level. It became popular to designate natural areas as "protected," though the exact level of protection afforded would vary considerably and local populations could be displaced by the designation. Still, by the year 2000, terrestrial and marine reserves covered 7.9 per cent and 0.5 per cent of the earth's land and sea area, respectively, with many of the protected areas in the biodiversity-rich tropical zones (Blamford et al., 2004:8).[2] As well, ecotourism took off as a small-scale, viable economic alternative to forestry and fishing, though global tourism remains a serious threat to local ecology. The public concern for whales, gorillas, panda bears, and other charismatic species kept the issue of wildlife protection on the national agenda in many countries where a budding environmental movement was slowly becoming "mainstreamed" in policy circles. It would be a vast overstatement to claim that the 1970s and 1980s led inexorably to a heightened universal concern with biodiversity itself, however. Indeed, it was not a commonly used term, nor were most environmental groups focused on this theme, one we consider so integral to sustainability today.

The less-radical conservationist ethos also prompted the development of international arrangements, based largely on the gradual (and often arrested) recognition that economic activities shared by two or more states were driving certain species to extinction, especially birds, fish, and marine mammals. These agreements included the 1882 North Sea Fisheries Convention and the 1885 Convention for the Uniform Regulation of Fishing in the Rhine (Birnie et al., 2009:594); the Convention for the Preservation of Animals, Birds, and Fish in Africa was signed by colonial powers in 1900. Most arrangements have involved regulating the utilization of natural resources and not the proscription of their use. However, one can clearly discern a preservationist streak in early American efforts. These were inspired by the works of Ralph Waldo Emerson, Henry David Thoreau, and Walt Whitman, who were themselves inspired by nature and "endowed it with moral and spiritual significance" (Epstein, 2006:35–36). By 1872, the lobbying of John Muir cumulated in the creation of the Yellowstone National Park in Wyoming, for example, and the pro-conservationist Sierra Club was created in 1892 and is one of the most influential NGOs in operation today.

International conservation efforts were institutionalized to a limited degree with the founding of the International Office for the Protection of Nature (IOPN) in 1934, following the adoption of the 1933 International Convention on the Preservation of Fauna and Flora in their Natural State. After the tumultuous events of World War II, the International Union for the Protection of Nature (IUPN) was founded with Swiss support in 1948. Its focus would evolve from a preservationist view of mammal protection to that of a full-fledged scientific body involving state and non-state actors with a conservationist view; in 1956, the IUPN became the International Union for the *Conservation* of Nature *and Natural Resources* (IUCN). The IUCN is better known as the World Conservation Union today, and, before the advent of the CBD, it was seen as the "lynchpin of the system" (Boardman, 1981). Its work remains vital. It is best described as a vast network of scientific and policy experts, with both state and non-state members; and it has commissions on law, policy, ecosystem management, endangered species, protected areas, and education (full disclosure: I belong to the last one). The IUCN maintains the famous Red List, which lists thousands of endangered species, from the Arabian oryx to the Bolivian chinchilla rat, the blue-throated macaw, and the candelabra tree.[3] The World Wildlife Fund emerged from a British initiative in 1961, led partly by famous wildlife painter and conservationist Sir Peter Scott, to work on funding issues related to the IUCN's agenda; it soon became an autonomous, transnational organization with considerable economic clout, now known as the World Wide Fund for Nature or the WWF. The creation of the UNEP in the 1970s and a myriad of other biodiversity-related institutions would culminate in the adoption of a trade-related agreement, CITES (described later in this chapter), and the CBD, which surfaced as the primary international arrangement for biodiversity protection by the mid-1990s.

There are several other important biodiversity-related conventions. The UNFCCC on climate change and the UNCCD on desertification, both covered in other chapters, are highly relevant. The Ramsar Convention is on wetland protection and though marshlands are still highly threatened on a global scale, the Ramsar Secretariat is generally appreciated for its effectiveness. The UNESCO World Heritage Convention has had some success in establishing protected areas, though it is primarily concerned with human artifacts; and UNESCO's Man and the Biosphere Programme was essential in developing a realistic model for area protection. The Bonn Convention on the Conservation of Migratory Species of Wild Animals of 1979 serves as a framework convention under which many states have signed agreements or a memorandum of understanding related to joint efforts to conserve endangered migratory species. The 1951 International Plant Protection Convention (IPPC) is aimed at protecting plants by preventing the introduction of pests, while the Codex Alimentarius Commission deals with trade in food, including sensitive products such as meat.

Put together, these arrangements reflect and generate considerable activity, commitment, and energy; coupled with organizations such as the IUCN, their role in the dispersal of scientific knowledge is quite beneficial. And there are many arrangements related to specific species as well, from whales (the International Whaling Commission was established in 1946) to polar bears (the International Agreement on the Conservation of Polar Bears was signed in 1973). Countless regional, national, and municipal organizations interact with governments on a daily basis to conserve biodiversity today; as environmental impact assessment (EIA) becomes a standard prefix to development projects, funding decisions, and even tourism destinations, there is more action on this portfolio than many of the others examined in this book. The heart of global governance efforts, however, remains the often-beleaguered CBD and its secretariat, located in Montreal—a short walk from the powerful St. Lawrence River, where the beautiful beluga whale is no longer considered doomed (though it remains highly vulnerable).

The Convention on Biological Diversity

The CBD was negotiated before the 1992 United Nations Conference on the Environment and Development (UNCED); it was signed by 157 countries at the time, and, by December 1993, the required number of countries had ratified it, bringing it into force. Contrary to some early predictions (Raustiala and Victor, 1996), its large number of signatories and its somewhat vague language have not left it ineffectual, though, as we shall see, there are certainly divergent opinions on just how effective this arrangement has proven (see LePrestre, 2002, for an authoritative overview).

The process leading to the CBD was not exactly uncharted diplomatic territory, but it was a change from the norm nonetheless. Because the most biodiverse regions are in the equatorial regions and southern hemisphere, southern states, which collectively hold roughly four-fifths of the world's biodiversity, held uncharacteristically efficacious bargaining power. Also, as the CBD addressed both social and economic issues from its onset, it became a unique convention with a crosscutting approach to conservation, a model later mirrored by the UN

Convention to Combat Desertification. The CBD has multiple agendas and implications for "intellectual property rights, trade, technology [transfer], human health, and culture" (McGraw, 2002:18). It emerged as a compromise document, marrying the demands of southern states for greater recognition of their legal jurisdiction over genetic resources with northern demands to advance the cause of protecting highly biodiverse regions, such as tropical forests. Because the UNCED was being held in Rio de Janeiro, its host country, Brazil, had the opportunity to move diplomatically toward reconciling environmental protection and social-economic development, as embodied in the "sustainable development" paradigm (CBD, 2004). On the other hand, the United States, which had originally wanted the CBD to be a largely science-based convention, did not agree with the southern advocacy for sustainable development and especially with the equitable sharing of genetic resources. At present (2012), the United States has yet to ratify the convention although it has signed it. Canadian Prime Minister Brian Mulroney was the first to sign the convention, and Canada lobbied hard to host the secretariat in Montreal. Japan played a major role leading up to the tenth CBD conference of the parties (COP 10) in Nagoya, but after the tumultuous events there in October 2011 much less can be expected.

The main "framework principals" of the CBD are the implementation of national strategy and action plans that are to be developed by each country that has ratified the convention, cooperation with other conventions and organizations through memorandums of understanding, and negotiation of future binding and nonbinding agreements. The complexity of the CBD, as well as its framework nature, is immediately evident: there are not only thematic work areas (such as agricultural biodiversity or marine biodiversity) but also crosscutting issues (such as the ecosystem approach and environmental impact assessment) and economic and legal matters (such as access and benefit sharing or technology transfer and cooperation). Although the CBD Secretariat is located in Montreal, it is under the management of the UNEP in Nairobi, Kenya, which can impede or slow down some processes. For example, further complicating the matter of chronic understaffing are the impediments and delays to the hiring process, which is set by UN procedures and overviewed by the UNEP in Nairobi. Some efforts to overcome this phenomenon were initiated by the charismatic former executive secretary of the CBD, Dr. Ahmed Djoghlaf, who has gained some leverage in hiring short-term contract people to fill immediate needs. Djoghlaf, an Algerian with previous experience at the GEF and UNEP, has done much to turn the secretariat into a more professional, expanded organization, though there are limits to what can be done with limited resources and so many competing or crosscutting agencies. A tireless diplomat, known for marathon work sessions during the CBD COPs, he has a flare for public relations. Whenever I took a senior class to the CBD Secretariat for a visit, I could be sure that, travel demands permitting, they would get to meet, greet, and listen to the executive secretary of a major international organization, which is quite remarkable. Brazilian Braulio Ferreira de Souza Dias replaced Djoghlaf in February 2012.

In Siebenhüner's analysis of the Secretariat of the Convention on Biological Diversity, he notes that as a "comparatively small convention secretariat formally under the auspices of UNEP, one would expect rather limited effects of this intergovernmental bureaucracy on the outside world" (Siebenhüner, 2007:260). Building on LePrestre's examination of the role of the secretariat, he concludes:

> The ... CBD Secretariat was able to generate external effects that can mainly be explained by three sets of factors: formal autonomy, internal management and leadership, and problem complexity. The larger picture shows modest effects that the Secretariat has on external stakeholders and other actors such as national governments, businesses and NGOs. This is, however, consistent with its limited formal autonomy. By contrast, the Secretariat itself seems to be well organised and leaders show effective management skills. Over time, the Secretariat has developed functioning practices in facilitating international negotiations and in promoting the objectives of the Convention. (Siebenhüner, 2007:271–272)

Many elements of the CBD are based on social commitments rooted in soft law. The main goal, as stated in Article 1 is "the conservation of biological diversity, the sustainable use of its components and the fair and equitable sharing of the benefits arising out of the utilization of genetic resources" (CBD, 2005:5). In the 2010 COP, the Strategic Plan for Biodiversity 2010–2020 aims to "take effective and urgent action to halt the loss of biodiversity in order to ensure that by 2020 ecosystems are resilient and continue to provide essential services, thereby securing the planet's variety of life, and contributing to human well-being, and poverty eradication" (COP 10 Decision X/2). The text of the convention establishes the formation of working groups and ad hoc committees as necessary for the implementation of the CBD. Expert groups usually "reflect a narrow range of expertise, comprising of mostly scientists, career diplomats and programme officers with little experience in developing education or communication programmes" (McGraw, 2002:24). The resultant texts can be vague and difficult to understand.[4]

The CBD's Cartagena Protocol on Biosafety deals with the international transfer of living modified organisms (LMOs). Burgiel (2002) notes that "the negotiation of the Cartagena Protocol on Biosafety (the Protocol) became a flashpoint for an evolving trade-environment debate, which has proliferated in both policy and academic circles" (p. 53). The protocol demands advanced and "informed" agreement from the importing country before the exchange of any LMOs, which includes GMOs such as seeds. Fears of importing transgenic species of seeds capable of harming local biodiversity drove southern states to seek this formal protocol so that they could not be punished for violating trade agreements (similar to the WTO's SPS agreement, discussed in Chapter 8).

Gupta and Falkner (2006) suggest the following in their assessment of the influence of the Cartagena Protocol in China, Mexico, and South Africa:

> Market and trade dynamics and/or a general overarching concern with technological leadership and international competitiveness are driving policy choices in the three countries. In a domestic environment largely supportive of the use of transgenic technology in agriculture, the Cartagena Protocol has, nonetheless, influenced policy debates and regulatory and institutional developments in these key countries. Their prominent role in agricultural biotechnology application makes them important reference points for how the Protocol might shape domestic policy choices. (P.49)

According to Gupta and Falkner (2006), the main *influences* of the protocol are "enhanced choices as an avenue of influence," "enhanced access to information as an avenue of influence," "enhanced capacity as an avenue of influence," "domestic discursive and institutional change" as a regime influence, and "harmonization versus regulatory diversity" as a regime influence (p. 49–51). In the fifth meeting of the parties (MOP 5) in Nagoya, Japan, the Nagoya–Kuala Lumpur Supplementary Protocol on Liability and Redress to the Cartagena Protocol on Biosafety was adopted and was open for signature until March 2012 (CBD, 2011a). The adopted text brought an end to six years of negotiation and set the international stage with rules and procedures on liability and redress for damages to biodiversity resulting from living modified organisms. MOP 5 also adopted a 10-year strategic plan for the implementation of the Cartagena Protocol and a program of work on public awareness, education, and participation for biosafety.

The Nagoya Protocol on Access to Genetic Resources and the Fair and Equitable Sharing of Benefits Arising from their Utilization to the Convention on Biological Diversity was adopted at COP 10 and was open for signature until 1 February 2012. At the time of closing there were 92 signatories. The negotiations of this protocol were heated from the beginning; in the nine meetings preceding COP 10, the CBD Working Group on Access and Benefit-Sharing (ABS) failed to prepare an adequate draft of the protocol. The adopted text—a compromise between the demands of developing and developed countries—was agreed upon in the "final minutes of the final plenary in the early hours of 30 October when, after 2 weeks of negotiations, the package was adopted, helped by the high-level segment attended by 122 environment and other ministers and five Heads of State" (Herkenrath and Harrison, 2011:1). The Nagoya Protocol establishes a framework for the sharing of benefits arising from the utilization of genetic resources in a fair and equitable way, including the transfer of relevant technologies, which directly aims to curb biopiracy and promote good sharing terms in future bioprospecting agreements.[5] Whether this framework will actually benefit indigenous peoples and forest dwellers remains to be seen, but it removes considerable uncertainty in this area and at least makes a strong rhetorical gesture toward the goals of advancing democratic and social equality.

The development of national biodiversity strategies and action plans (NBSAPs) is a requirement of the convention as set out in Article 6(a). Currently, the CBD has 173 countries that have submitted reports (CBD, 2011b). In a review of the NBSAPs, Herkenrath (2002:36) points out that implementation must be accompanied by a favorable policy environment at the national as well as international level, with strong support from executive decision makers; and NBSAPs need to be integrated with other national programs, such as poverty reduction strategies, national strategies for sustainable development, and plans to implement other conventions such as Ramsar and the UNCCD (see the next chapter). The reports are decidedly uneven in terms of both progress claimed and quality of presentation. But this limitation should not lead to a negative conclusion about the overall effectiveness of the CBD. It has managed to assert "the principle of sovereign rights over natural resources and that access to genetic resources is subject to prior informed consent," reflecting the precautionary principle, and to integrate "environmental impact assessment (EIA) for the first time in a global convention in a non-transboundary context" (Koester, 2002:101). Perhaps the greatest area of success for the CBD is an increase in land converted to protected areas, though just how equitably these areas are being managed, using the guidelines of the convention such as Article 8(j), remains under review.[6]

Though the IUCN and UNEP remain central, the CBD Secretariat is now widely recognized as the flagship institution in the global quest for the protection of biodiversity. The International Day on Biological Diversity (May 22) of every year was designated to raise awareness about biodiversity and its various issues. In the beginning, not many countries actually celebrated the international day for biodiversity; the website lists five examples of countries' activities for 2006 (CBD, 2006b). However, 2010 celebrations list 19 countries (CBD, 2010b). No doubt great strides have been made in terms of the cognitive evolution on biodiversity, though it must be admitted that encouraging people to take action to save non-cuddly creatures is a difficult feat. It is easier for the public's imagination to be caught by charismatic animals, such as dolphins and gorillas, than to facilitate connections with frogs or obscure fungi, for example (McGraw, 2002), or to achieve the even more important intellectual appreciation of ecosystem services and integrity. As always, advocacy for biodiversity becomes more difficult when people are preoccupied by the worries of a recession-prone global economy.

The democratic legitimacy of the convention has improved with the remarkable increase in participation of indigenous and nongovernmental groups, especially after the successful negotiations on the multiyear program of work on Article 8(j) at COP 10 in Nagoya in October of 2010. Furthermore, COP 10 has also strengthened the links between biodiversity and development agendas "with development agencies, banks and policy institutions adopting a declaration for the mainstreaming of the biodiversity agenda into development plans" (Herkenrath and Harrison, 2011:2). The Global Environment Facility (GEF) has been a crucial instrument in this regard, as has Japanese funding. Many of the national reports, such as national biodiversity strategies and action plans, were developed from GEF grants. Since 1991, the GEF has financed over 500 projects relating to biodiversity, with a combined value of $6.5 billion, focused on 290 "enabling activities" (CBD, 2006a:22).[7] More directly, COP 9 in Bonn, Germany, established the Life Web Initiative, a platform for the creation of financing partnerships that aim to conserve biodiversity, secure livelihoods, and address climate change through the implementation of the CBD Programme of Work on Protected Areas. The coordination office of the platform, primarily funded by Germany, matches donors and recipients for project implementation; with 50 matches by May 2011, this understaffed program was off to a good start.

The CBD's external effects remain limited to the promotion of international cooperation and the selective diffusion of knowledge, mainly among scientific audiences, but the complexity of the underlying problem and the secretariat's limited formal autonomy should impose realistic expectations on any evaluation of its impact as a knowledge broker and even more so as a capacity builder. However, new implementation challenges such as biosafety and access and benefit sharing are more closely linked to other issues of high relevance in national and international public and policy discourses, for example, global trade, north-south conflicts, and the modification of genetic resources. The increasing activities of the CBD Secretariat in these fields give rise to the expectation of greater effects as a knowledge broker. It is also vital to have an international organization that can integrate serious new concerns, such as colony collapse disorder, into its agenda.[8] The effects of the secretariat as capacity builder remain severely limited by its formal autonomy as detailed in its mandate, and increased funding and support will be vital in the future. And, though the CBD's focus on habitat protection is laudable, we must also look at specific species in terms of their own immediate survival as well. For this, the international arrangement discussed next is an important platform.

The Convention on International Trade in Endangered Species of Wild Flora and Fauna

I first attended a CITES COP in the year 2000, at UNEP headquarters near Nairobi, Kenya. It was a memorable week for me: my first time in endlessly fascinating Africa, with its proud cultures and ancient bastions of wildlife; the mix of beauty and anxiety that Nairobi imparts on the northern visitor; and (as the Canadian delegation was kind enough to permit it) an inside view of how countries operate at COPs, beyond the final communiqué and the short media bites. Greenpeace members inflated a whale on the front yard and then rubbed shoulders with traditionally dressed Norwegian dancers from "Friends of Whalers." Hours were spent debating the future of hawksbill turtles, Nile crocodiles, and hundreds of less illustrious species. People were there to study topics such as "elephant politics"; NGOs such as Operation Campfire were there to coalesce African positions; Cuba and others played their usual outlier roles; representatives from the ornamental plant and aquarium industries expressed their views. It was a virtual smorgasbord of global environmental governance actors and actions, and I emerged with a newfound appreciation for its complexity and, to be honest, caught up in the excitement of it all—even as the long evening sessions dragged on far past the time any sensible jetlagged person would be in bed after enjoying a classic red sub-Saharan sunset.

We've long known that our voracious appetite for things natural, from ivory to fur to exotic parrots, can be disastrous for those nonhuman species on the receiving end of this lust. CITES was first drafted as a resolution at a meeting of the IUCN as far back as 1963. The text of the convention was then agreed upon by 80 countries in Washington, DC, and the Convention on International Trade in Endangered Species of Wild Flora and Fauna came into force in 1975 with 175 member countries. It remains one of the most widely ratified international conventions today. It aims to limit the international trade of species and their parts to ensure that their survival is not threatened. International trade of flora and fauna is estimated to be worth billions of dollars and includes hundreds of millions of species and species parts, including food products, artistic ornaments, and traditional medicines (many of which are highly questionable in terms of their effectiveness). Although most traded species are not endangered, the CITES agreement aims to ensure sustainable trade so as to safeguard resources for the future; it is a conservationist instrument not a preservationist one, though many would argue it should become the latter or that it occasionally assumes a preservationist position for political purposes (see Stoett, 2007). Today, the agreement assigns varying degrees of protection to an astounding variety of species, roughly 5,000 animal and 28,000 plant species. While several species-specific conventions and regionally based organizations exist, CITES is the only true effort at global governance in this context.

Species listed in CITES that are traded across borders are subject to certain controls through a licensing system managed by member countries. Scientists, especially those linked to the IUCN Species Survival Programme, play a key role here. CITES species are listed in three appendices attached to the convention: Appendix I provides the highest degree of protection, effectively banning all trade in live or dead species or species' parts; Appendix II limits trade to exceptional circumstances (the vast majority of listed species are in fact plant species); Appendix III indicates a country has unilaterally declared a certain species endangered and is asking for help in limiting trade in that species. The variation in species is quite interesting; examples of species on Appendix I in late 2011 included sturgeons, various butterflies, the monkey-puzzle tree, orchids, the blue whale, the Tasmanian wolf, the volcano rabbit, zebras, rhinoceroses, falcons, cockatoos, and the red rain frog. Members vote on whether or not to put species on Appendix II or to move them from there to Appendix I. Obviously, the big debates involve deciding which species are placed on Appendix I, and, in some cases (e.g., blue fin tuna, hawksbill turtles, sharks, gray whales), these debates themselves generate the only serious press coverage of CITES COPs. Also, importantly, species can be downgraded when recovery is accelerated. A number of species that have received protection under Appendix I have been downgraded to Appendix II, the most notable example being certain African elephants. Resolution Conf. 7.9 lays out the terms of reference for downgrading these African elephant populations from Appendix I to II, terms which are based upon "the status of the elephant populations, the effectiveness of elephant conservation measures, and the degree of control of the movement of ivory within and through the [states]" (Wijnstekers, 2005).

The broad legal recognition the convention has received is demonstrated by the widespread establishment of what are at least semi-effective licensing systems for the export and import of specimens. Countries have the right to issue export permits for Appendix I and II species if they determine that the export of the species will not be detrimental to its survival, the specimen was not obtained in contravention of the laws of that state, and any living specimen will be appropriately prepared and shipped so as to minimize the risk of injury (Article III [2]). Member countries may also enter a "reservation" exempting themselves from the permit requirements for a particular species (Article XXIII). Japan did this with regard to sea turtles (the green, hawksbill, and olive ridley turtles, which are listed in Appendix I); it withdrew the reservation in 1994 (Stoett, 2002). Temporary liftings of the ban on ivory (or, more specifically, the trade in the African elephant) have been orchestrated, largely as a political compromise between, on one side, sub-Saharan and Asian states and, on the other, Kenya, the United States, and Europe. Under Article III, an Appendix I specimen can be granted an import permit if the following conditions are met: the import will be for purposes that are not detrimental to the survival of the species, the recipient of a living specimen is suitably equipped to house and care for it, and the specimen is not to be used for primarily commercial purposes. For certain species, obtaining permits can pose practical difficulties, as with the case of approved quotas for hunting trophies of Appendix 1 species in which the hunter is obligated to obtain an import permit before an export permit is issued. Export quotas are established (for live species as well as specimen parts) unilaterally by each state, but the COP can also set them.

Arguably, the biggest problem this arrangement faces on a daily basis is the need for vigilant enforcement by border and customs agents, though false and invalid permits are becoming so problematic that the 13th conference of the parties to CITES recognized the need for appropriate measures (Wijnstekers, 2005). Training customs agents to detect listed species is no easy matter: there are thousands of species listed, and most agents are focused on illegal migration, illicit drugs, and concealed weapons as their main concerns.[9] Similarly, there is widespread corruption related to this issue across the globe. Indeed, the lucrative, billion-dollar trade in endangered wildlife would not exist if not for the price commanded by rare species and the lure of cash payments upon delivery, which tempt potential poachers. Many conclude that the only real way to deal with the trade is to remove the monetary incentive to get involved in it, but that would require large-scale development projects quite out of the range of CITES (though discussions do occur within several working groups on the socioeconomic implications of trade bans, and NGOs have a considerable presence at CITES COPs; see Dickson, 2008; Mathur, 2009).

Effectiveness in stemming the trade in endangered species and their parts can only be facilitated by adequate reporting and monitoring mechanisms, which are notably insufficient for marine biodiversity.[10] Baker (2008) notes that the "government of Japan recently acknowledged systematic under-reporting of catches of southern bluefin tuna (*Thunnus maccoyii*) over the last 20 years" (p. 3985–86). During the Soviet Union era Russian scientists aboard factory whaling vessels falsified nearly 30 years of reports to the International Whaling Commission. The full impacts of illegal, unreported, or unregulated fishing are only now being investigated. Of course, no one ever said all governments should be trusted, all the time—certainly no self-respecting political scientist would teach his or her students such an absurdity. But, given the chronic shortage and funding for adequate border control, which exacerbates the potential for corruption (the classic "turning of the blind eye" in this case), and the temptation to underreport the harvesting of mammals or plant products, it is clear that a non-state entity might be the best bet for accurate reporting.

The organization TRAFFIC, a wildlife trade monitoring partnership between WWF and IUCN that works closely with CITES, conducts multidisciplinary research regarding the monitoring of trade in endangered species and its historical impact and contemporary social significance, as well as on the importance of sustainable trade for ecosystem services and human well-being. In an effort to narrow the informational gap, TRAFFIC provides assistance to the decision-making processes at CITES under the guidance of a memorandum of understanding for joint activities. Other organizations, such as the Environmental Defense Fund, have employed clandestine techniques to detect and expose trade in endangered species; and still others attempt to physically intervene to protect hunted marine mammals, such as the Greenpeace offshoot the Sea Shepherd Conservation Society. INTERPOL is involved in tracking the links between transnational organized crime and the trade as well. But it persists, in depressing fashion.

At the CITES COPs themselves, a polemical, "virtual battleground" or normative separation between preservationists (species are off limits) and conservationists (sustainable use advocates) has become standard. While preservationists typically favor "no-go" green zones and Appendix I species preservation, conservationists believe that species will only be used sustainably if they are viewed as valuable and that local human populations should be rewarded, not punished, for conserving endangered species. If that entails some measure of harvest and commerce in that species, so be it.[11] In the best known and controversial example, the inclusion of the African elephant in Appendix I was initially based on the need to control the ivory trade. The establishment of ivory export quotas based on "scientifically established management programs" (Wijnstekers, 2005) at the fifth COP and its refinement in the sixth was followed by the monitoring mechanism of MIKE (Monitoring the Illegal Killing of Elephants) and ETIS (Elephant Trade Information System) at the tenth meeting. Both systems track illegal elephant activities with the overall objective of obtaining more information to support decision making and, thus, reduce the polarity of opinions among countries. Local farmers in some areas, notably South Africa, are dealing with rising elephant populations that have expanded beyond protected areas, leaving them to contend with eaten harvests and destroyed crops. But the authority to keep animal populations in check remains at the national level. Although most countries continue to ban trade in ivory, some have set quotas in regards to trophy tusks, the hunting of which is an acceptable Western sport; South Africa, for instance, has set a quota of 300 tusks as trophies (from 150 animals) for 2011 but does not allow any other form of ivory exports (CITES, 2011a). Conservationists (Japan, Norway, Iceland, and others) are content to resume a sustainable trade in these great beasts, and they are especially determined to drop certain whale species from Appendix I; preservationists argue that some creatures, including bears, whales, gorillas, and elephants, are too special for us to kill and trade regardless of how endangered they have become and that accepting their further commodification would be a giant leap backward.

The system of soft global governance instigated by CITES highlights issues of legitimacy: the ability of "far-off institutions" to make decisions regarding the use or nonuse of natural resources at the local level and the "diplomatic context in which they operate" (Stoett, 2002:196; see also Dickson, 2008). The adoption of an Appendix I species listing can be culturally insensitive and can fail to address adequately the need for an appreciation of local issues, let alone offer compensation for those whose livelihoods are affected in the process (Mathur, 2009). The appendices are contentious given they are developed by (country) expert groups and CITES expert committees, with no specifications for the involvement of the people who use or are affected by these species. This lack of adaptive policy making is often viewed as either a serious gap in effective governance or, worse, a manifestation of cultural imperialism. Aboriginal groups, in particular, reject the idea that Eurocentric organizations should have any right to tell them what sustainable development entails. For many of these communities, the local control of resources is a vital aspect of physical health and cultural survival. So the endless quest for a balance between local and global imperatives continues, in stark form, through the CITES arrangement; similar questions habitually arise in the International Whaling Convention, the Convention on the Conservation of Migratory Species of Wild Animals, the International Plant Protection Convention, and other wildlife and flora conservation arrangements.

The future of CITES may very well depend on its ability to promote the conservation of species as a universal value across all countries, cultures, and ecosystems, without imposing a preservationist agenda or prioritizing charismatic megafauna over equally important plant, reptilian, and insect species. But, most important, it must reconcile its current soft cultural imperialist system with the dire need to reduce the great peril that hundreds of thousands of species face, and it must come to this reconciliation without threatening the survival of local peoples. Not a small order for an organization with a pathetic annual budget and limited legitimacy. But it has made great strides in policy implementation and in assisting the cognitive evolution of an emerging environmentalism that is sensitive to local conditions. We should not underestimate the impact of CITES, which even has a mechanism to enforce compliance through the justified use of trade sanctions (Reeve, 2006). But we must also acknowledge that it does not encompass the bigger question of habitat conservation. In the end, CITES remains a trade treaty, and that is never forgotten by its members states; its aim is to permit trade in wildlife and other species to continue, not to abolish it. But it is part of the bigger puzzle of global environmental governance, which is slowly coming together.

Redefining the Wealth

We are just beginning to witness the colossal extinction staring us in the face. Every life support system on earth is at stake, but biodiversity-rich tropical regions and marine environments are especially threatened. The need for a sustained response is obvious and well advanced by scientists and environmentalists alike, though we need more public education about the nasty details: invasive species, the complex intricacies of forest and marine area protection, the opportunity costs of leaving prime real estate alone, the violence sometimes necessary to ward off impoverished poachers, and the endless need for updated training of underpaid border guards. If Free Willy and other popular cultural icons, as well as zoos and ecotourism, can get people interested, they are certainly welcome. But we must move beyond this often casual and fleeting interest to more concrete measures. The CBD and CITES secretariats and COPs are physical manifestations of international arrangements that face adaptive governance challenges everyday, and, though neither has direct sway over national or local governments, they can certainly influence thinking at both those levels. Importantly, they have some capacity to integrate new challenges, such as the impact of climate change, into their agendas. They serve as meeting places for the exchange of ideas, science, and normative positions. And because they are, invariably, sites of controversy, they generate press. They have achieved broad (if not deep) legal effectiveness, have had a real but necessarily limited environmental impact, have certainly achieved cognitive success (including the generation of related controversies), and (especially in the case of the CBD) have pushed the discussion of democratic legitimacy and social justice even more firmly onto the global governance agenda.

Meaningful conservation will ultimately be a function of the successful integration of local and global communities, values, funding, and legal actions that will stop the tide of habitat destruction. Similarly, wildlife conservation will have to pay for itself to be successful; ecotourism and even trophy hunting must be part of the solution. Incentives need to be realistically developed to encourage people to save wildlife from overexploitation, to avoid excessive mono-cropping and pesticide use, to resist the urge to turn marshland into condo complexes. We will return to the topic of habitat preservation in subsequent chapters, beginning with the next, which focuses on deforestation and desertification. But there are indeed international arrangements in place—this chapter has barely touched on their breadth and depth—that, while incapable of affecting such change on their own, can serve as catalysts, information banks, and embryonic global regulatory structures.

The continued decline of biodiversity is frightening, shameful, and simply unnecessary for human survival. It is not a pretty picture, but that should not resign us to the impoverishment of earth's remarkable biodiversity. One thing we need to establish at the start is that we are not discussing a luxury item here: biodiversity is essential to human physical and psychological health. Yes, psychological: anyone doubting its fundamental importance should read Wilson's classic text on "biophilia" (Wilson, 1984), extolling our emotional needs for the natural world, and the more recent edited text by Chivian and Bernstein (2008), which demonstrates the link between our health and the earth's in beautiful detail. The recognition of this connection will not ensure effective collective action on these issues, but it is a good starting point. So is the establishment of an Intergovernmental Platform on Biodiversity and Ecosystem Services (IPBES) to help co-ordinate the science–policy interface at an international level. Although it would be ridiculous to even consider the idea that global governance can overcome human population and resource pressure, the level of public awareness about biodiversity has doubtlessly increased over the last two decades, thanks in part to the work of those engaging the issue at the global level. At the same time, as with all of our case studies, this is an area where solutions obviously demand a determined, multilevel adaptive governance approach, one that encourages active work on the threatened ground we seek to protect.

Notes

1. "Intensification of agricultural systems, coupled with specialization by plant breeders and the harmonizing effect of globalization, has led to a substantial reduction in the genetic diversity of domesticated plants and animals in agricultural systems" (MEA, 2005a:5). Of course, organic farming and ecologically sensitive animal husbandry can be used to reverse this trend and actually increase genetic diversity, as one of the reviewers of this book reminded me.

2. See the World Database on Protected Areas for updates: http://www.wdpa.org.

3. Species are listed by ascending categories of danger, ranging through these designations: "least concern," "near threatened," "vulnerable," "endangered," "critically endangered," "extinct in the wild" (extirpated), and, finally, "extinct"; see http://www.iucnredlist.org.

4. For example the "Kon voluntary guidelines for the conduct of cultural, environmental and social impact assessments regarding developments proposed to take place on, or which are likely to impact on, sacred sites and on lands and waters traditionally occupied or used by indigenous and local communities" is a 25-page guideline document aiming to "provide general advice on the incorporation of cultural, environmental, [...] and social considerations of indigenous and local communities into new or existing impact-assessment procedures" (CBD, 2005:1165). This example not only emphasizes the complexity and vagueness of the soft laws of the convention but also its combination of social and scientific issues. For more on social impact assessment, see Stabinsky (2000).

5. Biopiracy occurs when northern pharmaceutical companies take advantage of the dense biodiversity in southern states and extract marketable genetic compounds without compensating the local population. See Mulligan (1999) and Stoett and Mulligan (2000).

6. Article 8(j) states that the practices of indigenous and local communities relating to the conservation and sustainable use of biodiversity are to be respected, encouraged, and promoted for the benefits arising from their use (CBD, 2005;119). Ironically, countries may try to out-compete one another in the formation of larger and larger nature reserves, which suits the goals of the convention but is not a result of its objectives. For example, in 2006, the former Bush administration of the United States created the largest marine protected area in the world in Hawaii, as an effort to gain a more credible reputation in the environment and to compete against Australia's Great Barrier Reef reserve, even as it steadfastly refused to enter the CBD officially.

7. Many of these projects were developed when CBD Executive Secretary Ahmed Djoghlaf, described above, was the director and coordinator of UNEP Division of the GEF.

8. The rapid decline in bee populations, especially in North America, has startled the scientific community, and, because bees act as primary pollinators, this decline represents a serious threat to food security. Although viruses are the suspected cause, others, such as pesticide use and climate change, have been suggested. The Food and Agriculture Organization (FAO) and CBD have been working together on an International Initiative for the Conservation and Sustainable Use of Pollinators.

9. I can with authority state that some agents do take trade in species quite seriously; I learned this when returning to Canada from Costa Rica. Having declared I was transporting butterflies (they were mounted in a souvenir piece and not endangered!), I was sent to the long line of people marked for closer inspection, whereupon the butterflies were examined with the aid of a guidebook. As inconvenient as this was (but then air travel and inconvenience are synonymous today), I was relieved that the agents did take the time to investigate!

10. To make matters worse, "few of the over 5,000 animal species and none of the 28,000 plant species listed under CITES are marine" (Doukakis et al., 2009). This is a very problematic lacuna given our knowledge of the threats faced by marine mammals and plants (see Chapter 6).

11. I have personally visited trophy hunting ranges in Namibia and eastern Africa where the money generated by several hunts per month covers the costs of protecting thousands of mammals and birds, and it is hard to argue with such success—regardless of one's opinion of the "sport" of trophy hunting.

CHAPTER FOUR

Deforestation and Land Degradation

*"... the line between reversible and irreversible damage for
some resources is not always clear, and in some cases, such as
old-growth ecosystems and severely eroded land, restoration
may require hundreds or even thousands of years.... [Such]
damage must be regarded as irreversible within the
context of the present and near future generations."*

RAYMOND MIKESELL (1992:13)

I THOUGHT OF MIKESELL'S TERRIBLE WARNING AS I ENTERED MY FIRST
Costa Rican rainforest path. Walking in a rainforest is a surreal experience for
a Canadian accustomed to open space, even for one who has already had the
pleasure of long treks in the beautiful old-growth forests of Vancouver Island.
The intricacies of such overwhelming biodiversity, the dense canopy above and
carpet of insects below, the strangely refreshing humidity and mist, the sneak-
ing suspicion that everything has its place here: if all this conjures one word,
that word is irreplaceability. I had a similar experience looking at the astounding termite mounds popping out of the drylands of northern Namibia, where
one hardly expects such abundance of life. If Mikesell's worst fears are realized,
these places could be lost for hundreds of future generations. Some aspects

might persist, but in diminished, unrecognizable form. Already, the signs of ecological compromise are unavoidable, and it is highly questionable whether or not this loss is truly benefiting the human population.

The causal pathways of deforestation and desertification are complex, related to natural cycles (nitrogen, carbon, and hydrogen), wind, population pressure, overgrazing, mining, agriculture, development, and many other factors. The human cost is high: as land is degraded, we lose valuable food security potential; as forests are mowed down for timber or burned for short-term farming, we lose biodiversity and the carbon absorption offered by displaced vegetation (roughly half of the dry weight of a tree is stored carbon). Even seemingly impervious mountain ranges, such as the Andes, the Himalayas, and the Rockies (one of North America's true ecological gems) are threatened by the impact of climate change, encroaching human population, invasive alien species, and deforestation. Throw social conflict and military destruction in the mix, and you have a recipe for disaster. Indeed, there are few areas on earth, from arctic tundra to antarctic ice sheets, that are not threatened by human activities and political inaction. Severe cases include sand dunes in Syria, mountain slopes in Nepal and hillsides in Haiti, Australian deserts, and the deforested highlands of Laos.

Cumulatively, we've cut down at least half of the world's forest area. Yet forests and the soil beneath them absorb about a quarter of all carbon emissions; are home to roughly half the earth's insect, bird, and animal species; regulate water cycles; and provide livelihoods for roughly 400 million of the world's lowest income earners (Astill, 2010:4). Meanwhile, close to a fifth of the world's population faces the stress associated with living in dryland areas; and yet, through excessive soil use ("peak soil" has emerged as a serious term, referring to the phase after which soil is rendered virtually useless through overuse), deforestation, and policy neglect, we are turning more of the earth's terrestrial surface into drylands, and vulnerable drylands into outright desert. Assisted by climate change—which can extend their habitat range—invasive alien species lay havoc to agriculture, aquaculture, islands, and forests.[1] Put bluntly, we seem to have trouble controlling the voracious twin appetites of population growth and economic progress, and, overall, we continue to accelerate the devastation of invaluable ecosystem services, resources, and habitats. Global political history is omnipresent in the grand arc of environmental degradation, and resource extraction was a staple of colonial domination. Debates over "differentiated responsibilities" are omnipresent and the broader north-south conflict casts a very long shadow on all international diplomacy related to trees, soil, and mountains alike. But there is plenty of responsibility to go around, as the quest for capital accumulation and material production drives deforestation and desertification throughout the world today.

Yet there is certainly hope. Policies aimed at the conservation of forests and agricultural lands have taken root in most states. Brazil, which has sovereign jurisdiction over nearly a third of all earth's rainforest, has given protected status to 500,000 sq km of the Amazon. Awareness of the tragedy of tropical deforestation is quite high, though fewer people are fully aware of the equally great dangers of desertification. A relatively strong secretariat promotes efforts to avoid desertification, and, though no such global institution exists to promote forests or reforestation, a range of regulatory and voluntary measures are arguably beginning to have some impact. Linking deforestation to climate change, the international community has embarked on an ambitious, if also controversial, and potentially well-funded program designed to reward states for avoiding deforestation (this is known as REDD, or Reducing Emissions from Deforestation and Forest Degradation). The Ramsar Convention Secretariat has promoted sound policy on wetlands protection, with mixed results. Land-use decisions are generally made at the local level, but global governance structures, such as the WTO's promotion of open agricultural production, not only invite foreign investment (and thus either continue or introduce foreign decision making) but also direct production toward global markets and nitrogen-heavy, chemical farming. Can an architectural structure of incentives be advanced that encourages states to avoid further deforestation when possible and to protect soil from unnecessary erosion, while respecting local human rights and security?

This question is ultimately about our own habitat preservation, for the ecosystem services provided by soil, forests, and mountain ranges are, as Mikesell implies, irreplaceable, including freshwater, oxygen, food, fiber, timber, fuel, atmospheric and climate regulation, flood and storm protection, erosion prevention, and nutrient cycling. We often think of things only when something goes wrong, much as we are most grateful for good health when unhealthy; the perennial complaint of offensive linemen in professional football applies—announcers rarely call their names unless they have made a mistake and taken a team penalty. Yet we would be remiss not to mention the positive contributions of hundreds of groups and millions of individuals. A proactive stance toward protecting the capacity of nature to protect communities has been a mainstay of indigenous cultures, as well as the goal of the Chipko movement in India and of many other NGOs, such as Wangari Muta Maathai's Green Belt Movement in Africa. Creating protected areas is an increasingly popular option, especially in mountainous regions where there are fewer humans to worry about. But, ultimately, the preservationist dream of leaving large swaths of nature untouched is a thing of the past; as the ultimate invasive species, we have made that a phantasmal notion. Learning to live within the limits suggested by a realistic assessment of nature's ability to absorb our consumption habits is the only sensible option at this point.

People of a certain age—mine included—will likely recall the startling images of burning Amazon jungle featured on many newsmagazine covers in the weeks leading up to the UNCED in 1992, and sustained awareness of the dilemmas associated with deforestation has made it a top priority issue ever since that ultimately disappointing summit in Rio de Janeiro, Brazil. As was the case with much of the burning of the Amazon rainforest, deforestation is as often about clearing ground for planting new trees or agriculture, or for gaining access to valuable minerals or oil, as it is about actually harvesting timber. The problem is only accelerated by population and income growth and the suddenly urgent quest for biofuels, which, in an ugly spurt of irony, is contributing to deforestation in the name of green energy.[2] Palm oil plantations are in especially high demand in southern states such as Indonesia (the oil is used for cooking, cosmetics, and biofuel), while temperate boreal forest is chopped down to develop the tar sands oil projects in Canada. Forestry is less about lumber than it is about opportunity cost avoidance: if we don't use this land for something other than birds' nests and Saturday strolls, it is wasted. However, the global timber industry is still a driving force behind deforestation, and it remains an example of utilitarian peril.

Europe's monumental deforestation is an often under-recognized aspect of its early development, and the southern state representatives at international conferences have typically argued that they should not be denied the opportunity to use their natural resources to seek better lives, even if, in doing so, they are diminishing what is an incomparable level of biodiversity. Of course, northern firms are often keen to invest in and import the results of large-scale and clear-cut logging, and countries such as Canada, Japan, and the United States are no strangers to controversies over the forestry industry. In terms of global governance, however, forestry has become a north-south fixation. As David Humphreys writes in his excellent summary of international forest politics, in

> the negotiations that took place before the 1992 UNCED ... it was suggested by developed country governments and the UN FAO that a third convention should be agreed, a global forests convention, that would support the forest-related provisions of the biodiversity and climate change conventions and promote the conservation and sustainable management of forests. However, states failed even to commence negotiations for a convention, eventually agreeing only to a non-legally binding instrument commonly called the Forest Principles. (Humphreys, 2011:137)

Periodic efforts to institutionalize a forum for global discussions proved largely fruitless. The creation of a resourceless UN Forum on Forests in 2000 did not succeed in convincing southern states that a global convention is necessary or desirable, though a weak-willed "Non-Legally Binding Instrument on All Types of Forests" was signed in 2007. To find an extant arrangement—albeit one aimed at both conserving and exploiting forests—we must turn to what Humphreys (2011) asserts is the "first, and so far the only, international commodity organization with a conservation mandate" (p. 143); which, some would argue, is itself a contradiction in terms. Nonetheless, the International Tropical Timber Agreement (ITTA) offers several important lessons for global environmental governance and illustrates the north-south diplomatic context.

The International Tropical Timber Agreement

The ITTA was first ratified on April 1, 1985, following a long chain of diplomatic events beginning with discussions at the United Nations Conference on Trade and Development (UNCTAD) in 1966. There have been two successor agreements, one in 1994 and the other in 2006 (Poore, 2003:27). Previous to the ITTA's ratification, evidence suggests that low-income tropical timber exporter states were colluding to form a cartel that would resemble the oil-rich OPEC (Nagtzaam, 2009:253). As with coffee, tea, bauxite, and other commodities, this aspect of efforts to establish a "new international economic order" went, basically, nowhere at the time. But the idea of a bureau that could facilitate trade in tropical timber slowly gained momentum, culminating in a series of successive plenary sessions over a six-year period beginning in 1977 (Poore, 2003:32). This project was explicitly utilitarian: discussions had little to do with conservation but focused on facilitating the processing and export of timber in producer countries. This focus did change during the fourth round of plenary sessions, where four topics of immediate concern were decided, as Poore (2003) lists: "improved market intelligence; increased processing in producer countries; research and development; and reforestation and management" (p.33). Reforestation is not the same thing as avoiding deforestation, but it is surely a necessary step, if only to allow forestry to assume a less omnivorous approach toward harvesting timber and become a more sustainable industry.

After a failed start, it appeared an ITTA was unlikely in February of 1985. In March that year, several key states came together in London, including Japan, the United Kingdom, Malaysia, Indonesia, Brazil, and the Netherlands, at the invitation of the International Institute for Environment and Development (IIED; see Chase, 1993:757). They released a statement acknowledging that trade and environmental sustainability need not be mutually exclusive goals, and they gained the number of votes necessary to ratify the agreement, which went into force on April 1, 1985. The agreement created both the International Tropical Timber Council, which consisted of representatives of each state's respective forestry departments or other appointed proxies, and the International Tropical Timber Organization (ITTO). The arrangement recognizes separate groups (producers and consumers) and provides a complicated weighted voting procedure that rewards high levels of production (Brazil, Indonesia, and Malaysia are the leaders) and high levels of consumption (Johnson, 1985:42). As Nagtzaam (2009) observes, "The quicker a state destroys its forests, the more votes it gets, leading to the absurd situation where exploiting states carry disproportionate weight in council deliberations" (p. 271). At the same time, however, the ITTA is one of the first multilateral arrangements to incorporate the concept of sustainability (Chase, 1993:757) and to encourage reforestation. In response to this objective, the agreement also established the Committee on Reforestation and Forest Management, which would disseminate information and facilitate in the transfer of knowledge on best practices. Chase (1993) described the blending of commodities with environmental concerns as a new "hybrid-agreement" (p. 757).

Of course, this arrangement focuses only on tropical timber (ITTO, 1994). Exporting states initially sought to exclude temperate forest products. As time went by, however, a role reversal occurred, and, by the early 2000s, there had been much pressure to expand the scope of future arrangements with regard to territory and species (Flejzor, 2005:22). In the most recent 2006 ITTA update, coniferous species were added in addition to hardwoods, as well as "tropical timber" products, which Article 2.1 lists as including "logs, sawnwood, veneer sheets, and plywood" derived from any timber originating between the Tropic of Cancer and the Tropic of Capricorn. But we do not have a global instrument or an international secretariat regulating the global timber trade. Meanwhile, in Asia, deforestation is occurring at a quicker pace than it had been before the ITTO even existed. The 2009 ITTO report indicates that the production of tropical timber products has grown slightly between 2006 and 2008 with 136.7 and 143.7 cubic meters being processed respectively (ITTO, 2009:34).[3] Funding for reforestation-related projects dropped, and the ITTO itself has struggled with a deficit budget (ITTO, 2008). The global recession of 2009 certainly compounded this ongoing financial weakness.

If we are concerned with limiting global deforestation, the ITTA evinces structurally limited effectiveness because it encourages growth in the forestry sector, even if it seeks to protect the endangered species listed under CITES and to promote reforestation. Indeed, one can point to the ITTA as a classic case of the double-edged sword, which critics insist serves to legitimize a destructive industry, casting a veneer of corporate and state responsibility over a habitual pattern of unsustainable overexploitation. Nagtzaam (2009) argues that producer states "have constantly sought to dilute even the weak environmental constraints suggested by the ITTO" (p. 303–4). For example, in the early 1990s, Austria advanced national legislation that would require all imported timber products to be identified as one of the 50 types of acceptable timber originating from a sustainably managed forest (Poore, 2003:110). This proposal was quickly attacked by both producers and other consumers, and the status quo remained intact. But the ITTO also faces the undeniable reality of widespread corruption in this sector. In the large Indonesian forestry industry, for example, illicit logging has been historically prevalent (Poore, 2003:218–19). Clearly, when a "special relationship" between members of government and the logging industry exists, compliance reports to the ITTO based on self-appraisals mean very little. However, the inclusion of a call to combat illicit logging in the 2006 ITTA appears a step in the right direction.

Dauvergne and Lister (2011) argue that private global governance provides a possible answer to the limitations of state-centered programs and international agreements. Indeed, there are several arrangements, such as the United Nations Global Compact, ISO 14000, the Global Reporting Initiative, and the Forest Stewardship Council, which, in cooperation with NGOs and many northern multinational producers and manufacturers, allow market players to raise standards that can, in turn, be championed by leading multinational corporations. Within this (admittedly) rather optimistic context, the ITTO can play an instrumental role in the dissemination of information and in the concrete spread of education through what is known as the "Bali Fund." As of 2006, the ITTO had funded over 800 projects, with 80 per cent including some kind of educational component and community participation (Aoki, 2008:32). This initiative is hardly akin to promoting environmental justice, of course.

Indeed, the ITTA has limited democratic legitimacy. Its weighted voting structure encourages regional inequality: Brazil dominates the South American and Caribbean region with 157 votes (more than six times as many as the next vote-rich country, Peru), while Malaysia and Indonesia dominate Asia, with 105 and 131 votes respectively (ITTO, 2006:Annex A). Africa, by contrast, has no comparative leverage whatsoever. The current arrangement essentially provides a select few states with *de facto* veto powers. Consumer members are not immune to such power politics either: Japan, the European Union, and the United States, combined with the leading export countries, have created a powerful veto coalition that places conservation secondary to exploitation (Nagtzaam, 2009:273). The development of regional offices in Gabon, Africa and in Brasilia for Latin America and the Caribbean should encourage some decentralization (Ze Meka and Johnson 2008:263); head offices are in Yokohama, Japan. And though the 2006 ITTA stresses the importance of collaborating with indigenous peoples, it stops short of saying that they should be included in any kind of decision and policy making, instead focusing on inclusion in programs and strategies for capacity building. Similarly, NGOs do not have standing before the ITTC either, although some do have observer status. NGOs were actually quite influential in the earlier days of the ITTA and, in particular, in the development and inclusion of a sustainability component in the 1983 ITTA, but their collaborations tapered out by the mid-1990s (Grainger, 2005:343).[4] Humphreys (2004) concludes that "NGO influence has been slight on the ITTO. Confronting a powerful coalition of timber trade federations and timber producing states, NGOs have been unable to ensure that environmental considerations prevailed over timber exploitation" (p. 57).

It may be that the ITTA will remain a relatively ineffective vehicle for conservation. Perhaps a more promising venture will be the REDD project. REDD is an acronym for Reduced Emissions from Deforestation and Forest Degradation, and the initiative was launched recently to encourage states to avoid deforestation so as to maintain the carbon sink potential of standing forests; as Humphreys (2011) puts it, REDD entails the "incentivizing of conservation through valuing the carbon that is stored in forests in order to prevent deforestation" (p. 146). Reducing deforestation rates will be rewarded with carbon credits, which can be sold on global markets; this reward system is similar to the one established by the Clean Development Mechanism (CDM) discussed in the next chapter. The problems are that this type of scheme does not prevent further pollution or overconsumption by states willing to pay less industrialized states; there is, at present, no effective global carbon market; and financial benefits will generally bypass indigenous peoples and other groups, mostly "flowing to national treasuries rather than to communities" (Humphreys 2011:147). Indeed, it has been suggested that such arrangements are, in effect, a new form of "carbon colonialism," using southern labor and land to preserve pollution patterns in the north. According to Isaac Osuoka (2010),

> Examinations of particular carbon offset projects within the context of the CDM (Bohm and Dabhi, 2009) and the Reduce Emissions from Deforestation and Degradation program (REDD) ... have shown that in most cases emissions have increased, while corporations make extra profits by selling the offset credits that are obtained by presenting claims of "hypo-thetical" emissions reduction. (P. 168)

The ITTA and REDD are international arrangements that reflect widespread concern with the impact of deforestation on the global commons, but there is simply no stomach for taking the next step and declaring the word's forests part of those commons. Sovereignty over natural resources, often viewed as a victory over colonialism, precludes such thinking. The northern public's concern with the atmosphere and biodiversity, while laudable, does not seem to extend to a concrete willingness to even negotiate a serious convention on forestry that would include temperate forests. Meanwhile, southern states, and forest dwellers and indigenous people within those states, are understandably reluctant to part with sovereign jurisdiction over any part of their territory, much less with what is in many cases the most valuable part on the world market. As highly endangered species of trees are listed in CITES, they can be taken off the trade circuit, but this step alone will not stop their illicit exploitation, nor will it curb unsustainable, boom-and-bust forestry practices. More transparency, vigilance, fortitude, and financial commitment will be needed from all concerned parties to improve on this situation.

Desertification

The nasty twin sibling of deforestation is desertification, and the two are often strongly linked. An endless debate rages over whether the term should refer simply to the spread of deserts or whether we should take a more encompassing view that includes land degradation in general (Batterbury and Warren, 2001). I take the latter approach here; though the primary related international arrangement refers specifically to desertification, it clearly treats land degradation as the main problem—and sustainable development as the primary solution. Plans for solar power exports aside, no one would seriously discuss the sustainable development of deserts at the local level. They are, by definition, largely uninhabitable. Desertification was first conceptualized as an issue in need of global political attention following the severe drought and associated famine in the Sudano-Sahelian region of Africa between 1968 and 1974 (Geist, 2005; Mortimore, 1998; Thomas and Middleton, 1994). It would again become a popular theme after the Ethiopian famine of 1984. Blaming famines on nature has a long tradition, of course, but, as Amartya Sen (1981) and many others have tried to teach us, famine is a political disaster.

Nevertheless, a weak natural resource base will, without question, either trigger or exacerbate famine conditions. People living in drylands are especially vulnerable in this context: they have limited access to fertile soil and often rely on external production for basic food consumption. Drylands include "all terrestrial regions where the production of crops, forage, wood and other ecosystem services are limited by water [including] all lands where the climate is classified as dry subhumid, semiarid, arid or hyper-arid" (Adeel et al., 2008: Appendix A). Every continent, including Australia, contains inhabited drylands. Desertification refers to the processes whereby the quality of land is degraded to the point where it can no longer sustain agricultural activity. There is much we know, and more we do not know, about how, when, and why this occurs, but that it is occurring at historically unprecedented rates is undeniable. With rising human consumption rates and population levels, this escalation of desertification comes at a rather bad time! It is no surprise, then, that desertification became a major topic in international decision-making forums nor that, much like the ITTA discussed above, the north-south dynamic was the central animating context.

The United Nations Convention to Combat Desertification

Though UNESCO developed an arid zone program in 1952, it took serious African drought and famine in the late 1960s for an Inter-state Permanent Committee on Desertification in the Sahel to be created in 1973 among nine Sahelian countries. And it was not until 1977, following continuous drought and famine in dryland Africa, that the United Nations convened the United Nations Conference on Desertification (UNCOD) in Nairobi. The meeting's participants concluded that desertification was not just a natural process: the driving agents included farmers and local decisions that led to poor soil conservation efforts (Batterbury and Warren, 2001). The UNCOD adopted a nonbinding "Plan of Action to Combat Desertification" (PACD), which served as the defining framework for national and international action (and inaction) over the following 15 years under the UNEP, but it showed few concrete results. As long as desertification was effectively framed as a local problem, directing any serious global governance efforts its way was unlikely (UNEP, 2002). This configuration follows a broader northern pattern of eschewing admissions of complicity in the degenerative ecological and social processes of the decolonized world, or what many theorists have referred to as the periphery of the world economy, an increasingly untenable position.

Dejected by the failure of the PACD, many African countries garnered support from other G77 countries to push for an agreement during the June 1992 Earth Summit in Rio de Janeiro. Later in 1992, following extensive lobbying and deliberation among the parties, the UN General Assembly accepted the proposition for a desertification convention and simultaneously established the Intergovernmental Negotiating Committee for the Elaboration of a Convention to Combat Desertification (known, thankfully, as INCD). From 1993 to 1994, the INCD deliberated five times to prepare a text for the convention, which saw light in 1994 (see Batterbury and Warren, 2001; Corell, 1999; Martello, 2004; Najam, 2004). The UNCCD legally came into force when the 50th signatory ratified the agreement in December 1996. Several of the UNCCD articles are legally binding on contracting parties, and special mechanisms (annexes) are included for parts of the world where desertification has had area-specific impacts, including Africa, Latin America, the northern Mediterranean, and Asia. Yet, largely because of a shortage of funds to support the UNCCD in poor countries, as well as local indifference and even corruption, widespread implementation has been uneven at best (Batterbury and Warren, 2001).

Southern states had pushed hard for the UNCCD. In 1991, they adopted two key agreements, the Abidjan Declaration and the African Common Proposition on Environment and Development; yet northern states rejected a call for a UNCED-related convention as late as March 1992, not wanting to tie this seemingly local problem to a global agenda for sustainable development (Ortiz and Tang, 2005). Knowing that both sides had reached an impasse, the European Union extended its reach to the southern countries in return for their pledge of a forest convention (only a nonbinding declaration emerged on forestry, as mentioned previously). After the expected bickering among southern states, it was finally agreed that the severe situation in Africa (which contains over a third of the earth's drylands) warranted that the region emerge as the main focus of the convention. An agreement was finally reached on the establishment of a "global mechanism" for funding as well. The UNCCD defines desertification as "land degradation in arid, semi-arid and dry sub-humid areas resulting from various factors, including climatic variations and human activities" (UN, 1994, Article 1 of the UNCCD).

This precludes the more common perception of desertification as the natural expansion of wind-swept deserts. (Indeed the term "land degradation" may have been a better choice for the convention itself, but political forces from various angles conspired to use the less precise term instead.) The UNCCD stands alone in one important aspect: it was called for and designed for southern hemispheric states, labeled by many a "sustainable development treaty" instead of an international environmental agreement (Chasek, 1997:147).[5] As such, it maintains one fairly unique feature, and that is the surprisingly active, openly "pro-development" UNCCD Secretariat located in Bonn. As Steffen Bauer (2009) suggests, the secretariat "even boasts to have been influential on specific matters. This is a remarkable difference from most other international bureaucracies ... which generally maintain to scrupulously abide by the instructions of governments" (p. 310).

Bruyninckx (2004) notes that the participatory dimension of the UNCCD framework not only welcomes public input but, in fact, characterizes local knowledge as an invaluable asset in the fight against desertification. Moreover, the UNCCD has the inherent capacity to influence the way states behave by establishing legal obligations in national legislatures, demanding action plans and reports if affected countries wish to be on the receiving end of related funding. For example, the implementation of the UNCCD has had a behavior-changing impact on the governance structure in Burkina Faso, a land-locked West African nation that, despite poor soil conditions, relies extensively on agriculture, which constitutes roughly 85 per cent of its economic activity. Agriculture is practiced against a backdrop of a degrading environment, climate change impacts, steady annual population growth, and poor methods of cultivation, as well as the cause-effect cycle of major internal migration. In the mid-1980s and early 1990s, approximately 10 per cent of the total population was forced to relocate to areas with arable lands, yet the relocation itself triggered natural resource degradation. We return to the theme of environmental refugees later in this book, but we should note here that internal displacement is one of the gravest threats to human rights related to land degradation, and, exacerbated by internal conflicts, often results in what I have labeled "ecopolitical displacees" crossing borders and having fair claim to refugee status (Stoett, 1994b). This link between conflict, migration, and desertification gives international organizations such as the UN High Commissioner for Refugees and the International Organization for Migration, regional organizations such as the African Union, and weary national governments good cause to support the UNCCD program.

The UNCCD's website lists and describes several impressive success stories in Syria, China, India, Ethiopia, Turkey, Brazil, and Ecuador.[6] Although it is easy to exaggerate the impact of an international arrangement, it does appear that the UNCCD has played a major role encouraging states to develop "national action programmes" (NAPs) on desertification, an essential first step toward a national policy (in the previous chapter, we learned that the CBD makes a similar, though sometimes unfulfilled, demand from member states). Burkina Faso's national government adopted a NAP in the late 1990s, presenting two scenarios for the long term. The first takes a passive stance on governance, viewing continued desertification, migration, and lowered food security as inevitable (or a self-fulfilling prophecy). The second is far more optimistic. It calls for a trajectory of substantial planning programs in line with a larger national strategy aimed at bucking the trend of desertification, with the intent of making the decision-making process open to public input. The latter scenario demands extensive coordination between the national government and local interest groups, such as farmers. Bruyninckx (2005) thinks that the emergence of the NAP in Burkina Faso can be summarized as an historic achievement. Unlike past national development initiatives that have been mired in institutional disinterest and poor implementation, the NAP establishes a decentralized, participatory institutional arrangement and decision-making process coupled with legislative support for environmental interests. However, there is always room for improvement. Though the NAP appears to contain the required elements under the UNCCD, it lacks clear goals, and more could be done to improve transparency and debate within the Burkina Faso context, which involves a largely illiterate rural population. But its call for the decentralization of resource-related authority and for local participation is heartening.

Again, some progress against severe land degradation has been seen. China has had a favorable outcome in a five-decade program aimed at curtailing land degradation, which has expanded the socioeconomic benefits in many dryland areas (Stringer, 2008). On the heels of positive results, the Chinese govern ment adopted the UNCCD during the past decade. Of the few studies loosely addressing the connection between the UNCCD and its impact on the restoration of degraded land, the one by Su et al. (2007) has pointed to the effects of the Chinese effort in the Hexi Corridor in the northwest part of China, where shelterbelt integration, land framing, and shrub and forest regeneration correlate with the reduced wind erosion via increased surface stabilization. Similarly, Manu et al. (2000) found that, in a Sahelian watershed, the use of eroded soils and run-off water to grow herbaceous species to replace traditional fodder for livestock decreased pressure on and facilitated the recovery of poor soils.

Indeed, the UNCCD, unlike most other international arrangements, calls for the development of a decentralized, participatory approach toward its implementation, with the intent of empowering local populations and incorporating both traditional and scientific knowledge in the development of NAPs at the local level. There are over 900 civil society organizations accredited to the UNCCD today, and NGOs are eligible for funding to help them attend COPs and other functions. This not atypical of an international environmental arrangement, but the role of NGOs and of civil society seems especially pronounced at the UNCCD, perhaps because it is known as a pro-development forum and not a space that states and MNCs take great care to influence (these have focused primarily on agribusiness concerns such as pesticide regulations and GMO policy at the FAO and elsewhere). The UNCCD has permitted space for the discussion of gender, children's rights, workplace issues, and other crosscutting themes and concerns.[7] (To be fair, the ITTO discussed earlier in this chapter involves many partner organizations and implementing agencies with little direct links to corporate interests as well.)

Several concerns about the future of the UNCCD are easily discerned from the literature today. The most important, beyond the perpetual lack of funding only exacerbated by the global financial crisis of 2008–10, is that Article 1 of the convention states that land degradation is bound by specific climatic zones (Stringer, 2008). Despite widespread acceptance (the convention is in force in 194 states— every UN member), the convention targets Africa, where approximately 65 per cent of the land is at risk of desertification; yet many countries that do not meet the climatic zone criteria, such as Gabon, Slovenia, and Iceland, as well as the United States and Australia, face serious problems of degradation.[8] The emphasis on Africa was reasonable in the UNCCD's infancy, but the convention needs to grow without risking its vital pro-development character. If it is becoming in danger of losing its openly pro-development stance, it may be because of the logical, yet limiting, effort to link desertification too closely with climate change. Indeed, the UNCCD Secretariat has been publicly occupied with explaining the link between climate change and desertification; in nearly 98 per cent of the UNCCD Executive Secretary's recent speeches, climate change is mentioned (Conliffe, 2011).[9] No doubt, some UNCCD contracting parties put disproportionate emphasis on the link between desertification and climate change in the hope that such a linkage may lead to additional financing. Other members oppose that perspective and argue that climate change represents but one of many pressing threats to drylands; the prospect of developing access to a strong base of climate funds must be weighed against the fact that preventing desertification cannot be accomplished with a singular source of funding (Conliffe, 2011). Alternative sources of funding exist in the private sector and for the protection and promotion of ecosystem services and food security.

And the centrality of climate change raises another dilemma: to mitigate or adapt? We'll return to this theme in the next chapter, but suffice to say here that many advocates of strong climate change policy have, until fairly recently, treated serious discussions about adaptation as a sign of resignation and failure: we should be stopping the problem, not learning to live with it. Of course, those who have struggled to survive encroaching sand dunes or deforested peaked soil have not had to wrestle with the philosophical dimensions of this dilemma. By 2010, it appeared that contracting parties and other UNCCD actors had reached consensus on the need for adaptation measures. Indeed, for most northern member states, mitigation is a nonstarter if it entails a strict greenhouse gas reduction arrangement. Backtracking to 2009, we see that the UNCCD Secretariat had recognized that, in light of the emerging Copenhagen Accord (on climate change) and the new menu of desertification-adaptation linkages, the UN Framework Convention on Climate Change (UNFCCC) would place less interest on pursuing mitigation objectives. Tellingly, the UNCCD Secretariat reorganized its agenda to place desertification-adaptation linkages among its top priorities. Indeed, pursuing adaptation mirrors the UNCCD aim to better the livelihoods of those affected by land degradation, while the UNFCCC calls for adaptation measures in countries suffering the most from desertification. The actions of the UNCCD Secretariat combined with the shift in climate change ideology of member countries—as well as growing interest in requesting additional linkages with the UNFCCC—suggest a greater probability of achieving UNCCD governance goals, but these undertakings and changes also limit, to some degree, the legitimacy of the broader development agenda that has animated the UNCCD since Rio.

In 2003 the UNCCD adopted the Global Environment Facility (GEF) as an official financial mechanism (it also serves the CBD, the UNFCCC, and the Stockholm

Convention on Persistent Organic Pollutants in this capacity). Parties to the UNCCD could apply for GEF funding to develop national capacity. A more recent fund makes a small amount available for members wishing to align their NAPs with the latest UNCCD ten-year strategy. Bauer (2009) refers to this as a "paradigmatic shift ... [a] striking example for the power of discourse. Acknowledging that desertification is a global issue, at least politically ... reflects a major concession of donor countries vis-à-vis affected countries" (p. 299). Indeed, one might argue that the GEF's acceptance in 2002 of land degradation as a focal point is evidence of the cognitive effect of the UNCCD. The UN declaration of 2006 as the International Year of Deserts and Desertification also helped, and we are currently living in the UN-declared Decade for Deserts and the Fight against Desertification (2010–20). Yet recent estimates indicate that up to 12 million hectares of land become arid each year (Bodansky, 2010:260). With a growing world population, it is quite irrational to tolerate this situation; with increased levels of rainfall in many parts of the world, it seems bitterly unfair that climate change may well be responsible for increased aridity as well. The UNCCD offers one of the interlinked arrangements that can at least provide a normative—and necessarily contested—platform from which we can work to rectify this.

Taking Root

As a graduate student in the early 1990s, I helped organize a conference on environmental problems in Asia and had the pleasure of picking up a solitary, wrinkled, humble but revered Gandhi-like figure at the train station, Sunderlal Bahuguna. He was one of the leaders of the famous Chipko movement in India, which has been fighting to preserve Himalayan forests for decades; he's often been imprisoned as a result. In 1981, he embarked on a 5,000-kilometer march across the Himalayas. He was the stuff of legend, and I can still recall the moment he took the podium in front of an audience of largely blue-suited government officials and tired academics and exhorted us to chant "yes to life!" with him. The equation is a simple one, but quite accurate: forests provide life for people and are one of the most important sources of what we, in typical economistic terms have labeled *ecosystem services*. The Chipko movement began in the 1700s, when women sacrificed their lives to defend locally valued Khejri trees. Bahuguna and others—mostly courageous women who wanted to protect their natural heritage and livelihoods—revived the practice of peaceful resistance to logging in the early 1970s and, arguably, met with some success, including a 15-year ban on logging in the Himalayan region imposed by Indian Prime Minister Indira Gandhi. Though most of us chanted along with him, I am not sure most us—urban creatures of modern society—understood the fundamental message he was conveying; I am unsure now, 20 years later, that it is any better understood.

Of course, back then, we did not have the UNCCD, and the ITTO was in its infancy. Nor did many observers face the realization that climate change is a major, global issue affecting all others. Indeed, on both the deforestation and desertification issues, climate change has emerged as the main connecting theme. The next chapter, on the atmosphere, will address this linkage more closely. In this chapter, we focused on the more conventional reasons for threats to land: the overexploitation of soil (leading to peak soil), trade in agricultural or forest products, the use of slash-and-burn agriculture, and other causes, such as invasive alien species and human population pressure. We looked also at two international UN-based arrangements, neither of which has succeeded in its stated goals but both of which have certainly been influential. The ITTA has had limited success in conserving rare tropical timber and stands accused by many activists and forestry experts as an example of an international arrangement designed to facilitate an industry rather than conserve a natural resource, much like the original International Convention on the Regulation of Whaling initially served to conserve whalers, not cetaceans. It has achieved limited legal efficacy, limited environmental impact, some measure of cognitive success, and rather little democratic legitimacy. The UNCCD, on the other hand, has a much more explicit mandate to curb desertification and even contribute to the development process at the same time, but it is limited by its central focus on Africa. It has surprisingly widespread legal efficacy, but (understandably enough) has yet to achieve marked environmental impact, despite its demonstrable cognitive success and open pursuit of democratic legitimacy. In both cases the north-south divide is axiomatic and far from being a relic of the cold war past. But both the ITTA and the UNCCD have quite different points of focus and legal demands.

There is much room for improvement. Shockingly, as Humphreys (2011) reminds us, there is "no multilateral agreement to ban the trade in illegally logged timber" (p. 144); such an agreement, at least, should be a realizable goal. In fact, international criminal law has referred to illegal logging in the case, for example, of former Liberian dictator Charles Taylor, as a means to prop up bloody dictatorships. Yet, without a multilateral ban, "no state can impose a unilateral ban without falling foul of the WTO" (p. 144), though there has been some welcome European Union movement in this direction. A global forestry convention that includes temperate forests still seems a long way off, however; and although the REDD mechanism, if carefully applied, could yield some positive benefits in the future, it will lack democratic legitimacy if it serves to reinforce northern pollution rights while denying southerners access to resources or perpetuating unsustainable and harsh employment conditions. Ultimately, we must work— using a combination of local, national, and global incentives—to reduce demand for rare timber and, more generally, to reduce the willingness to engage in clear-cut harvesting everywhere. The year 2011 was indeed the UN International Year of Forests, an apt time to begin resolute work on this issue. The CBD LifeWeb Initiative described in the previous chapter and other efforts to ensure that conservation is rewarded are certainly steps in the right direction.

Meanwhile, land degradation is such a serious issue on a hungry planet that it is rather unbelievable how little attention it garners, and how we often fall prey to common misunderstandings and orthodoxies that do not appreciate the value of local knowledge. As the UNCED took place in 1992, it became apparent that global trade and climate patterns affected the aridity of land as much as local negligence or shortsighted thinking. Desertification was still viewed primarily as an African problem, and, indeed, African states were the main proponents of a convention at Rio; yet it was also evident that desertification (or land degradation) was becoming a first-order issue in the United States, Mexico, China, Brazil, Iceland, and elsewhere. There is little doubt that the UNCCD has resulted in increased knowledge about desertification, though it is not one of the better-known conventions. If a clear understanding of desertification is still rather murky in the public eye, this should hardly surprise us: the experts themselves often disagree on what it is, what causes it, and its true extent (see Bodansky, 2010:281n43).[10] And since land degradation is linked to agricultural demand and export production, we should bear in mind that all of this takes place within the context of ongoing debates over the benefits and costs of liberalizing trade in agriculture, as witnessed in the stalled Doha Round of WTO negotiations (see Williams, 2011 and Chapter 7).

So we have a regrettable combination of weak environmental governance at the international level and a problematic reliance on unsustainable practices, including an insatiable demand for palm oil in the south and tar sand oil in the north, leading to the destruction of forests and increased demand for agricultural products to feed a global food and fuel market; this causal chain gives rise to the evolution of "peak soil" conditions. And it is abundantly clear that, as with biodiversity, the causal and normative linkages between desertification and deforestation and other global ecopolitical concerns, such as environmental security, food security, conflict, migration, and health, are in need of enhanced international attention by actors in these arrangements, whether they are diplomats, activists, farmers, or scientists. An explicit recognition of these linkages and the need for urgent action are at the core of efforts to achieve the beleaguered Millennium Development Goals, which have been all but abandoned. Although it is unlikely that the related conventions will get any stronger in the near future, there has been much progress at the local level that we should not overlook. At the international level, the UNEP, CBD, FAO, IPPC, UNESCO, and other institutions and arrangements are deeply involved in the quest to conserve arable land and forests. They contribute also to the cognitive evolution of these needs. A recent bilateral arrangement between oil-rich Norway and forestry giant Indonesia will freeze clearance permits on 64 million hectares of forest and peat land.[11] Nevertheless, we need to strengthen extant arrangements—give them some regulatory teeth and more funding for equality issues—and to limit the seemingly inexorable appetite for the commoditization of nature that continues to scar the land on which we are fortunate to walk with the likes of Wangari Muta Maathai and Sunderlal Bahuguna. Ultimately, we need to take our roots seriously—not just our historical roots but the ones in the soils of the earth that nourish the vegetation sustaining life on this challenged planet.

Notes

1. Canada lost approximately 5.2 per cent of tree cover between 2000 and 2005, "partly because of a plague of bark-beetles in its temperate and boreal zones, a record number of which have been surviving the recent mild winters. By 2009, they had devastated over 16m hectares of Canadian pine forest" (Astill, 2010:5).

2. On biofuels, journalist George Monbiot (2008) sums it up nicely: "The reason governments are so enthusiastic about biofuels is that they don't upset drivers. They appear to reduce the amount of carbon from our cars, without requiring new taxes. It's an illusion sustained by the fact that only the emissions produced at home count towards our national total. The forest clearance in Malaysia doesn't increase our official impact by a gram" (p. 41).

3. Readers should bear in mind that commodity export figures are always less than perfectly accurate, as they are subject to both accidental and deliberate under- and overreporting. Further, the global recession of 2008 and subsequent market turbulence may have resulted in what was essentially a temporary dip in consumption as housing markets tumbled in the United States, Japan, and elsewhere.

4. Generally, the kinds of environmental NGOs that attended ITTC meetings were conservation oriented, as opposed to those that were seen as more activist and extreme, such as Greenpeace. Common collaborators in the 1980s were the World Wildlife Fund (WWF), Friend of the Earth (FoE), and, especially, the International Institute for Environment and Development, which performed many independent reviews and assessments for the ITTO (see Poore, 2003).

5. As Bauer (2009) puts it, "Many stakeholders of [the UNCCD] do not necessarily view the fight against desertification as an environmental issue or conceive of the convention as an environmental treaty. Rather, they consider it a development convention and an instrument to fight poverty in the developing world" (p. 293).

6. The UNCCD website (http://www.unccd.int/main.php) was accessed May 16, 2011.

7. "The recommendations and guidance emerging from the International Year on Deserts and Desertification events target not only the problem of desertification as a form of environmental degradation, but also as a broader, cross-cutting development issue in desert regions. For example, 'women' and 'young people' were highlighted as key stakeholder groups that should be encouraged to become more involved in environmental decision-making and activities to combat desertification" (Stringer, 2008:2070).

8. Stringer refers to the UNCCD as boasting "the most universal membership any comparable international environmental agreement has achieved to date. However, despite such absolute endorsement, the UNCCD and moreover, the desertification issue, remains an important site of tension and north-south cleavage" (Stringer, 2008:2067).

9. Of course, this number is probably typical of most speeches related to international environmental issues today, which raises the broader question of whether climate change has, in effect, crowded out other issues worthy of collective concern. We will return to this question in later chapters.

10. As Bauer (2009) assures us, however, "the achievement of wide-spread scientific consensus on the phenomenon has been fairly straightforward—at least, it has been agreed for several decades that desertification describes a process of severe land degradation that is primarily anthropogenic and that expands into regions where it would climatically not be expected" (p. 304).

11. This is in exchange for one billion dollars of development aid. However, it seems unlikely that OPEC countries will follow suit, and the palm oil industry has largely escaped efforts to halt its tremendous growth—a theme we will return to in our discussion of energy governance. See Koswanage and Taylor (2011).

CHAPTER FIVE

Air Pollution
and Climate Change

"We are now realizing that we may be on the threshold of changes
to our climate, changes which are so extensive and immediate
that they will profoundly affect the life of the human race."

GRO HARLEM BRUNDTLAND, AT THE TORONTO

CONFERENCE, 1988 (QUOTED IN CAMPBELL, 2008:3)

IT IS HARD TO BELIEVE THAT 25 YEARS HAVE PASSED SINCE GRO HARLEM Brundtland, former prime minister of Norway, director-general of the World Health Organization, and lead author of the seminal *Report of the World Commission on Environment and Development* (Brundtland et al., 1987), made this statement.[1] Much later, Canada's most (deservedly) famous environmental scientist and media pundit, David Suzuki, would add these words: "in the late '80s when I began to take climate change seriously, we referred to global warming as a 'slow motion catastrophe,' one we expected to kick in perhaps generations later. Instead, the signs of change have accelerated alarmingly" (quoted in Brown, 2007:48). Such is the impact of the age of the Anthropocene.

Air pollution is a major problem wherever heavy industry, mechanized transportation, and energy production occur, and, as we will see in this chapter, strong international efforts have resulted. Yet global air pollution policy is, in essence, a tale of two efforts, and the second—the need to combat global warming—has been much less successful. Climate change is caused by atmospheric pollution from heavily industrialized regions, clogged highways, fossil fuel power plants, and many other sources, and even the Environmental Protection Agency in the United States has taken the conceptual step of defining excessive carbon dioxide as a pollutant. International environmental diplomacy has struggled to find relief for the local communities most heavily affected, though there have been many efforts in this regard. This chapter will examine some of the causes of atmospheric pollution and global governance efforts to manage it. Included is a section on the ozone layer and on the relative success story of the Montreal Protocol. Today, many people would accept the claim that, short of nuclear Armageddon, climate change is the most serious threat faced by humankind and the planet itself. For the purpose of this chapter, however, I will treat it as another form of atmospheric pollution, albeit one that results from the continued spread of many others.

Nothing is as physically immediate to us as individuals as the air we breathe. In the Canadian province of Ontario alone, the Ontario Medical Association estimated that 1,900 deaths, 13,000 emergency department visits, 9,800 hospital admissions, and 46 million illnesses were due to air pollution in the year 2000 (Molina and Molina, 2004:649–50); in 2006, the WHO estimated that air pollution in earth's cities caused two million "premature deaths" each year (Environment News Service, 2006). Yet few things could be further from most people's daily lives than multilateral atmospheric pollution and climate change talks. In between, there is a world of regulation, budding regulatory designs, heavily politicized scientific debates, and energy needs. This chapter will introduce atmospheric pollution and climate change as problems inherently in need of multilevel governance, and it will consider international agreements that have had some success in preventing a worse situation but that have clearly failed at the broader task of mitigating climate change. The cognitive issues discussed in other chapters certainly apply here because it is so difficult to frame a climate change agreement that manages to take into account sharply differing viewpoints of climate justice. But we can look with some optimism at treaties and networks engaged in the task of limiting atmospheric pollution in Europe, North America, and elsewhere.

Although global warming is a function of atmospheric pollution due to excessive release of carbon, methane, and other greenhouse gases, it is common to discuss climate change separately from the other forms of atmospheric pollution, such as persistent organic pollutants, and international law has largely maintained this separation. I will begin, therefore, with a discussion of air pollution before discussing climate change, but bear in mind these are all problems of the commons, demanding collective action. Though the level of complexity differs, the essential fact remains: what we put in the air does not disappear into a void—neither an ecological nor a political one.

Atmospheric Pollution

Atmospheric pollution is a broad term defined by Environment Canada as "any chemical, physical, or biological agent that modifies the natural characteristics of the atmosphere" (Environment Canada, 2010a). More tangibly, it refers to the heightened presence in the air of solid particulate matter, gases, metals and chemicals harmful to both human health and the environment, and attributed to human activities. Atmospheric pollutants can be grouped into four main categories: criteria air contaminants, heavy metals, persistent organic pollutants, and toxics. Criteria air contaminants are what cause acid rain and smog, and they comprise compounds such as sulfur dioxide (SO_2), nitrogen oxides (NO), ground-level ozone (O_3), and volatile organic compounds (Environment Canada, 2011). They are produced by various means, notably the burning of fossil fuels. Heavy metals include such elements as lead and mercury, which, while needed by our bodies in trace amounts, can be poisonous in larger concentrations. They can bio-accumulate in body tissues, enter the water and food supply, and be transported by air. Persistent organic pollutants (or POPs) are chemical substances that persist for long durations in the environment. They, too, can enter the food supply and bioaccumulate in body tissues, and they pose severe risks to human health and ecosystems, even in minimal concentrations. They are known, as well, to travel far from their sources and across international boundaries, so they are frequently found in places where they have never been used or produced; they are the subject of international negotiations and a major global arrangement, the Stockholm Convention (Bilcke, 2002). The primary substances of concern in this category are pesticides such as DDT, industrial chemicals such as polychlorinated biphenyls or PCBs, and by-products of various industrial processes such as dioxins and furans (Environment Canada, 2011). The discovery of PCBs in the breast milk of Inuit women in northern Canada in the 1980s was a major moment for the public acknowledgment of these problems (see Dewailly et al., 1989). Toxic pollutants, lastly, are a broad category, comprising some substances already noted in other categories here (such as POPs and mercury), but also other toxic substances such as asbestos.

I once taught at Simon Fraser University in Burnaby, which sits on an elevated mini-mountain looking over beautiful Vancouver. This afforded a wonderful view but, by late afternoon, it was a frightening one, as the city—buffeted by mountains and seawater—was invariably enveloped in thick smog, looking more like a bowl of nasty pea soup than a modern metropolis. Anyone who has read Dickens has imagined the smog-choked cities of the industrial revolution, with their "satanic mills," dark skies, and dirty faces. Today, countries such as China, India, and Brazil are industrializing at a breakneck pace and massive populations are flooding into the cities in search of economic and educational opportunities. Indeed, few images speak more potently to this than the now familiar sight, delivered courtesy of media coverage of the summer 2008 Olympics, of Beijing residents donning facemasks on their daily commute to work or school. In Cairo, another of the world's most polluted cities, elevated lead content alone was responsible for between 15,000 and 20,000 deaths a year according to a 1996 report commissioned by the Egyptian government, the pollution being attributed mostly to motor vehicle emissions (Molina and Molina, 2004:662). In Mexico City, it is estimated that a mere 10 per cent cut in ambient particulate matter could save as many as 3,000 lives and prevent 10,000 new cases of chronic bronchitis a year (Mckinley et al., 2005:1954). In many regions, suspended dust clouds follow in the wake of poorly maintained and congested roads. I recall watching a car drive on a road near Dar el Salaam in Tanzania and thinking a small tornado was following it! Meanwhile, the global consumption of solid coal, perhaps the dirtiest of fossil fuels, is only increasing as economic development continues to rely on this antiquated source of energy (Chow et al., 2004). Policy makers in different cities around the world, especially in the largest cities where the crisis is most acute, have begun to take the issue of air pollution seriously and, in particular, to attack the underlying source of much air pollution: the automobile. In London, for instance, the municipal government established a cordon around much of the inner city known as the congestion charge, and drivers must pay for access to the inner core. Intergovernmental cooperation in Mexico City, Bus Rapid Transit in Santiago, switching to natural gas in Delhi, public rentals of bicycles in Montreal, or stringent fuel efficiency standards in Beijing: the cities of the world are taking up the challenge. But international initiatives are also vital.

Air quality is, after all, a transboundary issue: borders might be able to stop migration, but they are useless against atmospheric pollution. Canada and the United States have a history of cooperation on air quality, including the Canada–United States Air Quality Agreement signed in 1991 primarily to address the issue of transboundary air pollution. More recently, in 2003, the governments of the United States and Canada announced three joint projects under the Canada–United States Border Air Quality Strategy, all of which provide interesting and innovative lessons on the importance and promise of transboundary cooperation on matters of air quality (and the environment more generally). Jointly piloted by Environment Canada and the United States Environmental Protection Agency (EPA) and targeting specific geographical regions (or "airsheds"), the projects sought to include a comprehensive array of key stakeholders, from provincial and state environmental agencies on both sides of the border to municipal environmental agencies in the cities within the defined area, as well as the International Joint Commission. Most crucially, a joint steering committee was established to provide oversight and leadership to the numerous partners and to organize the work and implement the suggestions of various workshops (Barton, 2008). However, this regional approach within a neighborly context is insufficient for dealing with the truly global phenomenon of atmospheric pollution, which demands a multilateral arrangement that can permit some sacrifices of sovereignty.

The Convention on Long-Range Transboundary Air Pollution (CLRTAP)

The CLRTAP is a regional treaty signed in 1979 by members of the United Nations Economic Commission for Europe (UNECE), which includes both Canada and the United States as well; through its various protocols, the CLRTAP targets all major air pollutants, from sulfur dioxide and nitrogen oxide to heavy metals and POPs (see Sliggers and Kakebeeke, 2004). The 2001 Stockholm Convention on Persistent Organic Pollutants, as the name implies, is more limited in scope, though it is also broader in geographical reach, encompassing a wider array of member countries spanning all continents.

The problem of atmospheric pollution began to appear on the radar of Scandinavian researchers as early as the late 1960s, when scientists began to note a marked decline in local fish populations. With the death of the fish soon linked to the growing acidification of the lakes, it wasn't long before acid rain was identified as the culprit (Kim, 2007:448) and researchers hypothesized a link between acid rain over Scandinavian lakes and sulfur dioxide emissions emanating from continental Europe. Although it may seem self-evident today, the idea of transboundary air pollution remained deeply controversial at the beginning of the 1970s, to both scientists and policy makers alike (Lidskog and Sundqvist, 2004:212). In North America, the acid rain debate became increasingly heated following similar discoveries by Canadian scientists that linked both acidified lakes and damaged forest areas in Canada—in particular on the sensitive Canadian Shield—to rising sulfur dioxide emissions coming from the northeastern United States.

In 1972, the United Nations Conference on the Human Environment in Stockholm, Sweden, furthered the transformation of the acid rain issue from an "esoteric research discipline" into a "household phrase" (Lidskog and Sundqvist, 2004:213). Two years later, a ministerial-level meeting was held in Geneva, Switzerland, culminating in the Convention on Long-Range Transboundary

Air Pollution (CLRTAP), signed by the European Community (EC) and 34 governments of the UNECE. It was the first ever legally binding instrument to address problems of air pollution on an international regional basis. The convention entered into force in 1983 and today encompasses 51 member states and eight separate protocols targeting a variety of specific measures, the most recent adopted in 1999 (ECE, 2010).

In the 1980s, Canadian scientists also began discovering troubling levels of contaminants in the arctic ecosystems of the Canadian north. The Canadian government responded with the creation of the Northern Contaminants Program in 1991 (Government of Canada, 2006:24). And soon after, at a meeting of the Arctic Council (see Chapter 6) held in Reykjavik in 1994, Canada pushed the issue of toxic chemicals onto the global agenda. In the 1995 Washington Conference to Adopt the Global Programme of Action for the Protection of the Marine Environment from Land-Based Activities, the notion of developing a global tool to combat toxic chemicals in the environment was initially broached, and discussions began within the CLRTAP to develop an instrument to control POPs, the fruits of which emerged in 1998 with the signing of the convention's Protocol on Persistent Organic Pollutants. In June of that year, negotiations commenced in Montreal under the auspices of the UNEP. The aim was to replace the regional CLRTAP, which was confined to Europe and North America, with a truly global treaty to target POPs (Environment Canada, 2010b). Two and a half years later, the 2001 Stockholm Convention was signed by 91 parties across all continents; it entered into force in 2004. Today, the convention counts 170 parties.

Chronology of Major Events on Air Pollution, sans Climate Change

1968	Scandinavian researchers discover decline in local fish populations is linked to acidification of lakes caused by rising sulfur dioxide emissions from continental Europe.
1972	United Nations Conference on the Human Environment is held in Stockholm, Sweden.
1972–77	Several studies add further evidence to the theory of the transboundary deposition of air pollutants.
1979	A high-level meeting on the protection of the environment is held in Geneva, Switzerland to address rising concerns pertaining to air pollution. The meeting, which is convened within the framework of the UN Economic Commission

	for Europe, results in the adoption of the CLRTAP, signed by 34 governments of the UNECE and the European Community (EC).
1983	The CLRTAP enters into force.
1985	CLRTAP: The Protocol on the Reduction of Sulphur Emissions or Their Transboundary Fluxes by at Least 30 Per Cent is adopted.
1988	CLRTAP: The Protocol Concerning the Control of Emissions of Nitrogen Oxides or their Transboundary Fluxes is adopted.
1991	CLRTAP: The Protocol Concerning the Control of Emissions of Volatile Organic Compounds or their Transboundary Fluxes is adopted.
1992	Agenda 21 is adopted at the United Nations Conference on Environment and Development (UNCED), also known as the Earth Summit, which was held in Rio de Janeiro, Brazil. The statement calls for action to curb the use of and exposure to toxic chemicals.
1994	CLRTAP: The Oslo Protocol on Further Reductions of Sulphur Emissions is adopted.
1994	Reykjavik meeting of the Arctic Council. Canada plays a pivotal role in getting POPs on the agenda in the run-up to the Washington Conference (described below).
1995	Washington Conference to Adopt the Global Programme of Action for the Protection of the Marine Environment from Land-Based Activities, wherein the adoption of a global instrument to curb persistent organic pollutants (POPs) is broached.
1998	CLRTAP: The Protocol on Heavy Metals is adopted.
1998	CLRTAP: The Protocol on Persistent Organic Pollutants is signed, effectively laying the groundwork for the future Stockholm Convention.
1998–2000	Intergovernmental negotiations take place on a new global treaty targeting POPs.
1999	The Gothenburg Protocol to Abate Acidification, Eutrophication and Ground-Level Ozone is adopted.
21 May, 2001	91 countries sign the Stockholm Convention on Persistent Organic Pollutants.
2004	The Stockholm Convention enters into force (US EPA, 2011).
2010	The number of parties to the Stockholm Convention sits at 170. Parties to the CLRTAP number 51 (ECE, 2010).

Progress on achieving the targets listed in the protocols has been quite good, and the CLRTAP is generally considered a success, with all parties together reducing overall emissions by over 50 per cent (Lidskog and Sundqvist, 2004:211). Sulfur emissions, targeted for a 30 per cent cut under the convention's first protocol in 1985, have dropped by 60 per cent in Europe from 1980 levels (Bull, Johansson, and Krzyzanowski, 2008), and, by 2004, at least 20 of the 25 parties to the subsequent 1994 Oslo Protocol on Further Reductions of Sulfur Emissions had reportedly met their targets as well (ECE, 2007:29). Pursuant to the 1998 Protocol on Persistent Organic Pollutants, 15 of the 28 parties to the protocol had ceased all or virtually all production and use of pollutants listed in annexes I and II (targeted for elimination and restriction, respectively), and overall emissions within the treaty area decreased 18 per cent compared to 1990 levels (ECE, 2007:9). There is a need to ensure greater compliance, while certain issues, such as particulate matter, require revisions to extant protocols or, even, new ones (Bull et al., 2008:55).

An interesting component of the umbrella CLRTAP regime, and a deep nod to the reality of sovereignty in environmental diplomacy, is the way in which the protocols are developed apart from the core convention, with member states freely selecting which protocols they prefer to join. As Björkbom (1999) has remarked, "each Protocol is thus a separate international agreement, with various groups of countries as parties or signatories," and none of the protocols boasts complete membership by all parties to the convention (p. 390). This innate flexibility may be seen as a strength or a weakness. It encourages inclusiveness (at least within the UNECE region, Canada, and the United States) and has thus strengthened its participatory nature and legitimacy. On the other hand, the ease with which a country can choose not to be part of a particularly inconvenient or demanding protocol might also serve to hinder its effectiveness greatly. This being said, the number of signatories to each protocol has actually been increasing steadily over time, due perhaps to what Björkbom (1999) labels a "change of attitude" on the part of member states toward taking environmental concerns more seriously.

The successes of the CLRTAP treaty—as well as its failures—must now serve as a foundation for a truly global, comprehensive treaty to combat air pollution, one beyond the limited scope of the Stockholm Convention on POPs. Such a treaty becomes more necessary as China, India, Indonesia, Brazil, South Africa, and other states continue to industrialize and export atmospheric pollution elsewhere in the process. If no such eventuality awaits in the near future, whether due to lack of political will or lack of a sense of urgency among politicians and civilians alike, a second option might be the development of separate regional umbrella agreements, also modeled on the success of the CLRTAP, each seeking similar objectives within their own broad-based territories. In 2002, the ten-member Association of Southeast Asian Nations (ASEAN) signed the Agreement on

Transboundary Haze Pollution, a legally binding environmental treaty designed (as the title suggests) to combat haze pollution (ASEAN, 2010). However, the treaty, which entered into force in November of 2003, has been criticized for a lack of adequate mechanisms pertaining to monitoring, inspection, standards, liability, and compliance, leading some to dismiss it as a "blind and toothless paper tiger" (Florano, 2003:142).

The Ozone Layer Arrangement

As a prelude to the wider discussion on climate change, I should first mention negotiations on the conservation of the ozone layer, that stratospheric shield 18–20 kilometers high that protects us from the sun's radiation. Because this topic has been covered in great detail elsewhere, I will not go into significant detail, saving space for the broader discussion of climate change (see Benedict, 1991; Grundmann, 2001; Litfin, 1994). Today, it is easy to forget how ubiquitous chlorofluorocarbons (CFCs) were in the 1960s and 1970s. These compounds were used as propellants in spray cans, as coolants in refrigeration and air conditioning, within insulation, and for cleaning in electronics manufacturing. In 1974, the Molina-Rowland hypothesis was advanced, which argued that CFCs, when released into the atmosphere, rose to the stratosphere and diminished the ozone layer (Molina and Rowland, 1974). Their effect, demonstrated empirically by 1985 over Antarctica, was to create a noticeable hole in the ozone layer itself, permitting more ultraviolet rays to enter the earth's atmosphere and leading to increasing skin cancer rates, diminished agriculture and algae, and—though it was not often discussed at this time—increased global warming.

Scientists played a leading role here, publicizing the threat posed by the diminishment of the ozone layer as well as the theory that CFCs were the major cause. Indeed, it could be argued that, in this precedent-setting case, scientists set the agenda for the subsequent public debate. Initial reluctance to meddle with a staple of modern industry eventually gave way to concern and even enthusiastic support for strong regulatory methods and an international arrangement. The major industries involved in CFC production and use, including the chemical manufacturing giant Du Pont, were initially reluctant to implement such a sea change, but, eventually, they also were recruited to the cause, and they invested in the development of alternative technologies. As Grundmann (2001) writes, the "most important reason for the change in the long-term company policy ... was the fact that, even if attempts at international regulations fell through, the company would have to consider unilateral American regulations or even legal proceedings from skin cancer patients who could sue the polluters for compensation" (p. 151).

However, international regulations did not "fall through"; on the contrary, they were immensely successful. Spurred by the UNEP, led with determination by its energetic executive director (from 1975 to 1992!) Egyptian scientist Mostafa Tolba, and urged on by concerned NGOs and by private companies wanting to create an even playing field, countries signed the Vienna Convention for the Protection of the Ozone Layer in 1985; it identified the problem but was short on specifics. In 1987, the same year as the release of the Brundtland Report, the Montreal Protocol on Substances that Deplete the Ozone Layer was adopted to reduce substances "that contribute to the radiative forcing of climate change"; the focus of the protocol was on chlorofluorocarbons, methyl chloroform, and other ozone depleting substances, as well as on the provision of mechanisms to reduce the intensity of these substances (Velders et al., 2007:1). As there was limited evidence of ozone holes, the convention and protocol were, in effect, preventive initiatives. Northern industrialized states were to phase out most of these chemicals immediately, while southern states were given more time as well as access to substitute technology being developed in the north. This political compromise, later replicated in climate change negotiations, is certainly understandable, though, in retrospect, any effort to phase out CFCs completely would have been worth the cost. Since 1987, four amendments have been adopted, adding new chemicals to the regulatory regime and quickening the phase-out schedule for CFCs and halons. Importantly, the first amendment, in 1990, also established a multilateral fund of US$240 million to provide financial and technological support to developing countries complying with the provisions of the protocol. Canada contributes approximately US$6 million per year to the Multilateral Fund for the Implementation of the Montreal Protocol, in addition to providing office space in Montreal for the fund's international secretariat.[2]

Many scientists and scholars consider this a landmark agreement and think that "without the reductions achieved under the Montreal Protocol, the amount of heat trapped due to [ozone-depleting substances] ... would be about twice as high as present levels" (European Commission, 2007). Without question, the protocol delayed the process of ozone layer destruction, saving millions from skin cancer and helping to curb the upward trend toward global warming. Also, as R.E. Benedict (1991) concludes, the precedent set by the ozone issue was that "the richer nations for the first time acknowledged a responsibility to help developing countries to implement needed environmental policies without sacrificing aspirations for improved standards of living" (p. 207). However, this story is far from over. Because the ozone-destroying compounds are long lived, they will stay in the atmosphere for decades to come. The ozone hole over the Antarctic goes through periodic expansions, and scientists reported in 2011 that a "huge Arctic ozone hole opened up over the Northern Hemisphere ... for the first time in the observation record comparable to that in the Antarctic" (Munro, 2011:A3). We are uncertain as to how, exactly, ozone layer depletion and climate change feed into each other, but it is self-evident that the loop is a positive one. (And, in this case, a positive loop is a negative thing!) Illegal trade in CFCs and other products continues. And the political conditions which rendered the Montreal Protocol possible—willing industries, scientific certainty about causation, mass fear of skin cancer, the willingness of northern states to pay into a technology adaptation fund—are difficult to replicate.

The UN Framework
Convention on Climate Change

"The record shows that greenhouse gases, carbon dioxide in particular, did not go above 280 parts per million over the last 650,000 years. We're now more than 400 parts per million, coming close to what many scientists are now referring to as a tipping point ... [when the] Katrina scale of events will become simply the norm."

STEPHEN HAWKING (2007)[3]

It became painfully obvious in the 1990s that the issue of climate change would present a much deeper challenge to the international community than atmospheric pollution or ozone layer depletion. Climate change is one of those monster topics that permeate everything on the environmental agenda today. It is also a primary human rights concern (so much so that the phrase "climate justice" has become popular in recent years; see Adger et al., 2006 and Sandberg and Sandberg, 2010). Although long-term variations in climate are quite normal, most scientists agree that anthropogenic contributors, such as the exponential increase of fossil fuel burning and land-use changes, are driving the trend of global warming today. Greenhouse gases include carbon dioxide, methane, and nitrous oxide, among many others (United Nations Framework Convention on Climate Change, 2007:8).

In its 2007 synthesis report, the Intergovernmental Panel on Climate Change (IPCC) deemed carbon dioxide to be the most "important" anthropogenic gas; its annual emissions "grew by about 80% between 1970 and 2004" (IPCC, 2008:5). Carbon dioxide is emitted primarily through the use of fossil fuels and secondarily through land-use change. Emissions of methane are "pre-dominantly due to agriculture and fossil fuel use" while concentrations of nitrous oxide are also the result of agriculture. All regions of the world will face the impact of climate change. *Africa* will face water stress, reductions in yields from rain-fed agriculture, increases in arid or semiarid land, and sea level rise. *Asia* will have less freshwater availability, flooding in coastal areas, stress on natural resources, as well as increased mortality due to diarrheal diseases associated with floods and droughts. *Europe* is at risk of inland flashfloods, coastal flooding, and increased erosion as a result of storms and sea level rise. *Latin America* will have less tropical forest cover—replaced by savanna in eastern Amazonia—and will experience biodiversity loss through species extinction, decreased crop yields and livestock productivity, and changes in precipitation patterns, "with the disappearance of glaciers" to affect freshwater supplies. (IPCC, 2008:50). Canada's permafrost is melting, which in turn releases even more greenhouse gases into the atmosphere; the ice caps are melting at an accelerated rate as well. These are merely some examples of the potential burden that climate change can cause, to which we must at least add human migration (within and across borders; see Martin, 2010), frequent heat waves, the salinization of drinking water, coral bleaching, rising food prices, intense floods and droughts, and the spread of diseases and invasive species previously constrained by weather patterns (see Schneider and Lane, 2006 and Stern, 2007). Small island developing states (SIDs) are particularly vulnerable to the effects of climate change.[4] Because most of their economic and social activities are located along the coastline, their arable land, water resources, and biodiversity are highly vulnerable to sea level rise. Other indigenous communities, such as the Inuit of Canada, are also vulnerable to climatic disruptions (see Ford et al., 2010). But if worst-case scenarios are realized and the Great Ocean Conveyer is seriously disrupted, we might even be on the way toward another ice age (see Homer-Dixon, 2006:170–72).

One might surmise that, even if a small proportion of these threats were serious possibilities, we would be doing all we could to avert further climate change. Yet the international arrangements related to this issue are among the most ineffective ever devised. The problem is not a new one. Nobel Prize winner Svante Arrhenius was one of the first scientists to write of the greenhouse effect (Arrhenius, 1896); in the 1950s, Gilbert Plass showed how fossil fuel burning, deforestation, and the 6 billion tons of carbon dioxide emitted annually into the atmosphere could change earth's temperatures (Plass, 1956). In 1988, NASA scientist James Hansen testified "with 99 percent confidence" before a US Senate Committee that global warming was underway; his allegations were given credibility when heat waves swept the United States Midwest, generating sudden public awareness (Parsons, 1995:7). During the same year, amid the enthusiasm of a successful Montreal Protocol, the World Meteorological Organization and the UNEP created the IPCC, and the Toronto Conference on the Changing Atmosphere began the diplomatic process of climate change negotiations. When the first IPCC assessment report was published, the United Nations General Assembly subsequently negotiated the creation of the United Nations Framework Convention on Climate

Change in 1992. It took two years of negotiations (see von Stein, 2008:245) but did not call for legally binding regulatory measures; these measures were established five years later at Kyoto, though that protocol has not been met by any measurable standard.

The UNFCCC enjoys nearly universal membership: 195 countries are members (193 are party to the Kyoto Protocol, the United States is the main absentee). The secretariat, headed at present by Costa Rican Executive Secretary Christiana Figueres, is located in Bonn—fittingly enough, near to the Secretariat of the Convention to Combat Desertification discussed in the previous chapter. Under the Kyoto Protocol, industrialized countries were required to reduce collective emissions of the six greenhouse gases by at least 5 per cent from their 1990 baseline by the period of 2008–12.[5] Percentages differed between states. For example, the United States had to decrease by 7 per cent, Canada by 6 per cent, and the European Union by 8 per cent. Other countries, such as Australia, could actually increase temporarily. The 90-day countdown until the Kyoto Protocol officially entered into force began after Russia ratified the treaty on November 18, 2004.

Although governments must meet their targets primarily through national measures, the protocol also introduced three market-based mechanisms, which were pushed by the American delegation. These included emissions trading, the Clean Development Mechanism (CDM), and Joint Implementation (JI). One can now add REDD, discussed in Chapter 4, to this list. Emissions trading takes place when one country provides another country with financial or other considerations in exchange for that country taking a portion of their Kyoto-assigned reduction in emissions; under a *cap and trade* system, if a country (or, with the extant systems in place, a company) produces less than its share of emissions, it may trade its remaining permits with heavier polluters. Ideally, the price of such permits depends on the market.[6] Carbon trading takes place among European states and within some parts of North America (the Obama administration has called for a nation-wide system within the United States), but we are far from an operational global emissions trading arrangement. Most trading takes place in derivative contracts and involves large emitting private companies buying and selling permits electronically through either governments or the related exchange.[7] Some states, such as Canada, wanted to include carbon sinks (forests and lakes) as part of a tradable contribution to stemming climate change; this position is generally rejected by states with less natural carbon sink area, as we might expect. Indeed the controversy over carbon sinks, perhaps as much as any other issue, manages to bring national differences to the fore, even as "the construction of sinks as nationally territorial spaces is nevertheless undertaken with the understanding that the management of such sinks serves a universal order" (Paterson and Stripple, 2007:162).

The CDM allows governments and corporations from the Annex I countries to "invest in specific projects or contribute to funds, such as the World Bank's Carbon Investment Fund" in return for certified emission reduction credits "to achieve compliance with their emission limitation commitments" (Agriculture and Agri-Food Canada, 2000:5). The "emission reductions shall be certified on the basis of criteria including voluntary participation, 'real, measurable and long-term benefits' related to mitigating climate change, and emissions additionality ('reductions that are additional to any that would occur in the absence of the certified project activity')" (Grubb, 2003:153). Controversy swirls around some CDM projects, which are questionable in terms of their overall contribution to abatement; some argue this mechanism even creates an incentive to develop projects, such as monocultural eucalyptus farms, which are often considered inimical to the broader goal of sustainable development and may involve questionable labor standards (see Schreuder, 2009:163–93).[8] Joint Implementation permits Annex I countries to assist one another (and, especially, so-called economies in transition, such as the ex-Soviet bloc and Russia) by providing financial, technical, and other necessary assistance in return for "emission reduction units," which are credited to their targeted Kyoto GHG commitment (Grubb, 2003:154). In other words, the CDM facilitates development projects that, ideally, benefit the environment, while JI facilitates cross-investment among industrialized states that results in lowered overall emissions. Both are controversial (especially as they relate to the process of certifying individual projects), and neither has emerged as a popular mechanism to limit climate change.

The reasons certain countries like Australia, Russia, or the United States were so reluctant to ratify the Kyoto Protocol vary. People from the political left criticize the protocol for "having too many loopholes and inadequate compliance provisions, for undervaluing intergenerational equity" as well as for not being effective enough to reverse the impact of global warming; while from the political right, it is argued that measures under the Kyoto Protocol compromise economic growth and commercial interests, are based on uncertain scientific data, and do not provide equal responsibility among all countries (Zahran et al., 2007:38). Because developing countries did not have to reduce their emissions rate, many argue that the UNFCCC's call for a principle of "common but differentiated responsibilities and respective capacities" has been taken to an illogical extreme. All of these concerns are reasonable, but the absence of a serious architectural alternative has left us with Kyoto as the operational approach at the level of global governance since 1997.

Unsurprisingly, for most countries, implementing Kyoto has been much more difficult than signing or ratifying it. Canada's federalist system exemplifies associated problems. At Kyoto, Canada agreed to reduce emissions of carbon dioxide (and its equivalent in other GHGs) by 6 per cent from 1990 levels, in other words, by 240 megatonnes (Mt) CO_2 per year from 2008 to 2012 (Stoett, 2006:7). Subsequently, it gave its signature on April 29, 1998 and ratified the treaty on December 17, 2002 under former Canadian Prime Minister Jean Chrétien. At the same, Canada intended to maintain its reputation as a global leader and "multilateral citizen" in environmental negotiations. Prior to Kyoto, the Canadians had integrated the concept of "sustainable development" as an important criterion when calibrating environmental and economic policy, as well as environmental legislation (Bernstein, 2002:214). A Canadian government report published in 2002 suggested that "Canada's emissions of greenhouse gases … [were] about 19.6 per cent *higher* than they were in 1990" and estimated that, "if no action were taken to address climate change," they would be 33 per cent *higher* than Canada's Kyoto commitment by 2010 (Government of Canada, 2002:4, 12; emphasis is mine). In 2007, greenhouse gas emissions were measured at about 747 Mt CO_2 equivalent, which was an increase of 4 per cent from 200 (Bernstein, 2002:209). In 2006, the Conservative Canadian government under Prime Minister Steven Harper announced its intention to withdraw from the Kyoto Protocol and to pursue another alternative for combating climate change (CTV News, 2007). After the 2011 COP to the United Nations Framework Convention on Climate Change in Durban, South Africa, Canadian Environment Minister Peter Kent went all the way and announced that Canada would, indeed, withdraw from the Kyoto Protocol, referring to it as an "impediment" to further progress in climate change (Kennedy, 2011:A12).

The primary institutional constraint to implementation of environmental regulation lies in the complexities of Canadian federalism and its federal-provincial structure of government. Once an international treaty is signed, it must then be approved by the provincial governments to see what policy measures can be implemented. Environmental regulation occurs at the provincial and territorial level because provinces "own the land and natural resources within their territories, and have exclusive jurisdiction over non-renewable resources" (Bernstein, 2002:215). Some provinces, especially Alberta, are heavily dependent on the fossil fuel industry for economic growth. There are also inherent conflicts between the principles of Kyoto and the trade elements of NAFTA. According to NAFTA principles, "foreign investors should be given the same advantages as their domestic counterparts" (Hornsby, Summerlee, and Woodside, 2007:288). Canada's dependence on the American economy mirrors American dependence on Canadian energy exports—though, as Robert Paehlke (2008) and others argue, this mutual dependence could be used as leverage to encourage faster change in the United States (p. 124–26). It seems more likely that the economic recovery process will take precedence over concerns with carbon emissions.

Meanwhile, the United States signed and ratified the 1992 UNFCCC document at the Rio Earth Summit, but it did not legally mandate binding emissions reduction targets (Steurer, 2003:345). Former United States President Bill Clinton supported and signed the Kyoto Protocol in 1997. However, the Bush administration was reluctant to take any steps toward implementation, and the Obama administration has not placed the emphasis on Kyoto that many environmentalists had hoped for. Arguably, Kyoto itself never had a chance within the American system of checks and balances. While talks were taking place in Japan, members of Congress in the United States coupled with the US State Department delegation to observe the negotiations critically. In July 1997, the entire Senate, with a vote of 97–0, passed a nonbinding resolution stating that it would not ratify the protocol as it was. The Senate's reasons were twofold. Senators from both political parties believed that emissions reductions would result in severe economic costs. Second, they rejected the protocol because developing countries, such as India and China, did not have to cut emissions in the immediate future (Steurer, 2003:345–46). As a result of the Senate's position, the Clinton administration, upon its return to the United States, tried renegotiating certain points of the protocol instead of asking for ratification, but this strategy failed. The Bush administration announced its retreat from the Kyoto Protocol on March 28, 2001 (Steurer, 2003:350) and officially withdrew a day later. President Bush instead announced that he would propose the Clear Skies and Global Climate Change Initiative as a substitute for Kyoto. The Obama administration has sought clearer carbon policies but faces an uncooperative Congress.

In marked contrast, although some "individual EU countries may have difficulties achieving their Kyoto Protocol targets, the EU as a whole appears to be on course for meeting its Kyoto obligations" (van Kooten, 2003:410). EU countries decided to respect their Kyoto commitments as a collective effort and subsequently negotiated "an internal burden-sharing agreement and submitted their ratification on the same day" (von Stein, 2008:256). Some European member-states bear more responsibility than others. For example, Germany, the United Kingdom, and Luxembourg had to reduce amounts of greenhouse gas emissions quite drastically and have either exceeded or almost matched their target goals. On the other side of the world, in China, the Communist Party and state-controlled media have marked a shift in climate policy, actually admitting to the problem and openly pursuing alternative energy sources, though soft brown coal's abundance and China's reliance on massive industrial growth suggest that this carbon giant, which has overtaken the United States as the world's biggest emitter, has a long way to go before it can lay claim to the successes achieved in Europe. It is clear that a post-Kyoto arrangement will need to include reduction obligations on the part of China, India, Brazil, and other southern industrialized states, but getting there will not be a simple affair.

The 2009 Copenhagen Accord resulted from COP 15, largely on the strength of leadership from the United States, China, India, Brazil, and South Africa.

Along with the recognition that countries need to come together to "limit global temperatures rising no more than 2 degrees Celsius above pre-industrial levels," it was agreed that $100 billion needed to be mobilized to developing countries annually until 2020. In addition, countries would monitor their own efforts and report to the United Nations every second year, but no details were decided upon the implementation of international carbon markets (UNFCCC, 2009). These are voluntary commitments only; for example, the United States "pledged to reduce greenhouse gas emissions by about 17 percent by 2020 compared with 2005, contingent on Congress enacting climate change and energy legislation." Canada agreed to do the same. China agreed to "try to voluntarily reduce its emissions of carbon dioxide per unit of economic growth—a measure known as 'carbon intensity'—by 40 to 45 percent by 2020 compared with 2005 levels," while India "set a domestic emissions intensity reduction target by 20 to 25 percent by 2020 compared with 2005 levels, excluding its agricultural sector" (Broder, 2010). Nevertheless, although this response suggests that there is support for the Copenhagen Accord, the pledges made by the 100+ list of countries that have signed the agreement in sum could not possibly meet the accord's goal of holding warming to 2 degrees Celsius above preindustrial levels. Among those who did not support the Copenhagen Accord were Bolivia, Venezuela, Nicaragua, Cuba, Sudan, and Saudi Arabia. Saudi Arabia and other oil exporters fear a loss of oil revenues if the world shifts to renewable energies; others are concerned that the accord does not demand enough from northern states, given their historical record of greenhouse gas production.

Indeed, much as was the case with biodiversity, deforestation, and desertification, a large portion of the negotiations that took place at Copenhagen was aimed at diffusing the rift between north and south. Another way developing countries became involved was through the Adaptation Fund, "established to finance concrete adaptation projects and programmes in developing country Parties to the Kyoto Protocol that are particularly vulnerable to the adverse effects of climate change" (UNFCCC, 2011). The Global Environmental Facility's role as a funding mechanism for the Convention on Biological Diversity and the UN Convention to Combat Desertification is important here, but we have barely scratched the surface in terms of the amount of funding most experts envision will be necessary to give future climate change arrangements widespread legitimacy. We cannot erase the central historical fact that most greenhouse gas emissions were produced in the industrialized north, even if the table is slowly turning on modern production. That the UNFCCC, in which "adaptation is not addressed in any single article in a comprehensive way" (Mace, 2006:55) was not more prescient in this regard can be attributed to American reluctance to legitimize the theme with open talks. But under the rubric of "climate justice," which is generating exceptional policy linkages for the international development industry, small island states, human rights advocates, and many others, adaptation funding has emerged as a central point of debate and will not fade away. And, as there is much controversy about this point, there is also room for innovation. For example, "climate debt reparations" could involve more open migration and refugee policies, technology transfers, debt relief, and other issues typically framed within the north-south debate (see Klein, 2010, for a spirited discussion).

Some place greater faith in the role of technological improvements. Even if one accepts the idea that technological changes alone might suffice, these solutions still entail a serious reappraisal of current government spending and the distribution of wealth.[9] As E. Somanathan (2010) suggests, "the major action needed to realize [necessary] reductions involves promoting research and development that will make low-carbon and carbon-neutral energy sources competitive vis-à-vis fossil fuels. Developed countries will have to support this development not only through domestic regulation, taxes, and tradable permits for fossil-fuel use, but also by committing more government funds to R&D on non-carbon energy sources" (p. 615). Some of the more ambitious ideas about geo-engineering a solution, such as scattering sunlight by injecting particles into the atmosphere or fertilizing the oceans to stimulate phytoplankton blooms or using a chemical sorbet to remove carbon from the air directly, would involve unprecedented costs and shared risks and would need to be not only carefully negotiated but also paid for as well.

The Harvard Project on International Climate Agreements (Aldy and Stavins, 2010b) puts forth several potential global governance frameworks:

1. "Emissions caps established using a set of formulas that assign quantitative emissions limits to countries through 2100.... The caps would be implemented through a global system of linked national and regional cap-and-trade programs that would allow for trading among firms and sources."

2. A "system of linked international agreements that separately address mitigation in various sectors and gases, along with issues like adaptation, technology research and development, and geoengineering."

3. "Harmonized domestic taxes on emissions of GHGs from all sources, where the tax or charge would be internationally adjusted from time to time, and each country would collect and keep the revenues it generates."

4. "An architecture that ... links national and regional tradable permit systems only indirectly, through the global CDM [which] may already be evolving as the *de facto* post-Kyoto international climate policy architecture." (P. 53–59)

Ultimately a combination of global cap and trade and local carbon taxes holds the most promise for curbing climate change, but—and here some purists will beg to differ—it is clearly too late to obsess on stopping it altogether. I certainly agree with others that, "as in the case of transboundary air pollution and ozone depletion, legally binding standards for the abatement of greenhouse gas emissions can only come through agreement on detailed commitments and international supervisory mechanisms" (Birnie, Boyle, and Redgwell, 2009:340). But we will also need to agree to serious adaptation structures if we want to approach the goal of international democratic legitimacy within a humanistic ethos. In general, we will need to go beyond perpetually stalled international negotiations to see concrete action on climate change take root. On the political surface of things, it appears that much of the energy around climate change has been directed toward what Paehlke (2008) refers to as "climate change action avoidance" (p. 104). However, there is certainly a growing trend toward awareness of the issue in the private sector, where green initiatives serve to improve corporate public profiles and even energy companies are jumping on the bandwagon. However, global governance continues to prove elusive, due largely to the level of commitment demanded and rifts between northern industrialized states, oil-producing states, and southern, rapidly industrializing states. The agreement reached in Durban in late 2011 is, essentially, an agreement to agree later—to a global pact by 2015 that includes all states pledging to take effective action that would force them to cut emissions by 2020!

Deep Breaths

> "... in a way, it's a privilege to be at the heart of an intimate struggle internationally over the preservation of the planet. But the very real question is: can we reverse it now? Have we unleashed Armageddon? ... Must we now begin to contemplate measures of geo-engineering which were formerly thought to be faintly lunatic in their scientific prescriptions?"
>
> STEPHEN LEWIS, KEYNOTE ADDRESS TO THE 5TH WORLD ENVIRONMENTAL EDUCATION CONGRESS, MAY 10, 2009, MONTREAL (QUOTED IN SANDBERG AND SANDBERG, 2010: 30–1)

Perhaps more than any other topic covered in this book, climate change inspires the anxiety I discussed in Chapter 1; it is the heart of the megacrisis. The complexity of the issue is daunting, as every human action is of consequence. Consumers and diplomats alike share in the blame and the opportunities for positive change.

Yet nothing could be worse than giving in to futility on this issue; if we had done so with regard to other forms of atmospheric pollution, we would be choking on the consequences today. The relative successes of the CLRTAP and ozone arrangements suggest concrete collective action is possible, if complex. Now we need to adapt to this even bigger challenge.

The CLRTAP employs an effective umbrella mechanism that makes the adoption of future, refining protocols quite possible. It has proven to be both legally and environmentally effective and has sustained cognitive success, especially amongst policy makers. It has less of a mandate to approach democratic legitimacy or inequality issues, though it does operate by consensus. Similarly, the Montreal Protocol has enjoyed high levels of success in all the categories of our framework, though one might argue that the threat posed by ozone layer depletion was so dire, and the scientific consensus so strong, that success was embedded in the very process. Most notably, perhaps, the adaptation fund created by the protocol established a precedent (celebrated and lamented at the same time today) of transferring some wealth and technology to southern states in order to achieve realistic targets. The UNFCCC, by contrast, is so mired in acrimonious negotiations and in the spread of disinformation about the science of climate change that its relative failure in all of our categories should be no surprise. Climate change is an issue so large that it escapes the usual parameters of measurement by policy analysis.

The atmosphere may well be the purest form of the commons; unless we construct super-domed cities capable of producing their own oxygen, our fates are all tied together when it comes to the air we breathe, the ultraviolet radiation to which we are exposed, and the drought, excessive rain, and heavy storms we must respond to as climate change proceeds. As we have seen, there are a multitude of international commitments related to atmospheric pollution, and some, such as the Montreal Protocol on the Ozone Layer, have been exceptionally successful. Others, such as the Kyoto Protocol, have been much more difficult to implement and have left us with less optimism, though innovations such as REDD hold some promise, and a global cap and trade system combined with localized carbon taxes may be a real possibility if increased public awareness can help push politicians further in this direction and corporations are mindful of the fact that there is money in progress on this front. At the local level, however, cities and villages have shown much more promise in terms of abating climate change. Indeed, a wealth of scholarly literature is emerging that examines the increasingly progressive roles played by cities, including the international Cities for Climate Protection Campaign (Betsill and Bulkeley, 2004; Gore, 2010; Lindseth, 2004).

The precautionary principle suggests we should avoid any unnecessary risks (necessity, one assumes, is defined in relation to human survival). Where are we heading with atmospheric pollution and climate change if not into a great, unknown epoch? Or, as Thomas Homer-Dixon (2006) puts it, "walking toward a cliff" (p. 168)? Birnie, Boyle, and Redgwell (2009) suggest that, if left "unchecked," climate change "may change the world as we know it irreversibly. Tackling it represents probably the greatest challenge the UN system has ever faced" (p. 378). Indeed, the problem is not just one for the UN but for all of us, every minute of every day; we are all potential system-disturbing butterflies in this great chaotic chain of events. We should not walk in fear but in quiet respect of this fact, resolute in a commitment to keep working toward solutions.

Notes

1. This report, published under the title *Our Common Future*, was instrumental in awakening European, North American, and other publics to environmental issues. It was controversial, dismissed as alarmist by some and as naïve by others critical of its faith in long-term economic growth. Little would change were such a report to emerge today, though it would be largely superfluous, as its central claims about environmental pressures are hardly controversial today.

2. For a review of Canada's environmental agreements related to air pollution and the ozone, see the Foreign Affairs and International Trade Canada website: http://www.international.gc.ca/enviro/agreements-ententes/waste-dechets.aspx?view=d.

3. Quoted in the film *The 11th Hour*; excerpts were published in the *New Perspectives Quarterly* 24 (4), retrieved December 4, 2011 from http://www.digitalnpq.org/archive/2007_fall/12_dicaprio_etal.html.

4. According to the UN Department of Social and Economic Affairs, SIDs are made up of 52 states and territories extending from the Pacific, Indian, and Atlantic Oceans and the Caribbean Sea, including regions such as Haiti, Fiji, and the Seychelles; many of them have formed the Alliance of Small Island States to collectively urge industrialized countries to curb greenhouse gas emissions. See http://www.sidsnet.org/aosis/index.html and Strauss (2009).

5. These six gases are carbon dioxide (CO_2), methane (CH_4), nitrous oxide (N_{20}), hydrofluorocarbons (HFCs), perfluorocarbons (PFCs), and sulphur hexafluoride (SF_6).

6. For a compact discussion of the market mechanisms associated with the Kyoto Protocol, see Grubb (2003).

7. However, as *The Economist* reports, the EU's Emissions Trading Scheme is certainly taken seriously, so much so that thieves have begun to steal carbon credits—as much as $62 million worth in 2011. See "Carbon Trading: Green Fleeces, Red Faces," *The Economist*, February 5, 2011:88.

8. "A particular concern is the exclusion of marginalized groups from their own forest resources once they become the property of a distant carbon trader for whom they represent a valuable investment opportunity" (Bulkeley and Newell, 2010:49).

9. As Beth DeSombre (2011) writes, "[o]ne of the (many) reasons ... that climate change is such a difficult problem of international cooperation is that substitute technologies or chemicals are not easily available; addressing the problem adequately will require fundamentally changing our relationship with fossil fuels" (p. 140). Or, as Yda Schreuder (2009) intones, a "business-as-usual scenario, based on the IEA's World Energy Outlook projection, is not an option for future generations" (p. 197).

CHAPTER SIX

Blue Peril:
Oceans and Rivers

*"She is called Mother Earth because from her come
all living things. Water is her lifeblood. It flows
through her, nourishes her, and purifies her."*

THE OJIBWE CREATION STORY[1]

I WAS FORTUNATE ENOUGH TO SPEND MOST OF MY CHILDHOOD SUMMERS
at a cottage on Lake Huron in Ontario. Everything in life seemed to revolve
around the lake, which is immense, deep, and beautiful: local fishing boats,
the tourist industry, swimming lessons, golden sunsets on the horizon, terrific
storms that flung crashing waves on shore. The lake was always there, one constant in a fast-changing small town. One of the North American Great Lakes,
Huron was less damaged by industrialization than its cousins to the south, such
as Lake Erie or Lake Ontario. But it was always evident to me that this precious
source of water, fish, and inspiration, despite its size and depth, was a fragile
and vulnerable thing, one that it would be foolish to take for granted; and
rarely a day would pass when some form of garbage would not wash up on
shore, from plastic bottles to the occasional dead cow that had wandered too

far from a farmer's field. Of course in my youthful ignorance I had no idea how much worse things would get for the earth's water sources.

Satellite photos and astronaut testimony indicate that, viewed from space, the earth looks rather blue. Water is without doubt the most valuable natural resource we share, one we will need long after the last barrel of oil has been extracted from the ground (unfortunately, we now use copious amounts of water to produce oil!). As a species, we are a consequence of the global oceans, and our local habitats spring forth from riverbeds and shorelines. The provision of water is one of the more obvious ecosystem services offered by nature, and our symbiotic relationship with it has shaped our history, culture, science, and today's local and global economies.

Indeed, water is so central to our lives that future generations may ask themselves how we could treat such a vital resource with such systemic negligence. This chapter will examine several global and regional governance issues related to water management, including international cooperation in the polar regions, the oceans crises, and freshwater sharing arrangements. I conclude that we are making some progress in many areas, but it is coming at an inadequate pace and is often devoid of the deep-rooted democratic legitimacy we need to instill in related arrangements and institutions.

We face several simultaneous water crises. Freshwater—vital, potable, agriculture-ready—is an inspiration for poet and politician alike. Shared rivers and lakes are sites of international controversy and intrigue: if ever there was a test of our ability to forge cooperative relationships, including the more ambitious neofunctionalist designs discussed in earlier chapters, water would seem to raise it. Indeed, many studies have concluded that the fears of "water wars," once so popular in the media and among scholars concerned with "new" security issues, are overrated and that water has, in fact, provided ample opportunities for peaceful solutions (Wolf et al., 2005). Shared rivers are perhaps the most obvious example, and I will discuss several of them in this chapter. Some optimism emerges, though it is not enough to give us any serious cause for celebration at this stage. And successes must be weighed against dwindling freshwater glaciers, lakes, and aquifers, the source of most of our drinking, cleaning, and agricultural water.

The oceans crisis, however, is quite possibly the most serious collective action problem we face, period. It is amazing to me, and no doubt a source of constant frustration to oceanographers, marine biologists, and their disciplinary associates, that most people seem to remain unaware of the crises (yes, that is plural) that the oceans face today; we still need a cognitive revolution on this front. Overfishing, induced by bottom trawling, ghost driftnets, wasted bycatch, and other practices that would not be followed by rational creatures, is only the most visible crisis involved.[2] Climate change threatens the very nature of ocean water and thus contributes to various feedback loops. The pollution entering our oceans every day from cities, farms, factories, ships, and other units is quite simply beyond me: Marine invasive alien species are spreading through both incidental comme trade routes and deliberate introductions (see Chapter 9). The fragile, biodiv coral reefs are threatened by acidification, the use of cyanide for ornamental tropical fish hunting, and careless tourists (Wilkinson, 2006). Warmer ocean water throws our understanding of planetary weather patterns into disarray and disrupts migratory patterns. All of this takes place in an adaptive multi-governance context in which it is clear that a longstanding tradition of super-exploiting the commons is the norm. How to overcome these crises without a central source of authority—and before it is too late? Before turning to the warmer oceans, we will briefly examine two decidedly colder areas where we have achieved some measure of adaptive governance success, though the unique circumstances in which this success was achieved mean that the agreements reached do not present much of a model for replication elsewhere.

The Poles

Two examples of international arrangements that involve ocean space literally sit at polar opposites. The Antarctic Treaty System governs Antarctica, which is vital for many ecological reasons and contains much of the world's ice, many of its whales, and most of its penguins. The Antarctic Treaty was signed December 1, 1959 by 12 states that had been active on the continent by that time, some of which lay claim to territory. There are now 28 consultative parties and 18 adherent parties.[3] This treaty was largely a function of cold war diplomacy, but it would evolve into a much more comprehensive governance system, and it came to include the Convention on the Conservation of Antarctic Marine Living Resources (1982) and, perhaps most important, the Protocol on Environmental Protection of 1991, which was so significant because it adopted an explicit ecosystem-wide approach. The latter encourages scientific exchange, forbids commercial mineral resource mining, and aims to prevent marine pollution. This shared governance approach is unique, though proponents of the "common heritage of mankind" principle and some ENGOs had advocated UN trusteeship or other models that would include all states rather than only the select few that can afford to conduct research in such a remote and hostile environment (see Herber, 1991). It also remains to be seen whether the protocol can actually conserve the Southern Ocean fishery, and Japanese and Norwegian whalers have continued limited whaling in the region.

The ATS's antipodal counterpart is very different in both form and function. The Arctic Council was created in Ottawa in 1996 and comprises Canada, Denmark (including Greenland and the Faroe Islands), Finland, Iceland, Norway, the Russian Federation, Sweden, and the United States. These arctic states created the council in an effort to coordinate policy in what is quickly emerging as an economically hypercompetitive region. Climate change is increasing commercial and extractive access to the polar circumference, transforming its landscape and terrestrial and aquatic species, raising new national security concerns, and complicating the lives of its inhabitants, in particular, the transnational circumpolar Inuit (Jeffers, 2010). The latter are granted an observer's seat on the Arctic Council (through several representative NGOs), but have no vote on collective matters.[4] The council implements the Arctic Environmental Protection Plan introduced by the eight arctic states in 1991. By no means has the council assumed the form of a supranational governance institution such as the European Union, however: it exists largely as a diplomatic channel for posturing and issuing occasional joint communiqués, with arguably little direct impact and with some items, such as national security concerns, off the table altogether. But at least such a forum exists, and it may prove instrumental in the near future as the ice melts and hazardous oil drilling proceeds. For the open seas, we have even less cooperation. Indeed both the ATS and the Arctic Council, despite their differences and the persistence of state authority as the main political variable in both regions, were relatively easy to effect in comparison to meeting a much more challenging test: collective governance over the oceans. This difficulty is most unfortunate because we presently face nothing less than an unprecedented, overlapping series of oceans crises.

The Oceans Crises

As Bodansky (2010) writes, "Resources in areas beyond national jurisdiction, such as the high seas, were generally seen as inexhaustible by classical writers on international law such as Pufendorf and Vattel, and thus not a source of conflict. They could be treated as *res nullius*—that is, belonging to no one and therefore open to all" (p. 21). With this intellectual framework in play, the current state of the oceans may be considered a true tragedy of the commons, as discussed in Chapter 2. The oceans cover 70 per cent of earth's surface, contain much of its biodiversity, and are a major food source for humans. Forty-four per cent of the world's population lives within 200 kilometers of a coastline (Parris, 2005). More than half of the world's people depend on seafood as their primary source of protein; and, as the International Maritime Organization (IMO) reports, "more than 90 percent of global trade is carried by sea." Fishing employs 15–20 million people worldwide and is the main source of protein for billions (Tibbetts, 1996). On a larger scale, the planet's ecosystems depend heavily on oceans, as they absorb and filter carbon: "The oceans also serve as an important sink, having absorbed over 80% of the heat added to the climate system and over one-half of all anthropogenic carbon emissions over the past 200 years, thus playing a key role in the mitigation of climate change" (Currie and Wowk, 2009:388). Of course, all of this carbon absorption is now posing serious threats to the oceans themselves, affecting marine life, the currents or vital underwater streams, and sea levels.

Exacerbating matters is our tendency to literally use the oceans as a giant liquid garbage dump. In the spring of 2010, a seemingly unstoppable oil leak in the Gulf of Mexico reminded us of how dangerous resource extraction can be in an aquatic environment. Indeed, the most publicized form of sea pollution is the dramatic and graphically portrayed oil spill. Among the most infamous incidents was the Exxon-Valdez oil spill that occurred in Alaska in 1989, when roughly 40,000 tons of crude oil was spilt along the Pacific coastline. Yet, in the 1980s, some 3.5 million metric tons of oil were being intentionally released into the oceans every year, divided almost equally between land and sea-based sources (Levy, 1984:231). The International Maritime Organization (IMO) has made efforts to regulate intentional oil dumping (caused when large ships change their engine oil at sea) and to reduce accidental discharges as well as the spread of invasive species through commercial shipping. But, beyond oil, we have been so prolific at dumping waste into the oceans that they are now littered with debris such as cigarette filters, baby diapers, six-pack rings, bottles and cans, plastic bags, fishing line and gear, retired ships, and even automobile parts (Tibbetts, 1996:80).[5] According to one study, the "major sources of this debris include storm water discharges, sewer overflows, litter, solid waste disposal and landfills, offshore mineral and oil exploration, industrial activities, and illegal dumping. The sheer volume and geographic range of marine debris is daunting: 14 billion pounds of garbage accumulates annually in oceans and travels around the globe" (Leous and Parry, 2005:257). Even more harmful is the pollution generated from "non-point" sources: human-caused increases in nutrient elements (e.g., nitrogen, phosphorous, and iron) that enter the oceans through rivers and air currents, causing massive changes in marine ecosystems. On-land sources of pollution, such as lawn fertilizers and agricultural runoff, have created areas with seasonally depleted oxygen levels (hypoxia), which in turn lead to so-called dead zones (places devoid of all marine life). Coastal zone development and the damming of rivers have also led to marine habitat destruction, often causing sedimentation problems in rivers and streams, beach erosion, and the near elimination of fisheries spawning in some areas (Pirages and DeGeest, 2004:65). Even before the BP oil spill of 2010 in the Gulf of Mexico, a dead zone covering over 18,000 square kilometers was found near the Mississippi River delta.[6] More signs of marine pollution are red and brown tides, areas of explosive and overwhelming algal growth, and the emergence of the microbial predators that attack fish species.

More generally, climate change and ocean acidification affect the health of the oceans. As mentioned, the oceans absorb most of the world's carbon dioxide, which slows down global warming but causes them to acidify rapidly (Borgerson, 2009:15). The excess heat created by global warming elevated ocean temperatures in the upper 700 meters by 0.1 degree Celsius between 1961 and 2003 (IPCC, 2008). The specific systems and sectors that were particularly vulnerable included water resources in midlatitudes and dry tropics (Draper and Kundell, 2007:406). Because warming water expands, sea level rise is a major threat to inhabitants of coastlines and small island states alike. Ocean phytoplankton, the vital link in the food chain and in carbon absorption, is becoming progressively less productive (Homer-Dixon, 2006:174). Coral reef bleaching is now common throughout the oceans and will drastically reduce biodiversity. However, we are also concerned about ocean *cooling* because the melting of polar glaciers could slow down or stop the warm Gulf Stream that forms part of the Great Ocean Conveyor and circulates the sun's energy; should the Gulf Stream be disrupted, we might face a regional ice age. Many of these processes would be difficult to stop even if we were able to halt all greenhouse gas emissions tomorrow.

Overfishing, however, is a more immediately preventable tragedy. Much of what we loosely refer to as "ocean governance" resulted from competition over fish: "The industrialization of fishing necessitated measures of conservation, which in turn required management and jurisdiction. Jurisdiction implied the expansion of national claims in ocean space" (Majumdar, 1990:2682). Commercial fishing has evolved from single-hooked lines to huge trawl nets that scrape the ocean floor (much as we have clear-cut forests and strip-mined land), mile-long drift-nets (and their eerie, deadly remnants, "ghost nets"), and long-line gear.[7] Factory ships are capable of producing 40,000 to 50,000 pounds of product per day, guided by global positioning satellites. It's estimated that "three quarters (75%) of the world's commercial marine fisheries are either fully exploited (50%) or overexploited (25%)" (MEA, 2005a:8). Cod, salmon, and swordfish are among the worst hit. And, as we saw with exotic timber in Chapter 4 and CFCs in Chapter 5, illegal activity—fishing without licenses, off the radar of regional fisheries organizations, or underreporting the catch and discarded bycatch of fishing and whaling operations—remains a large problem, no doubt increasing significantly the sheer volume of exploited marine life.

Early international fisheries arrangements include the 1882 North Sea Fisheries Convention, the 1948 Agreement for the Establishment of the Asia-Pacific Fishery Commission, and the 1949 International Convention for the Northwest Atlantic Fisheries (now known as the Northwest Atlantic Fisheries Commission or NAFO). The International Convention for the Conservation of Atlantic Tunas (ICCAT) was signed at Rio de Janeiro on May 14, 1966 and entered into force in 1969. It applies to the whole Atlantic Ocean and comprises both tuna and tuna-like fishes (more than 30 species, including swordfish). Headquartered in Madrid,

ICCAT regulates fishing of those species throughout the Atlantic north of the equator and in the Mediterranean, using fishing quotas and other regulations established by fisheries population biologists. ICCAT also directs catch reporting, trade monitoring, and population assessments. Members of ICCAT follow its guidelines to then allocate quotas to their fishermen, give licenses, and enforce regulations within their national boundaries. However, conservation groups have criticized ICCAT for not acting aggressively enough to protect the bluefin tuna.[8] Groups have lobbied to have bluefin tuna listed in the CITES appendices (see Chapter 3), but this action has been fiercely opposed by Japan. Instead, Japan and ICCAT have worked out a system to track and regulate the trade of tuna; unregulated fish from "flags-of-convenience" fishing fleets and states that aren't compliant with ICCAT regulations are banned from the Japanese market (Bestor, 2001), though monitoring this ban is another story.[9] Quotas have been regularly set higher than scientists advised, and there is no doubt that stocks of most species of tuna have been steadily declining. Other tuna commissions include the Indian Ocean Tuna Commission (IOTC), formed in 1993, and the Commission for the Conservation of Southern Bluefin Tuna (CCSBT) established in 1994 (see Allen, 2010). Another notable example of a contemporary fisheries arrangement is the Canada–United States Pacific Salmon Treaty of 1985, which struggles to regulate the take of a valuable anadromous species (it migrates not only between countries but between rivers and the ocean; see Yanagida, 1987). Meanwhile, the FAO's Fisheries and Aquaculture Department is aimed at facilitating and securing the "long-term sustainable development and utilization of the world's fisheries and aquaculture" (www.fao.org); through monitoring and scientific research by its Advisory Committee on Fishery Research (ACFR), it establishes guidelines to help in fisheries management. The FAO also provides a soft-law framework for considering the impacts of potentially destructive fishing practices on vulnerable marine ecosystems, through its Code of Conduct for Responsible Fisheries and the FAO Technical Guidelines for Responsible Fisheries. These are helpful forms of "soft law," which is certainly the operative phrase when it comes to ocean governance, as a cursory look at the United Nations Conference on the Law of the Sea (UNCLOS) indicates.

UNCLOS

The United Nations Convention on the Law of the Sea is, to date, the most complete and widely recognized treaty relating to all aspects of ocean management, and it took no less than nine years to negotiate (1973–82). It is best viewed as an ambitious umbrella agreement that promotes and legitimizes many other aspects of marine environmental governance. One hundred and fifty-nine parties initially signed the convention, and it became effective November 1994 after Guyana became the 60th state to ratify it. UNCLOS has generated what we recognize now as both formal and customary international ocean law and has triggered activity on many environmental issues, but it has hardly lived up to its initial, and overly optimistic, promise. Like many ecopolitical arrangements, it is a victim of great expectations.

Negotiations for UNCLOS were triggered by the Truman Declaration of 1945, which claimed the continental shelf as "an extension of the land-mass of the adjacent state and thus naturally appurtenant to it."[10] This explicated desire for sovereignty over shelf resources was a consequence of related discoveries in hydrocarbon reserves such as oil and gas. In 1947, primarily in order to protect its whaling and fishing industries, Chile unilaterally claimed jurisdiction over a 200-mile economic zone adjacent to its coast. Soon after, Peru and Ecuador made similar declarations. Predictably enough, these new claims to territorial waters led to international conflicts, and, at the first UN Conference on the Law of the Sea (held in 1958 in Geneva) conventions were adopted on freedom of navigation, fishing, overflight, the laying of submarine cables and pipelines, territorial seas, the freedom of fishing, and seabed exploitation rights. These arrangements were not widely accepted, and UNCLOS II began in 1960 with a mandate to move forward on coastal jurisdiction issues, but it again failed to reach consensus. (Major maritime states feared the extension of coastal jurisdiction would jeopardize their high-seas rights of free passage.) In 1967, the concept of a "common heritage of mankind" was popularized by Arvid Pardo (the Maltese permanent UN representative), who delivered a forceful speech proposing a "declaration or treaty concerning the reservation exclusively for peaceful purposes of the sea-bed and ocean floor underlying the seas beyond the present limits of national jurisdiction, and the use of their resources in the interest of mankind" (Majumdar, 1990:2683). This proposition was not popular among major Western powers, of course, but it resonated in much of the southern hemisphere, which was entering yet another decade of poverty and was looking at the seabed as a potential source of exploitable resources.

The third conference to draft UNCLOS, which ran from late 1973 to mid-1982, was a diplomatic marathon; indeed, it became a way of life for those most intimately involved in the negotiations. Comprised of 320 articles and 9 annexes, the convention addresses all issues pertaining to the delimitation of ocean space, environmental control, marine scientific research, economic and commercial activities, the transfer of technology, and dispute settlement; and it was ahead of UNCED (1992) by enshrining the precautionary principle as well. The UN Division of Ocean Affairs and the Law of the Sea monitors its uneven implementation.

Waters inside a 12-nautical-mile limit are designated territorial waters, while a "contiguous zone" contains waters within a 24-mile limit and the exclusive economic zone (EEZ) is within 200 nautical miles. Though continental shelves extending beyond the EEZ cloud the issue, water past the 200-mile mark is generally considered the common high seas, where all states are permitted to engage in lawful activities; within 200 miles, states have exclusive jurisdiction over commercial operations, though they do not have territorial rights. (If this sounds like a confusing compromise, this is often the case in global politics!) The International Tribunal for the Law of the Sea (ITLOS), sitting in Hamburg, Germany, serves to adjudicate international maritime disputes, though other legal avenues are also encouraged, which can lead to what Boyle refers to as "procedural fragmentation" (Boyle, 1997:54; see also Boyle, 2007 and Vicuna, 2007).

The seabed contains manganese or polymetallic nodules, which are rich in iron, nickel, copper, cobalt, and manganese, and this economic opportunity becomes increasingly attractive as the metal content of land-based ores declines. However, although the quantities of nodules on the ocean floor are astronomically large, only a fraction of them are of sufficiently high grade to suggest that they can be economically mined, and the technology for their exploitation is primitive. Nonetheless, the question facing the architects of UNCLOS was a stark one: should such riches be the property of whoever first discovers and extracts them (*res nullius*)? Or are they part of the common heritage of humankind (*res communis*), to be shared by all, including landlocked, non-maritime states? (See DeSombre, 2006:81.) The answer, which has yet to be accepted by many northern states, was the creation of the International Seabed Authority (ISA), located in Kingston, Jamaica and operational since 1996. Its purpose is to facilitate the sharing of deep-sea resources among states and oversee any extraction of minerals from the deep seabed. Under the ISA was to be another entity, the Enterprise, envisioned by UNCLOS as the result of a technology transfer plan; its task was to undertake the actual exploitation of deep-seabed minerals.

This aspect of the agreement was highly controversial. If in place, the envisioned Enterprise would benefit from competitive advantages such as guaranteed loans, direct subsidized funding, a ten-year exemption from royalty payments to the ISA, and a requirement that mining consortia relinquish to the Enterprise one-half of each claimed mine site (Pirages and DeGeest, 2004:67). In 1994, the treaty was revised to eliminate the technology transfer requirement, the restricted subsidies on seabed mining, and the ISA-imposed production limits on land-based producers. These 1994 revisions to UNCLOS changed the mandate of the ISA and set the course for its official operationalization in 1996.

Opposition to the inherent principle of wealth sharing is strong, however, despite the fact that deep seabed mining has largely been an unrealistic proposition. In particular, the United States has rejected UNCLOS partly because of the ISA, though it has recently flirted with the idea of ratification and would, in effect, have a veto right in the ISA's complex Governing Council, which is run by consensus (see Lodge, 2006). Canada, by contrast, finally ratified in 2003, though this had more to do with Canada's territorial interests, which can be pursued in the UNCLOS Commission on the Limits of the Continental Shelf. At any rate, the ISA is now receiving applications for deep-sea mining in two regions and may assume a more proactive role in the future. Beyond the question of sharing the mineral wealth of the oceans, however, it will be just as important that such operations are as environmentally sensitive and careful as possible; and the carbon emissions from this industrial activity will be significant.

UNCLOS also serves as a base architecture for the world's multilateral fishing and living marine resource arrangements. As up to 90 per cent of the ocean catch is within 200 miles of the coast, the advent of the EEZ (which, in contrast to the mandate of the ISA, is widely accepted as customary law) meant that most fishable stocks now fell under national states' jurisdiction. That led to increasing competition for the same fish between multiple individuals with licenses from the same country. Contrary to its goal of encouraging self-responsibility, acceptance of the exclusive economic zone principle generated the "incentive to use expensive technology to increase efficiency [which], combined with domestic subsidies in many states, created an overcapitalized domestic fishery within most EEZs, and dramatic depletion of fisheries within EEZs" (DeSombre, 2006:90). (To be fair, we are being speculative here, as we do not know what the world fishery would look like without the advent of the EEZ.) And it opened major disputes regarding fishing stocks because many species of fish migrate across EEZ lines. An infamous example was the so-called turbot war between Canada and Spain in the early 1990s, when Canada broke international law by seizing a Spanish trawler in the high seas off the eastern coast.

These conflicts gave rise to the 1995 Agreement on the Conservation and Management of Straddling and Highly Migratory Fish Stocks (Anderson, 1994, 1996; Stoett, 2001), which entered into force in 2001 and gives coastal states the right to take preventive action if straddling stocks are deemed to be endangered by foreign fishing vessels. One commentator has concluded that this arrangement "is evidence of the emergence of a general high-seas fisheries regime with rules, norms, principles, and procedures that are firm enough to be enforced" (Bailey, 1996:260), though this would seem an exaggeration.

The UN Fish Stock Agreement (UNFSA) is another UNCLOS-generated international instrument for fisheries management. It enumerates several general principles related to highly migratory fish stocks, and it reinforces the FAO view that regional fisheries management arrangements are the most effective means to conserve stocks and to ensure that states have an incentive to comply. This initiative mirrors the UNEP's efforts to create the Regional Seas Programme in the 1970s and 1980s (Barker, 2002:76). A notable exception to the regional approach has been the one taken in response to the whaling issue; a global International Whaling Commission (IWC) has survived internal turmoil and remains the main body dealing with this fishery (and this is enshrined in UNCLOS), though a regional pro-whaling organization, the North Atlantic Marine Mammal Commission, competes for legitimacy.[11] The 1989 and 1992 UN resolutions calling for global moratoria on high seas large-scale driftnets have had a positive impact, clearly establishing the fact that it is against customary international law to engage in this most destructive of fishing practices. However, comprehensive enforcement of this moratoria is expensive and problematic and, unfortunately, it does not apply to the EEZs (see Carr and Gianni, 1993).

While one shudders to think of how bare the oceans would be *sans* any regulation, fishing commissions frequently set catch limits that are higher than those suggested by their scientific committees. This was one of the reasons the IWC nearly orchestrated the extinction of the great whale species such as the blue, humpback, and sperm. Most arrangements give their member-states the possibility to opt out of any given regulation, arguably a necessary evil in a world of sovereign states. The processes "also allow for political factors (such as the interests states have in supporting their domestic fishers) to trump scientific ones in the setting of quotas, and allow for some member states to occasionally operate outside the regulatory system" (DeSombre, 2006:85). The lack of coordination between different fisheries management bodies is also problematic, as most organizations tend to focus on a specific species or geographical region. "You'll never have ecosystems management come to reality one species at a time because everything you do to one affects another" said Pew Commission member Pat White (Schrope, 2002).

And speaking of whales: though we have gone to great lengths to limit the number of whales we kill each year, after staring at their extinction for several decades, the biggest threat they face now is not the harpoon but the cacophony and pollution of human civilization. Long-term threats to whales include noise pollution, overfishing, and climate change. Shipping degrades the underwater acoustic environment that whales need for communicating and locating their prey; ship strikes and entanglement in fishing gear kill more whales every year than whaling. Cetologists (who engage in the scientific study of cetaceans) have long argued that organic pollutants found in the ocean, such as PCBs, DDT, dieldrin, and heptachlor, are harming marine mammal populations and are linked to "sterility, premature parturition, depression of reproductive rates, cancer, alteration of growth and bone development...." (Burns and Wandesforde-Smith,

2002:207).[12] Microscopic plants and animals ingest pollutants, including plastic particles and other toxic chemicals, which work their way up the food chain, with their concentration multiplying at each stage. Because whales are at the top, they are the most severely contaminated (though humans suffer from mercury poisoning as well). Yet, the "greatest long-term threat to the North Atlantic right whale and all cetaceans … is the synergistic effect of climate change" (Rieser, 2009:408); the warming of oceans and melting arctic ice is changing the abundance and distribution of zooplankton. So we learn that even these magnificent creatures, once used for everything from nightlights to women's corsets to feeding fur farm animals, then revered by so many and saved from the brink of extinction by concerted action, are at risk from our everyday behavior.

Unfortunately, UNCLOS has done even less to mitigate ocean pollution directly. Here we need to turn to the IMO, a UN specialized agency responsible for measures to improve international shipping safety and security and to prevent marine pollution from ships. The 1973 MARPOL Convention, or the Convention for the Prevention of Pollution from Ships, "has fundamentally changed the way ships are built and has dramatically decreased the extent of oil pollution" (DeSombre, 2006:75). It mandates equipment standards that oil tankers must adopt to prevent the operational discharge of oil and directs that specified chemicals can be discharged only at designated reception facilities and that their discharge is forbidden within 12 miles of land. Optional annexes attempt to minimize pollution by sewage, garbage, and harmful packaged substances, and a subsequent protocol attempts to reduce the possibility of the incidental transport of invasive alien species in ballast water.[13] In May 2005, a new annex entered into force to limit air pollution from ships as well. UNCLOS empowered the IMO to set minimum antipollution standards to be binding on all vessels, and it is, arguably, the current organization with the most direct responsibility for ocean governance.[14]

Much more needs to be done. We need to expand vastly the marine protected areas, which have been proven to protect seafloor habitats, coral reefs, and fish stocks (Currie and Wowk, 2009; Temple Swing, 2003:151). The CBD estimates that, globally, "of 232 marine ecoregions, only 18% meet the target for protected area coverage of at least 10%, while half have less than 1% protection" (CBD 2010a:49). Aquaculture—the farming of fish and shellfish—is a growth industry that needs international regulation, though the FAO is heavily engaged in this topic. By 2000, aquaculture was already producing a quarter of all the seafood consumed by humans, and the figure is expected to rise to more than a half by 2030 (Temple Swing, 2003:142). In our hungry world, with depleted ocean fisheries and the high environmental costs of agricultural meat production, the growth of aquacultural activity is a promising development, provided that sustainability and the precautionary principle can be operative principles and that related problems, such as invasive species, cross-species contamination, the salinization of marshlands, and wastage, can be minimized. Meanwhile, urban and agricultural waste disposal at sea remains a scourge on the oceans, and retrieving solid debris (including the floating plastic bag islands, which deposit small particles of plastic in the food chain) should be a priority.

UNCLOS did break important ground as the first treaty to encompass all matters relating to the oceans, and by gaining almost universal recognition, even from non-member states. Many provisions of UNCLOS have become customary law, thus binding even states that haven't ratified the treaty. But we have a long way to go before our collective actions reflect the severity of the oceans crisis and we embrace the need for some fundamental change in how we treat the beautiful seas that sustain us.

Freshwater Scarcity

We need to put the freshwater issue into perspective: only roughly 2.5 per cent of earth's water is freshwater, and two-thirds of that is frozen (ice and snow). This leaves less than 1 per cent of the earth's water resources for seven billion to share, much of which is "wasted or contaminated" (Hossay, 2006:161). As creatures entirely dependent on water's existence, we tend to take this vital resource for granted. I believe a day is fast approaching when we will see a major cultural shift toward (or back toward, in many cultural contexts) the inherent value of water. For the most part, the adaptive governance needed to secure clean water supplies is at the local level, but the privatization of water resources will change this if multinational firms become increasingly involved in exporting and importing water supplies. The commodification of water is, in my view, a dangerous trend because water—surely one of the most basic building blocks of human security—should be a public good, and it is ideological folly to insist that privatization holds the answer for natural resource collective action problems. But policies encouraging water conservation and equitable distribution won't come cheaply either.

One area where international arrangements have (often quietly) assumed long-term significance is in the contestation and cooperation over shared freshwater sources, especially rivers, and I turn to this ecopolitical context now. I had the pleasure of attending the 71st International Law Association's annual meeting in 2004 in Germany, where the Berlin Rules on Water Resources were adopted; these replaced the Helsinki Rules on the Uses of Waters of International Rivers, approved by the association in 1966 (ILA, 2004). This was an effort to codify the international customary laws that had evolved to ensure that upstream states do not pollute shared water and that states avoid military conflict over water resources. The Berlin Rules also addressed a plethora of other common collective action problems. It was interesting to watch international lawyers at work, and working in Berlin, a city so besieged by warfare, toward a lasting agreement on peaceful methods to resolve conflict. The truth is that this is one area in which we have seen limited success, though we should not be complacent about it nor ignore the impact of economic development along riversides on the human security of riparian peoples.

The Veins of Life: Shared River Arrangements

"From being the sewer of Europe in the 1970s, the
Rhine is now a clean transboundary river."

FRIJTERS AND LEENTVAAR (2003:29)

To demonstrate the breadth of transboundary cooperation on rivers, I will break with the previous approach here and discuss several international arrangements. We've long been warned about future water wars, driven by geopolitical competition and scarcity. Certainly, conflicts over water rights and access are real; for example, skirmishes over river rights and access took place in the summer of 2011 between two usually peaceful neighbors, Costa Rica and Nicaragua. In the Middle East, the Tigris and Euphrates rivers originate in southeastern Turkey, snake through Syria and Iraq where they join in the Shatt-al-Arab delta, and then flow into the Persian Gulf (Altinbilek, 2004:18; Freeman, 2001:129); downstream states are openly distrustful of Turkey's long-term intentions with regards to this primary water source. China's damming of the upper Mekong in southeast Asia rightly worries countries in the lower delta. Even Canadians are known for casting a wary eye south when it comes to the possibility of future water disputes with a parched superpower. Sharing coastlines, lakes, and rivers isn't inherently easy. We might expect more conflict, yet we see forms of cooperation almost everywhere we look. As Wolf et al. (2006) suggest, water is more likely to serve as a "pathway to peace" rather than to conflict, at least when we consider international negotiations related to river basins (see also Dinar, 2011). I turn now to brief expositions of several river-sharing arrangements.

The largest river in northwestern Europe, the Rhine, provides a long-term success story of not only transboundary resource cooperation but also ecosystem restoration. The Rhine River begins its journey at the Rheinwaldhorn in the Swiss Alps and continues north for over 1,200 km through several countries, including Switzerland, France, Germany, Luxembourg, and the Netherlands, finally flowing into the North Sea. It is "Europe's most densely navigated shipping route, connecting the world's largest seaport ... with the world['s] largest inland port" (Frijters and Leentvaar, 2003:3).[15] Continental Europe's heavy industries were built along the Rhine, and it played a major role in the development of German commerce; it was also a bountiful ecosystem for wildlife and fish. The former triumphed over the latter, however, and after two world wars and decades more of industrial waste, the Rhine became an ecological disaster. Cooperation on navigation rights was precedent setting for international law, and the International Convention for the Protection of the Rhine against Pollution (ICPR, also known as the Berne Convention) was signed by riparian states and the European Community in 1963—one of the first conventions to give NGOs and other actors explicit acknowledgment. However, collective efforts toward environmental protection would not appear in earnest until two near-cataclysmic events spurred a "rising degree of environmental awareness ... indicated by the growth of green NGOs and political parties ... [that] was probably the most import driving force behind the spectacular clean up of the Rhine" (Bernauer and Moser, 1996:410).

The first occurred in 1971, when scientists realized that "oxygen-consuming waste water and toxic substances reached such high levels that the Rhine lacked oxygen in its downstream sections [and almost] all aquatic life disappeared" (Huisman et al., 2000:90). Another catalyst was the Sandoz chemical accident of 1986, when a Swiss pesticide factory fire near Basel actually turned parts of the river red and killed even more downstream aquatic life (Frijters and Leentvaar, 2003:29). In response, the Rhine Action Programme of 1987 was created, and, with commendable application, the Rhine states limited pollution from industry and shipping and waste water to the point where salmon, once extinct in the river, have been successfully reintroduced. Importantly, Rhine restoration has taken place within the broader context of another major development in international environmental law, the signing of the Aarhus Convention on Access to Information, Public Participation in Decision-making and Access to Justice in Environmental Matters, negotiated through the UN Economic Commission for Europe (UNECE) in 1992. The Aarhus Convention is considered "the most impressive venture in the area of 'environmental democracy' [and public participation] so far undertaken under the auspices of the United Nations.... [It] links environmental rights and human rights ... acknowledges the rights for all citizens ... to live in a healthy environment ... [and] links governmental accountability and environmental protection" (Frijters and Leentvaar, 2003:18–19). Aarhus inspired the EU Water Framework Directive of 2000, which could emerge as a widely followed regional model of watershed governance.[16]

There are many other examples of states cooperating in order to share river resources. In Africa, the Nile River—the longest river in the world, though it competes with the Amazon for this distinct title and, at one point, is actually two rivers, the Blue and the White—is shared by ten states, including those of the Eastern Nile subbasin (Egypt, Ethiopia, Eritrea, and Sudan) and the Equatorial Lakes subbasin (Burundi, the Democratic Republic of the Congo, Kenya, Rwanda, Tanzania, and Uganda). Although the Egyptian stretch of the river was dammed as early as 1898, the Aswan High Dam was completed by the late 1960s in order to "fully control and regulate the river's flow... [and] enable states to maximize resource use efficiency"(Nicol, 2003:10). The dam was built at severe environmental and human cost, it gave Egypt an unfair advantage compared to upstream states, and it remains a monument to the hegemonic hold of large infrastructure developmentalism. However, in a region known for colonial domination (Kagwanja, 2007), intermittent warfare, and frequently severe water shortages, cooperation remains the driving force. After several attempts at negotiation and technical cooperation (Metawie, 2004), the 1999 Nile Basin Initiative (NBI) has proven a fairly successful multilateral arrangement. It includes almost all the riparian states (Eritrea sits as an observer), and it has a mandate to achieve "sustainable socio-economic development through the equitable utilization of ... the common Nile basin water resources" (quoted in Amer et al., 2005:4). Also, the Shared Vision Program component of the NBI emphasizes "integrated and participatory management" (Amer et al., 2005:4; Nicol, 2003:4). It is too early to say whether this program will actually improve the standard of living and opportunities for decision making for the millions of riparian people involved.

Other positive-sum ventures include the work that the United States and Mexico have undertaken in relation to the Rio Grande (Gensler, Oad, and Kinzli, 2009; Oad and Kullman, 2006; Patiño-Gomez et al., 2007) and cooperation between Brazil, Paraguay, and Argentina over the Paraná River (Da Rosa, 1983; De Las Carreras, 1987) and the Itaipú dam (Murphy and Sabadell, 1986), which was once the world's largest hydroelectric power dam (China's Three Gorges Dam on the Yangtze now holds that dubious distinction). Other cooperative arrangements exist for the Jordan River, shared by Syria, Lebanon, Jordan, Israel, and the Palestinian territory (Phillips et al., 2007); the Indus River, shared by India, Pakistan, China, and Afghanistan (Ali, 2008:178); and the Mekong, shared by Vietnam, Thailand, Cambodia, Laos, Burma, and China (Hensengerth, 2009). Indeed, the list is very long, and not all cases have permitted sustained institutional cooperation. Many of them have, however, and this is promising, though critics charge that some arrangements, such as Oslo-related efforts at Israeli-Palestinian water-sharing, are, in effect, "dressing up domination as cooperation" (Selby, 2003). And we must be aware, of course, that such arrangements do not guarantee civil liberties or even basic human security to those displaced by infrastructure development. My studies on the Mekong River Commission, for example, suggest that although it has generated remarkable levels of sustained interaction and even some policy integration amongst the lower delta states, it cannot bridge the gap in power between China and these states, nor has it yet proven to hold much democratic legitimacy amongst those most affected by major projects, such as the dynamiting of rapids to clear the way for large boats or the construction of dams along tributaries (see Stoett, 2005). It is always vital that civil society plays a major role in ensuring that these arrangements are not merely glossy brochures, complete with purchased environmental impact assessments (EIAs), used to justify power grabs and the marginalization of riparian peoples. (I return to the twin themes of environmental justice and human security in subsequent chapters.)

Beyond pollution, overfishing, and other threats, the biggest single alteration of river habitat occurs with the construction of large-scale dams, which effectively control the flow of the river and create massive reservoirs of still water. The World Commission on Dams (WCD) was established through the IUCN and the World Bank and was asked to write a report on the controversies associated with large dam construction.[17] Its report was a far-reaching discussion emphasizing the need for broad stakeholder consultation before and during dam construction, as well as a serious EIA.[18] Nonetheless, because of the human displacement associated with the construction of large reservoirs, dam construction remains one of most controversial of development projects. Indeed, I am not claiming that international arrangements are in and of themselves sufficient governance structures to deal with the complexities of freshwater management, a point Ken Conca makes in his brilliant book (Conca, 2005). Expert networks, citizen groups, fishermen and investors in market projects, and other actors with claims to representational legitimacy and authority will often have as much influence on events as the governments that have signed bilateral or multilateral agreements.

Nonetheless, the level of cooperation on shared rivers has been impressive. Closer to my own home, which is a short walk away from another great vestibule of water, the St. Lawrence River, Canada and the United States have institutionalized adaptive governance of the Great Lakes Basin, the largest freshwater source on earth, through the ongoing work of the highly regarded International Joint Commission, the Great Lakes Fishery Commission, and the state-provincial Great Lakes Commission.[19] Though the ravages of industrialization are still evident in the Great Lakes and the threats posed by climate change and invasive alien species are big challenges, the transborder governance architecture established over the last century will aid the two countries in the necessary diplomatic work to come. Achieving much wider cooperation on ocean sustainability is the next step, but it is a very big step indeed.

Surviving the Tides

"When the well's dry, we know the worth of water."

BENJAMIN FRANKLIN, *POOR RICHARD'S ALMANAC* (1746)

As I write this conclusion, I am sitting on the banks of the mighty St. Lawrence River in LaSalle, Quebec, within jumping distance of the Lachine Rapids. I have no intention of jumping, however! The river's muscular flow roars beside me, as the spring water feeds its many tributaries, some of which have experienced serious flooding this year, dislocating homeowners, farmers, and businesses. Several species of birds cross to and fro, stabbing at the ample offering of bug clouds filling patches of sky. It is hard to overestimate the cultural, economic, and environmental value of this beautiful watery beast. This river was once on the brink of ecological catastrophe, but we've managed to ward off the demons, with a concerted effort by Canadian and American, provincial and state, and municipal governments; local citizen's groups; scientists; industry; and others. Not that I would drink the water in untreated form; but, a few decades ago, it was widely felt that the St. Lawrence and, indeed, several of the Great Lakes were destined toward ecological death and that the smooth white beluga whales found in the eastern sections of the river were doomed to extinction. Room for improvement remains, and adjusting to climate change will be a challenge, but we should note success where we find it.

Can we do the same for the ocean into which many of the millions of liters of water passing beside me this morning will eventually spill? Can we make the global investment necessary to preserve the ecological and cultural heritage—the common heritage—of the interlinked systems of oceans, which determine so much of our terrestrial fate? While action on biodiversity, deforestation, land degradation, and atmospheric pollution is quite tangible and permits many rays of light to shine through the darkness of industrial impetus, and cooperation on shared river systems is heartening, the future of the oceans appears bleak if concerted action is not taken very soon in several key areas, even if we have largely put an end to the tragedy of uncontrolled whaling and have moved closer to controlling intentional releases of oil at sea. As with my beloved Lake Huron, it is hard to conceptualize the vast expanse of the oceans as vulnerable, fragile, and limited. Indeed, anyone who has been on a small ship in an ocean gale knows what it feels like to achieve temporary humility, if not insignificance, against the backdrop of such size and power. But the fact is that the oceans are in peril—they are to an unprecedented degree at our collective mercy in this Anthropocene era. As complex and comprehensive as UNCLOS appears, it is but a first step toward more effective ocean governance. It has had a wide legal impact, limited environmental efficacy, and some cognitive success, and it has made great strides in terms of democratic legitimacy by advocating the "common heritage of humankind" concept. Regional river agreements have generally been more effective, though the record is mixed when it comes to their ability to protect the human security of riparian communities. The Aarhus Convention is a strong precedent for establishing the environmental rights of citizens, but its protections are confined to European citizens and do not extend to those in areas where displacement and water shortages are everyday facts of life.

Indeed, water is already one of the most visible of human rights issues. To push a common water metaphor: a familiar saying, often favored by the market liberals, is that a rising tide lifts all boats. Regardless of the accuracy of such a grandiose justification for capital accumulation, one can with certainty argue that the oceans crisis will harm all of us: for the millions who live in coastal communities, especially in the small island states, rising tides may be the kiss of communal death. And yet the potential for the oceans, lakes, and rivers to continue to serve as the basis for all of human life remains tremendous.[20] In Chapter 10, we will return to global energy as an issue, but we have had little time here to discuss the benefits of small-scale hydroelectricity, including tidal and wave power. If we can rehabilitate the fisheries and properly regulate them and further develop sustainable aquaculture, we can provide healthy protein for billions. The biodiversity of the coral reef may yet reveal medical properties similar to those found in the tropical rain forests that we are, slowly, starting to protect. The litany of "ifs" is long, but the need for a passionate response is self-evident to most of us. We owe the water coursing through our veins this much, and more.

Notes

1. Excerpt from the *Mishomis Book* by Eddie Benton Banai found at http://www.real-dream-catchers.com/Native_American_origins/ojibwe_creation_story.htm.
2. Bycatch refers to unwanted species of fish and marine mammals that are caught in nets and then discarded, often after dying on deck; the estimated volume of discarded catches is around 7.3 million tonnes per year according to the Food and Agriculture Organization; see http://www.fao.org/fishery/topic/14832/en.
3. The original signatories were Argentina, Australia, Belgium, Chile, France, Japan, New Zealand, Norway, Russia (then the Soviet Union), South Africa, the United Kingdom, and the United States. Antarctica became the first designated nuclear weapons-free zone, though there was little at the time to fight over.
4. Though the inclusion of non-voting representation for indigenous people may seem like a cheap effort to gain some democratic legitimacy for the Arctic Council, in a diplomatic

world dominated by states and intergovernmental relations, it is a precedent-setting development. For more on the formation of the Arctic Council, see Stoett (2000b).

5. The "Eastern garbage patch," located in the middle of the Pacific, is an area of accumulated debris about the size of Texas. It is estimated to contain 3 million tons of debris (Leous and Parry, 2005:259). Innovative programs to pay economically dislocated fishermen to retrieve recyclable material are being developed.

6. On dead zones and hypoxia, see the Microbial Life Education Resources "Dead Zone General Collection" online at http://serc.carleton.edu/microbelife/topics/deadzone/general.html, accessed December 12, 2011.

7. The ghost net is perhaps an apt symbol for the careless treatment of the oceans, as it floats mercilessly through the dark underwater expanses, collecting marine life in its path for no beneficial purpose whatsoever.

8. Atlantic bluefin tuna are huge fish (averaging from 300 to 600 pounds), a pelagic species that lives from roughly the equator to Newfoundland and from Turkey to the Gulf of Mexico. Swimming at an average speed of 50 miles an hour across multiple national boundaries, they are classified as a highly migratory species. The high-end sushi trade has made this lucrative fish so desirable we have a repeat of earlier contests over whaling (see Bestor, 2001; on whaling, see Stoett, 1997).

9. The term "flags of convenience" refers to the practice of temporarily borrowing (in some cases, renting) flags from countries that do not participate in various marine arrangements so as to escape potential prosecution for violating those arrangements. It is a surprisingly common act of outright trickery.

10. "150. Proclamation 2667: Policy of the United States with Respect to the Natural Resources of the Subsoil and Sea Bed of the Continental Shelf," Harry Truman Library and Museum (http://trumanlibrary.org/publicpapers/viewpapers.php?pid=159). See also Pontecorvo (1986a, 1986b).

11. The reader is no doubt aware that cetaceans (whales) are mammals, not fish, but the term "fishery" has been applied to whaling operations for hundreds of years.

12. For a fascinating article on the role played by cetologists within the context of the IWC arrangement, see Peterson and Winter (1992).

13. Ballast water is taken in to help balance the hull of a large ship once it has offloaded its cargo; the water is released when the ship returns for reloading, sending invasive species such as zebra mussels into local waters.

14. The London Convention on the Prevention of Marine Pollution by Dumping of Wastes and Other Matter, which was adopted in 1972, and its 1996 Protocol established international regulations restricting the disposal of wastes from aircraft, platforms, and at-sea vessels, basically prohibiting all dumping of hazardous waste into the sea. However, it failed to address land-based sources of waste.

15. The authors are referring to Rotterdam and Duisburg (in the Netherlands and Germany, respectively), though we should note there is considerable controversy over whether these European ports are the biggest in the world.

16. See the European Commission's excellent Water Information System for Europe web-site (http://ec.europa.eu/environment/water/water-framework/index_en.html).

17. The WCD should not be confused with the International Commission on Large Dams, which was essentially an industry-based association with little legitimacy outside the dam-construction industry.

18. The WCD was disbanded in 2001 and was replaced with the UNEP's Dams and Development Project; see http://www.unep.org/dams/WCD/.

19. The NAFTA-based Commission on Environmental Cooperation (CEC) also plays a role here.

20. For rays of hope, visit the website of the World Water Council: http://www.world watercouncil.org/.

CHAPTER SEVEN

Trade and the Global Environment

"The one 'end-ism' that we often forget is the potential end of nature itself. Nature ... now needs our protection rather than offers us its shelter. It needs our protection from market forces."

MICHAEL DOYLE (1997:497)

IT WOULD BE RATHER SIMPLISTIC TO SUGGEST THAT ENVIRONMENTAL problems can be blamed directly on the trade of goods and services that cause ecological harm. Although it was fashionable for some time to draw a direct link between economic growth and environmental degradation, most environmentalists today would acknowledge that it is the type of economic growth—the precise configuration of investment and trade, regulation and implementation—that determines its ultimate environmental impact. (An unhealthy fixation on the myth of endless growth, however, is another thing, as Peter Brown and others remind us [Brown and Garver, 2009].) The benefits of trade are well known, and, indeed, one can quite plausibly argue that much of the material wealth many of us enjoy is the result of ongoing transactions between producers and consumers across borders. Although free trade might encourage a "race to the bottom" in terms of capital seeking low environmental and labor standards, it also has the potential to create employment and government revenue, which can, in turn, be helpful for mitigating environmental harm. Economic growth for its own sake is not desirable, but it can certainly be put to good use.

This chapter will examine two case studies that shed some light on progress made toward more effective, adaptive global governance arrangements designed to mitigate the ecological impact of trade. The first is trade in hazardous and toxic substances, which has generated uncountable local and national efforts as well as several major conventions; the second is an agreement reached by members of the World Trade Organization (WTO) to permit some level of domestic tampering with the freedom usually enjoyed by international traders, tampering to prevent environmental harm. Neither is perfect; neither is useless.

Dealing with trade puts us squarely in the intersection between the private sector and what governments can and cannot do in the contemporary international political economy. Today, trade in commodities has a very long product cycle ranging from the extraction of natural resources from the earth (land and water) to the disposal of end-product waste. Even trade in services demands the constant use of energy resources and the generation of e-waste (electronic waste such as discarded computers). Economic globalization spread, and then tightened, the web of interdependency that holds together the parts of trade and finance. Global ecopolitics has not been a dominant force in this development; on the contrary, most would agree, the intellectual hegemony of utilitarianism and liberalism and the legal institution of sovereignty have precluded strong regulatory action at the international level. Yet it is apparent that some form of regulation is necessary if we are to restrict trade to that which poses minimal risks to environmental and personal security. Even the relentlessly pro-trade WTO has mainstreamed this notion, establishing an ongoing Committee on Trade and Environment, which signifies a "reluctant acceptance of the environment as a legitimate issue for the trading system" (Williams, 2001:1); and the once highly controversial but now contextual North American Free Trade Agreement (NAFTA) has a side agreement and a Commission for Environmental Cooperation (CEC), located near my office in downtown Montreal. It is debatable whether or not, had "the problems of pollution and wastage of resources been dealt with before spreading industrial production around the globe, they would not threaten the survival of the planet" (Howes, 2005:176). But these problems must be addressed now, as we witness the continued development of a bifurcated world where "effective environmental regulation, exposure to deadly toxins, and the dumping of poisonous waste mirror the power and wealth inequities of the global society [in which] the poor struggle to survive in the toxic sludge of the rich" (Hossay, 2006:33).

Part of the solution to these problems may lie in the international financial institutions that seek to keep the world economy moving, such as the International Monetary Fund and the World Bank, as well as in regional development banks, which were introduced in Chapter 2. Most observers would agree that the record here is mixed: the history of the World Bank, for example, is replete with the imposition of structural adjustment programs that probably did more ecological harm than good as low-income countries struggled to deal with inherited national debt. Yet the Global Environmental Facility, which was originally formed partially through World Bank funding, is one of the most important funding mechanisms for global environmental governance today. Others have covered international financial institutions well (see, for example, Clapp and Dauvergne, 2008), so I will focus on trade issues in this chapter. But we should keep these institutions firmly in mind as we proceed.

Toxic Trade

A vivid example of this bifurcation is the transboundary trade in hazardous waste, which continues today despite one of the more robust efforts at global environmental governance. It is important to note, however, that most of the global trade in hazardous waste does not fit with this image. Greenpeace has estimated that only 2.5 million tonnes was exported from OECD member countries to the non-OECD countries of the developing world between 1989 and 1994 (Montgomery, 1995:5). However, this statistic belies the true extent of the hazard posed by this toxic refuse shipped to countries too often unable to manage it (Clapp, 1994:505), countries that "lack the human, technological, and financial resources to manage the transboundary movements of hazardous wastes" (Jurdi, 2002:12). Ecological modernization would demand the opposite: that toxic waste be moved from non-OECD countries to OECD countries, as the latter have the ability to "dispose" of it more effectively (Baggs, 2009). A further element compounding the dangers of the waste trade is its frequently clandestine nature. As opposition to the trade has grown, illegal waste traders have devised ever more creative means of disguising their shipments, including mislabeling cargo, nighttime dumping, and secret burial. One documented case involved an American company selling fertilizer to Bangladeshi farmers—but not before mixing it with 1,000 tonnes of copper smelter furnace dust, complete with high levels of lead. The "fertilizer" had already found its way to some farmers' fields before the scheme was eventually uncovered. Some shipments of hazardous waste have even been labeled as humanitarian assistance, including a European shipment of radioactive milk sent to Jamaica in 1987 and illegal pesticides sent by Germany to Albania in

1992 (Clapp, 1994:507–8). These cases probably signify only the tip of a clandestine iceberg whose extent we have yet to fully fathom. Of course, even perfectly legal transboundary waste movements can also serve as an effective disincentive toward decreasing domestic waste production.

To deal with national concerns pertaining to waste disposal, governments in the West first enacted more stringent regulations governing the treatment of waste. Consequently, the costs of disposing waste grew tremendously, soaring from $15/tonne in 1980 to approximately $250/tonne in 1988 (Clapp, 1994:506). As national debt skyrocketed, many southern countries, reeling under economic hardship, began to import toxic waste by-products from the industrialized world as a means of generating revenue. From a purely economic standpoint, the case seemed flawless. In 1991, a shocking internal memo composed by World Bank Chief Economist Lawrence Summers, presently President Obama's director of the National Economic Council, exposed such sentiments to broad daylight: "I think the economic logic behind dumping a load of toxic waste in the lowest wage country is impeccable," Mr. Summers opined, though most likely in a sarcastic, tongue-in-cheek manner, "and we should face up to that…. I've always thought that under-populated countries in Africa are vastly under-polluted" (quoted in Puckett, 1997). The memo was subsequently leaked to the world press, inviting outrage and derision and prompting Brazil's environment minister to respond in writing, calling Mr. Summers's reasoning "perfectly logical but totally insane" (Puckett, 1997).

The case of the *Khian Sea* ship serves as a notorious example of where we were heading. In August of 1986, the ship departed from the port of Philadelphia carrying 14,000 tonnes of toxic incinerator ash. After Greenpeace alerted all likely ports along the ship's route, the vessel, despite changing its name numerous times along the way, was repeatedly turned away from possible ports. Its "now legend" voyage lasted 27 months and took it to all 5 continents, after which the ship, unable to find a receptive port, is suspected of having dumped its waste in the Indian Ocean (Clapp, 1994:506). And, in 1987, a ship carrying 8,000 tonnes of radioactive and hazardous waste, ambiguously labeled "substances related to the building trade," made its way from Italy to the small port town of Koko, Nigeria. The waste was subsequently stored in drums in a farmer's backyard. After repackaging the waste for export back to Italy, Nigerian workers were hospitalized for severe chemical burns, nausea, vomiting blood, and partial paralysis, and a 500-meter radius area around the dump site was declared unsafe. In response, Nigeria recalled its ambassador to Italy, and the waste importers were sentenced to death by a Nigerian court (Krueger, 1998:12; Lipman, 2002:67; Puckett, 1997).

Beginning around 1987, there emerged what noted expert Jennifer Clapp refers to as a "Third World–NGO" alliance, which sought a ban on hazardous waste exports from rich to developing countries (Clapp, 1994:505). In June of that year, at the 14th Session of the UNEP Governing Council, the executive director was tasked with forming a working group consisting of technical and legal experts with the mandate of developing a global convention regulating the international trade in hazardous wastes. A month later, in July of 1987, Greenpeace published research revealing that waste exporters had by 1986 attempted to export upwards of 163 million tonnes of hazardous waste. While the drafting groups on a future waste trade convention were held throughout 1988 and 1989, several countries went ahead to enact unilateral import bans on hazardous waste. The number of bans rose from 3 in 1986 to 33 in 1988. (This number would continue to climb in the years to follow and was up to 88 in 1992 and more than 120 in 1995.) From the very beginning, the Basel negotiations were heated, with the debate quickly distilling into two opposing camps. On the one side was the Group of 77 (G-77) developing nations, which was in alliance with a network of environmental NGOs under the banner of the International Toxic Waste Action Network (ITWAN). This group demanded a total ban on the export of hazardous waste from high to low income countries. On the other side, the wealthy industrialized countries of the global north sought a more limited regulatory approach hinged on a system of prior and written informed consent roughly in keeping with the GATT.[1]

The final draft of the convention was submitted in March of 1989 at a conference held in Switzerland: pursuant to American-led opposition, the treaty shied away from including a ban on hazardous waste imports or exports. The Basel Convention on the Control of Transboundary Movements of Hazardous Wastes and Their Disposal, freshly signed, was instantly denounced by both Greenpeace and countries of the developing world, who saw it as a toothless and token reification of the status quo. African delegations walked out in protest. Fresh on the heels of Basel's perceived insult, both Africa, under the umbrella of the Organisation of African Unity (OAU—now the African Union) and the African, Caribbean, and Pacific (ACP) group of states came together to sign the Bamako and Lomé IV conventions, in 1989 and 1991, respectively. These conventions ban the import of toxic waste into the territories of member states. Lomé, signed between the European Community and the 69 countries of the ACP, thus became the first legally binding treaty prohibiting the export of hazardous waste, in this case from Europe to Africa, the Caribbean, and the Pacific. The Waigani Treaty followed. It was signed by the developing island countries of the South Pacific Forum (SPF) and banned all imports into the treaty area. On the more specific issue of trade in hazardous chemicals and pesticides, the Convention on the Prior Informed Consent Procedure for Certain Hazardous Chemicals and Pesticides in International Trade—also known as the Rotterdam Convention—was signed in 1998 under the joint auspices of the FAO and UNEP; the convention invokes the prior informed consent procedure with an eye to protecting especially southern countries from unwanted imports of hazardous chemicals (Kummer,

1999:323–24). The Rotterdam Convention entered into force in February of 2004, following sufficient ratifications, and currently counts 134 parties; it has been hailed as the "most significant development in the global governance of chemical pollutants" (Hough, 2011:184). The Stockholm Convention on Persistent Organic Pollutants, meanwhile, covers trade in specially designated chemicals such as aldrin, mirex, polychlorinated biphenyls (PCBs) and, partially and controversially, dichlorodiphenyltrichloroethane (DDT).[2]

The Basel Convention on Trade in Hazardous Substances

Public pressure against the toxic waste trade continued to build in OECD countries, and, in 1994, at the second COP to the Basel Convention, a ban on hazardous waste exports from OECD to non-OECD countries was finally adopted, to be made legally binding the following year as an amendment to the convention. To date, however, the United States, responsible for most (75–80 per cent) of the world's hazardous waste production (O'Neill, 2000:145), has still not ratified the Basel Convention and persists in its shipment of hazardous wastes to Asia and Africa (Dreher and Pulver, 2008:308), while the ban amendment continues to await sufficient ratifications for it to enter into force.[3]

The stated objectives of the Basel Convention are threefold: to minimize the transboundary movement of hazardous waste while reducing the overall volume produced at the source; to promote the "proximity principle," whereby waste is disposed of as near to its source as possible; and to prohibit the shipment of wastes to countries lacking the sufficient capacity to manage them in an environmentally sound manner. These principles, at least initially, however, lacked both legal teeth and incentives to reduce the production of hazardous wastes, and, in practice, the Basel Convention only prohibited exports to Antarctica and countries with their own national import bans. Importantly, however, the convention as adopted in 1989 hinges on the notion of "prior informed consent," so shipments, duly labeled and detailed, are permitted only after having received written authorization from a designated "competent authority" in the importing country while shipments to nonparties to the convention are disallowed unless covered by an agreement at least as stringent. Any contravention of the procedures consists of a breach of the convention and thereby becomes illegal trade (Krueger, 1998:120).

Beyond the absence of some key industrialized states, objections to the treaty stem from many sources. The complete lack of any ban led the environmental community to label it as the "legalization of 'toxic terror'" (Clapp, 1994:512); vague definitions on what constituted 'hazardous waste' or 'environmentally sound' further weakened the accord; a means of actually halting shipments that were refused prior consent was lacking; radioactive waste was excluded from the treaty, as were liability provisions; and insufficient attention was given to questions of enforcement and noncompliance (Sánchez, 1994:143). Ultimately, however, many of the convention's missing elements, such as a liability protocol, a compliance mechanism, and, most crucially, the advent of an eventual ban, would be dealt with at subsequent meetings of the conference of the parties (COPs).

Lauded by environmentalists as a triumph both for global democracy and environmental justice (Puckett and Fogel, 1994), a total ban on exports of hazardous waste from OECD to non-OECD countries was adopted in 1994 at the second COP. After some pushback by a small but powerful core of opponents (Japan, the United States, Canada, South Korea, New Zealand, and Australia), the ban was instead legally entrenched as an amendment to the Basel Convention at the third COP held the following year (BAN, 2011). Though the ambitious formal ban has yet to come into force, Greenpeace and the Basel Action Network claim it operates as customary international law and has helped avert untold catastrophes (Lipman, 2010; Puckett, 2000).

At the fourth COP in 1998, the parties addressed the issue of hazardous waste definitions and classed them into two separate categories, adjoined as annexes, but the adoption of a liability protocol had to wait until the COP held in 1999. The protocol, which attaches liability and compensation requirements for damages caused by the improper handling of hazardous waste shipments, has been both lauded by UNEP as a breakthrough in environmental law and lambasted by environmentalists who criticize its many loopholes (Choksi, 2001:524). Michael Tsimplis argues that, although "far from perfect," the protocol does nonetheless improve upon the original Basel Convention by providing compensation for damages caused by accidents or spills (Tsimplis, 2001:296). It also increases costs for insurance for unlimited liability, thereby rendering the local disposal of wastes more attractive, perhaps deterring future episodes such as the *Khian Sea* incident. In 2002, the parties to the convention finally adopted a compliance mechanism aimed at ensuring that countries live up to their obligations under the treaty (Shibata, 2003:183). Nevertheless, illegal trafficking continues to undermine the effectiveness of the convention, which leaves it to national governments to implement legislation pursuing such offenses (Kummer, 1998:233). As the UNEP wrote in 1995,

> While most of the developed industrial State Parties have adopted fairly elaborate legislation on most of these [implementation] issues, very few of the developing country Parties

have formulated adequate legislation or suitable administrative procedures on these subjects. In fact, many of these countries still lack the necessary legal and institutional framework to effectively control and prevent the dumping of hazardous wastes on their territories. (UNEP, 1995; quoted in Krueger, 1998:131)

Until such time as the ban receives sufficient ratifications to enter into force, the central operating principle of the Basel Convention remains the system of prior informed consent (PIC); and yet, capacity constraints in the Southern States too often impede non-OECD countries from making well-informed decisions regarding acceptance of a shipment and prevent them from being able to verify the accuracy of shipment details and contents before unloading (Krueger, 1998:121). In one particular instance in 1996, a German company was found to have shipped 560 tones of mixed and partly contaminated plastic waste to Beirut, having labeled the shipment as plastic "raw material for industrial production." As Krueger (1998) remarks, "If such fraud is not detected by the competent authority, or if the competent authority is in collusion with the illegal activity, then the notification scheme becomes useless" (p. 121). Further, the "chronic underfinancing" of the Basel Secretariat, located in Geneva, severely curtails its capacity to help parties adequately implement the PIC procedure (Krueger, 1998:123).

On another crucial front, however, the treaty's success has been far more certain. By shining a persistent and unforgiving light on some of the worst excesses of the industrialized world—and on their human cost, particularly to the world's poor—the Basel Convention and the processes surrounding it have succeeded in generating significant normative change. According to Jonathan Krueger (1999),

> The Basel Convention has been central to the elimination of some of the worst forms of toxic waste "dumping" by industrialized countries in developing countries. By publicizing and condemning this practice, the convention put a great deal of political pressure on exporting countries to stop it. Indeed, there is now an international consensus that rich countries should not send hazardous wastes to poor ones for final disposal, as exemplified by the ban in Decision III/1. Thus, the fact that the convention changed the norms of international behaviour was perhaps as important as the trade restrictions themselves. (P. 19)

Meanwhile, the meager group of initial signatories to the convention had by 1994 almost doubled to 65 parties and would continue to expand thereafter. By 2011, the Basel Convention numbered 175 parties, and 69 countries had ratified the ban amendment. Basel remains weakened by the exclusion of radioactive waste and electronic waste and by the possibility of countries exporting undetected hazardous waste by falsely labeling waste products as "destined for recycling" (however, several countries, including Canada, have made it clear that they will not ratify the ban amendment while it refers to recyclable material; see Kamuk and Hansen, 2007).

In comparison, the European Union has moved decisively to reflect the convention in its internal regulation. Many countries, such as Germany, have enforced provisions requiring producers to reduce waste generation, and monitor closely any movement of waste (O'Neill, 2000:144). Exports to developing countries are banned under German law and European Union directives, though the familiar story of inadequate enforcement has allowed for many instances of illegal exportations, including shipments of municipal solid waste sent to "black dumps" in the Czech Republic in 2005 and 2006 (Vail, 2008:828). Also, at least in EU forums, Germany continues to support the export of wastes destined for recycling, despite the inevitable opportunities this policy provides to illegal traffickers.

Despite an overall picture of success, we should not ignore remaining governance gaps when it comes to toxic trade. In informal discussions I had with many Bosnians and Croatians during my travels across these Balkan states in 2002, I was surprised how often the specter of organized crime and illegal toxic waste dumping came up as a serious local environmental challenge. Notwithstanding the protracted war in the 1990s, the countryside of Bosnia-Herzegovina is as beautiful as any in Europe, and it is shameful that parts of it have been used as a European dumping ground. Another major gap is the burgeoning trade in electronic waste (popularly known as "e-waste"). You are probably reading this text on an electronic device that you will need to discard in the future. I've certainly been through my share of computers before stopping to think about what happens to them when we throw them on the street as garbage or give them to recycling companies. Although some electronics are dismantled in North America or Europe, many of them are shipped to Africa and Asia, where they are stripped for reusable parts. This sounds like the responsible thing to do, but some of the electronic waste is, in fact, toxic, containing lead, cadmium, and mercury. "What's more," as Schmidt (2006) points out, "electronic components are usually housed in plastic casings that spew carcinogenic dioxins and polyaromatic hydrocarbons when burned" (p. 232). Basel does not ban trade in products destined for recycling or reuse, and it is unlikely that exporting states would accept it if it did (and less likely that the United States would ever ratify it). The Basel Action Network has devoted attention to a campaign to direct computer owners toward certified e-waste disposers to circumvent the convention's loophole on this issue; it is really up to us as consumers to move on this.[4]

The WTO and the Agreement
on the Application of Sanitary and
Phytosanitary Measures (SPS)

One of the reasons "prior informed consent" was used as a standard in the Basel Convention, and in many other multilateral and bilateral arrangements such as the Cartagena Protocol on Biosafety, is that it does not contravene the principles espoused by the GATT and WTO, providing it can be demonstrated that countries are taking scientifically determined defensive action and not simply protecting their economies from competitive imports. This is one of the greatest dilemmas of environmental policy making in the age of globalization: the world economic system is predicated on the acceptance of capital and product mobility, yet some investments and commodities present hazards to environmental security that should be unacceptable. At the same time, as Birnie, Boyle, and Redgwell (2009) write,

> WTO and GATT jurisprudence have tended to frown on unilateral action. However, there are at least two theoretical justifications for "creative" unilateral action. First, a unilateral act can be *de lege ferenda*, a new state practice that may mature into … custom under accepted norms of international law.… [And second,] a unilateral act may be a countermeasure … taken only under certain conditions. A countermeasure must be in response to a prior act contrary to international law; there must be a prior request for redress; and the measure taken by the aggrieved state must not be out of proportion to the gravity of the original wrongful act. (P. 776–77)

Environmental activists are often fond of pointing out that the WTO has generally stacked the deck against environmental policy considerations. There is no doubt that the fundamentally liberal perspective enshrined in the GATT dominates the international trade discourse, though occasional forays into protectionism look more like the realist paradigm resurgent. Yet, while researching international policy options related to invasive alien species in the summer of 2011, I found myself entering the WTO Secretariat in Geneva to interview two very enthusiastic WTO employees about how the organization can help countries deal with this potentially debilitating problem. There is a relatively unknown instrument within the WTO that, if used properly, could serve to solve the "environmental regulation versus open trade" dilemma posed by the organization's free-market bias, though the evidence so far suggests that this agreement still places the benefits of trade above the avoidance of environmental risks. The WTO succeeded the GATT in 1994, and Article 20 of its agreement allows states to make decisions based on the interest of human, animal, or plant life and health (Coleman and Gabler, 2002: 846). Both the SPS Agreement and the Technical Barriers to Trade (TBT) Agreement were crafted in response. At the end of the day, the SPS Agreement is still mainly a contract governing trade issues (Winham, 2009:415), designed to avoid and not encourage trade barriers, but it opens the door for environmental protection within the context of a liberal trading regime and is binding on all 153 (in 2011) WTO members.

Sanitary and phytosanitary measures are defined in Annex A of the SPS Agreement as measures with the intention

(a) to protect animal or plant life or health within the territory of the Member from risks arising from the entry, establishment or spread of pests, diseases, disease-carrying organisms or disease-causing organisms;

(b) to protect human or animal life or health within the territory of the Member from risks arising from additives, contaminants, toxins or disease-causing organisms in foods, beverages or feedstuffs;

(c) to protect human life or health within the territory of the Member from risks arising from diseases carried by animals, plants or products thereof, or from the entry, establishment or spread of pests; or

(d) to prevent or limit other damage within the territory of the Member from the entry, establishment or spread of pests.
(WTO, 1994:77)

Members are permitted to impose any limitation they see as necessary to combat serious risk to the environment or human health; however, the limitation must be reinforced by scientific evidence and constitute a minimal impairment on trade (Foster, 2008:456). Substantively, this language aims to have members set measures based on a "risk assessment paradigm," which serves to help set appropriate levels as well as guide policy maker's choices and to encourage the use of standards that, whenever possible, are expected to be internationally recognized (Coleman and Gabler, 2002:496; Roberts, 1998.)[5] The SPS Agreement encourages members to consult and contribute to the development of standards within the framework of the International Plant Protection Convention (IPPC), the World Organisation for Animal Health (known as the OIE because it was once called the Office International des Epizooties), and the Codex Alimentarius Commission (see Coleman and Gabler, 2002:496). Due to their frequent involvement with the SPS, the IPPC and Codex have "observer" status at all meetings of the SPS Committee, and the various international standards-setting organizations that are affiliated with the SPS Agreement are also all affiliated with the FAO (Coleman and Gabler, 2002:496–7).[6] All members can send delegates to the SPS Committee, which is mandated to help develop guidelines and sit as an informal dispute resolution body. Should disputants not wish to address the committee, they can also apply to the general WTO dispute mechanism, which consists of a panel, whose decisions can be binding, and an appellate body that is only accessible through unanimous approval by the SPS Committee (Roberts, 1998).

According to a WTO report released in March 2010, as of 2009 there had been 40 SPS disputes brought before WTO panels (WTO, 2010:31). The majority of the conflicts were resolved by mutual agreement with the help of the SPS panels, while five required official WTO panel reports that contained binding decisions. By far the most contentious grievance to date has occurred between the European Union (EU) and the United States (along with several other countries) over the EU's "*de facto* moratorium" on genetically modified agricultural products, which resulted in a three-year inquiry and the release of a panel report in 2006 (Foster, 2008; Peel, 2006). The pro-GMO side won the ruling overall (though GMO bans in many EU countries remain in place), but the case is significant for several reasons, including the explicit involvement of the *precautionary principle*. Peel (2006) observes that the initial scope of the agreement was so narrow that, unless matters were related to problems such as pests or disease due to plants and animals or their products, most items would fall under the scope of the TBT Agreement instead, which also had environmental provisions (p. 1016). In its report, however, the WTO Dispute Settlement Panel clarified the context of "environmental concerns" by establishing that the SPS Agreement would take precedence over other WTO agreements in any circumstances that related to the imposition of nontariff barriers on any sanitary or phytosanitary product or byproduct. This solidified the reach of the agreement to include any non-processed product derived from living organisms. It also clarified what is expected in regard to scientific evidence and the scientific assessment of risk, and it explained the WTO's stance on the SPS Agreement vis-à-vis other international agreements, such as the UN Cartagena Protocol on Biosafety.[7]

In the EU moratorium case, the WTO Dispute Settlement Panel ruled that, because none of the complaining parties were signatories to the Cartagena Protocol, that protocol had no relevance in WTO considerations (Winham, 2009:420). The result is that, unless all parties are the member of another treaty or agreement, its applicability is of no significance under the WTO. The immediate disadvantage for members that are a party to both the WTO's SPS Agreement and the Cartagena Protocol is to render the latter as subordinate to the WTO even if they stress the need to respect the Cartagena Protocol at least on an equal level as the SPS Agreement. Because the result of the panel decision also cemented the scope of the agreement as pertaining to all things environmental, upon hearing a dispute, the panel should automatically defer to the SPS Agreement. Some have argued that the result is an even more fragmented international environmental law system because of the conflicts that have emerged among the different international arrangements (Peel, 2006:1022).[8]

Regardless, the agreement provides room for negotiation and mandates the pursuit of scientific evidence, the harmonization of standards, regional considerations and disease-free areas, and transparency. All of these things could potentially lead to consensus on measures that actually would be environmentally beneficial. In order to effectively demonstrate the risks of trade in certain products, however, it is essential that scientific capacity building takes place in southern states in particular. How does the SPS Agreement address the uncertainty of scientific information? Article 5.7 of the SPS Agreement states the following:

> In cases where relevant scientific evidence is insufficient, a Member may provisionally adopt sanitary or phytosanitary measures on the basis of available pertinent information, including that from the relevant international organizations as well as from sanitary or phytosanitary measures applied by other Members. In such circumstances, Members shall seek to obtain the additional information necessary for a more objective assessment of risk and review the sanitary or phytosanitary measure accordingly within a reasonable period of time. (SPS Agreement, Article 5.7)

The substantive effect of this article is that it allows states latitude to temporarily impose appropriate sanitary and phytosanitary measures when scientific evidence is lacking in the causal relationship between the environmental or human health impacts of sanitary or phytosanitary products and their import and use. It has been said that this provision is reflective of the *precautionary principle*, which has arisen throughout this book (O'Riordan and Jordan, 1995:193). However, a WTO panel once opined that it does not want to import the entirety of the principle because it would run contrary to the *scientific* principles that underpin the rest of the agreement (Foster, 2009:51); in other words, whereas the precautionary principle demands caution in the event of *uncertainty of risk*, the SPS Agreement places *proof of risk* as the mechanism for exercising precaution (Kleinman, Kinchy, and Autry, 2009:363). The *proof of risk* is not the same thing as, and in fact runs contrary to, the expectation that one must be careful in a situation when not enough information exists to assess risk effectively. Thus, although Article 5.7 does address insufficiency of scientific evidence, it does not address uncertainty of risk, which is the primary driver of the precautionary principle.

These factors encouraged southern countries to form a coalition during the negotiation of the Cartagena Protocol on Biosafety to ensure that socioeconomic considerations ultimately garnered a place in that agreement (Kinchy, Kleinman, and Autry, 2008:169; Kleinman, Kinchy, and Autry, 2009:364). Indeed, Kleinman and his colleagues suggest that the Cartagena Protocol strikes a balance between socioeconomic development and environmental concerns related to biodiversity, which makes it more reflective of a sustainability paradigm. It could be argued that whereas the SPS Agreement was not able to facilitate cognitive evolution, those aspects that were stunted by the agreement were built into the Cartagena Protocol and flourished among its 130 signatories. At the same time, the evolution of the Cartagena Protocol was mired in conflicts of its own, and these are reflected in the fact that over the course of its development the number of items that touched upon socioeconomic subjects was reduced to one single article: Article 26 (Kinchy et al., 2008:170–71). It should also be pointed out that several prominent countries instrumental in whittling down the socioeconomic elements of the protocol did not even end up signing the agreement, including Canada and the United States.

It's often observed that arrangements formed under the WTO umbrella are inherently elitist, exclusionary, opaque, and, most of all, lacking in public input. Some of these shortcomings resonate through the SPS Agreement directly, while others are echoes of larger concerns about WTO norms in general. However, the arrangement does require consensus on all SPS Committee decisions, and this encourages internal dialogue. Of course, this consensus extends only to members of the agreement, namely to *states* and their delegates; and, by framing decision making strictly under the guise of Western scientific expertise, the enterprise of the SPS Agreement, as a whole, may be questionable because it intentionally seals the discussion from any larger dialogue, especially by the general public. Indeed, the SPS Committee could improve on transparency as well, by opening its discussions to more public scrutiny. Foster (2008) has pointed out that the use of public opinion in risk assessment may actually be compatible with the SPS Agreement if approached in the appropriate manner:

> [The] need to increase both the legitimacy and the functionality of the multilateral trade regime demands greater recognition of public opinion.... Greater emphasis must be placed in WTO jurisprudence on the acceptability, the importance, and even the necessity of encouraging the formation and expression of the public's diverse responses to risks. (Foster, 2008:456)

Winickoff and his colleagues go further, suggesting that panels should assess precaution along a continuum that can balance levels of scientific certainty at one end with levels of public concern on the other (Winickoff et al., 2005:115). Cardwell (2010) notes that public participation is condoned by other successful agreements, such as the Cartagena Protocol and the Aarhus Convention (the UNECE Convention on Access to Information, Public Participation in Decision-making and Access to Justice in Environmental Matters, discussed in the previous chapter), while the SPS Agreement has no such formal mechanisms in place (p. 13). For example, a 2005 Eurobarometer survey noted that nearly 60 per cent of all Europeans were opposed to GMOs; the French, in particular, held the highest opposition at 71 per cent (Cardwell, 2010:12). Little wonder the EU has refused to open its borders to most GMO imports. The SPS can operate as a potential check on the problems caused by trade in potentially dangerous goods, but it will only be effective if domestic constituencies pressure governments into actively pursuing such protection. Once again, we need consumer action.

Toward Ethical Investments

"Trading behavior occurs in many species but has a particularly elaborate form in humans. Trade is ... a biological phenomenon rather than an artefact of human civilisation.... The evolution of trading strategies is most likely in humans and social arthropods.... [T]rade can simultaneously increase consumption among populations and reduce pressure on locally scarce resources. This allows a species to increase its density and escape the constraints imposed by local resource limitations [and] represents a major ecological benefit to the trading species."

BRENDON MOYLE (2000:139)

Although I have problems with the bio-economic tone of this passage—any time someone compares human civilization with insects I am reminded of lab-coated technicians in dire need of a history book or two—it is certainly the case that human trade has had a beneficial effect as well as a displacement effect. There is little point adding to the endless debate about whether trade, itself, is a good or bad thing for the environment. Clearly, humans made the decision some time ago that trade is beneficial enough for people to justify the construction of an elaborate exchange system, complete with mechanisms to protect private property and finances, facilitate the physical and virtual transfer of goods and services, and aim to reduce protectionism over time. What matters is that we have arrangements in place, which offer room for decisive environmental governance at the national, local, and personal levels. And, though the Basel Convention and the SPS Agreement each has its own weaknesses, both certainly point us in the direction of that type of governance. Various EU bodies, as well as NAFTA's CEC offer examples of regional international arrangements with great potential to engage the public in research results and provide policy guidance, even if they lack sharp teeth. But global governance mechanisms are essential in a global economy.

Both Basel and the SPS Agreement offer important routes toward achieving greater control over the potential deleterious impact of trade. Basel has at least partial legal breadth, and we can argue it has had a positive environmental impact, great cognitive success, and is quite centered on the pursuit of democratic legitimacy. The impact of the SPS Agreement is less visible, but future applications are promising; it has had little cognitive success but does offer an avenue toward more democratic legitimacy for the WTO as a whole if it is not used solely to protect trade flow but also facilitates the protection of consumers and communities from environmental risk. Vigilance, as always, remains essential. We need to keep the pressure on large corporations that rely on trade and investment to accumulate capital and spread markets, while providing incentives toward green investment opportunities. We need to let governments know that we are watching the impact of trade in hazardous material and seek its ultimate elimination, while keeping a close eye also on how we are defining the term "hazardous." New technologies, such as nanotechnology and modern electronics, present new challenges to both Basel and SPS: scientific expertise and courageous voices will be needed to cope with these developments. On the crucial enforcement front, the Basel Secretariat continues to work in concert with both the World Customs Organization (WCO) and Interpol to try to thwart illegal trafficking of hazardous waste, though coordination structures and synergies between local, national, and international intelligence and enforcement bodies are still greatly underdeveloped.

Individuals will make investments that reflect their priorities and their willingness to take risks. Surely, we have a collective duty to make wise investment decisions, conduct legitimate environmental impact assessments, and consciously seek to minimize the impact of our actions. Surely, trade should continue to reflect the ingenuity of humanity and benefit the billions of people engaged in the global economy, while also reflecting international concerns with not just ecological damage but also social justice. The need for regulatory intervention is self-evident, as is the need for a concerted effort to steer our investments (financial as well as intellectual) toward ethical frameworks that support fairness and sustainability. Formal arrangements between states are both enabling and restrictive in this light.

Of course, one of the most widely touted benefits of international trade is the claim that it reduces the likelihood of war between states (a theory often referred to as commercial liberalism or, even, "commercial pacifism"; see Doyle,

1997). The validity of this claim is less clear than it sounds, of course, but there is little doubt that states having a mutual stake in economic prosperity will be less inclined to go to war against each other. However, the nexus between ecology and warfare is more complex than this, and we turn to this theme in our next chapter.

Notes

1. The GATT is the General Agreement of Tariffs and Trade, which forms the legal base of the WTO.
2. Representatives from several African states have argued that DDT imports are vital in their fight against malaria-carrying mosquitoes.
3. American policy on exporting hazardous waste is governed by both domestic laws and bilateral agreements between the United States and importing governments; most of the trade occurs with Canada, and the United States maintains bilateral waste trade agreements with Canada, Mexico, Costa Rica, and Malaysia, all of which rest on the principle of prior informed consent (US EPA, 1998:2). The United States is also party to an OECD agreement regulating the trade in recyclable wastes among its member states. Although violations continue to be discovered (see Hilz, 1992), there is little doubt that export regulations are tighter now than at any point in American history.
4. See the Basel Action Network website (BAN, 2010): http://www.ban.org/. Seattle-based NGO BAN has three priorities at present: stopping trade in e-waste; controlling the notorious trade in discarded ships, which are dismantled in Asia and elsewhere, releasing toxic substances; and implementing the Basel Convention throughout the world.
5. The emphasis on scientific evidence puts countries with limited capacity at a disadvantage, and it is often suggested that there needs to be a corresponding technology transfer and funding to help those countries implement standards as necessary (Mayeda, 2004:760). Indeed, the SPS Agreement has provisions for technology transfer and for the inclusion of southern countries in the development of international standards, such as Codex, IPPA, and IZO, and there has been some positive movement in this direction in recent years.
6. It is shameful, in my view, that the CBD does not have observer status at the SPS Committee, despite repeated attempts to obtain it. Most observers blame American obstinacy for this strange state of affairs.
7. The Cartagena Protocol is another multilateral agreement (see Chapter 3); however, it pertains strictly to living modified organisms (LMOs) and their safe transport between countries, as well as to the advanced notice of exporting countries to importing countries of LMO products. LMOs are similar to genetically modified organisms, but are only *living* organisms, such as seeds or plants, so the agreement does not extend to processed GMO products such as breakfast cereal or fabrics made from GMOs. A further contrast

can be drawn between the SPS Agreement and the Cartagena Protocol in regard to the fact that the former does not differentiate between LMOs and traditional organisms, while the latter does by virtue of the fact that it pertains only to LMOs.

8. The controversy over the threats posed by GMOs, including the socioeconomic dimension of farmer dependency, is another matter of course (see Kinchy, Kleinman, and Autry, 2008).

CHAPTER EIGHT

War and Peace and Justice

"The space programs and weapons systems of the great powers
alone burn up enough wealth and talent to underwrite the
intelligent development of whole nations. . . . It is out of such
routine extravagances that the technocracy weaves its spell over our
allegiance . . . and then assures us we are the hope of the world."

THEODORE ROSZAK (1973:406–7)

IT IS PERHAPS UNUSUAL TO GET THROUGH SO MUCH MATERIAL IN A TEXT on an aspect of international relations without spending much time on the subject of war. Military conflict lurks under the surface of everything done in the diplomatic realm; and militarism is the most expensive fixation of our time. It is estimated that "governments of the world spent US $1.339 trillion on their military readiness in 2007 ... or $202 for every person on the planet" (Barnett, Matthew, and O'Brien, 2010:5). And this is just "official" military spending: the illicit weapons market is impossible to quantify, but it is certainly well into the billions. Efforts to broaden the definition of national security (at times driven by realists, at others by liberals, and usually by critical theorists) have had some impact on our thinking, but they have displaced neither the central role of the state nor the tendency to place the protection of the security of individual states above all else. Sovereignty remains the central organizing concept of international relations, not collective security. Meanwhile, *human security* has ebbed and flowed as an operational concept in foreign policy formation, twinned with the "responsibility to protect" doctrine, which suggests that state governments failing to protect their citizens from egregious harm have lost the legitimacy to govern and should be subject to various forms of international intervention. Seemingly endless wars in Iraq and Afghanistan, with costs in the trillions of dollars, have sapped the will to intervene, and human security has all but collapsed as a foreign policy platform, even in states that once vocally espoused it, such as Canada. Nonetheless, peacekeeping remains a major aspect of United Nations activity, and, especially in the post–cold war era, the Security Council remains the center of international diplomacy.

Both the terrorist attacks of September 11, 2001, and the decidedly military response, revealed once again the violent context of international relations, despite the development of contemporary international law and various arrangements designed to curb or alter the use of violence. Environmental issues have a similar subtext, and violence often erupts as resource conflicts become unmanageable. Indeed an entire scholarly cottage industry exists that examines the hotly debated links between environmental change and violence. Generally, it is assumed that overcrowding increases the opportunity for friction and conflict; this idea seems logical enough, though the more advanced studies have come to mixed conclusions (Homer Dixon and Blitt, 1998). But there are certainly cases, both realized and potential, in which we can identify links between environmental problems, violent conflict, and human rights violations, such as the troubled history of the largely deforested Haitian hillsides. Resource scarcity, as we have seen, results from a variety of factors, including structural inequality and greed, irrational consumption habits, land degradation, natural disasters, and military conflict itself. Rightly, ecofeminists add gender discrimination to the list. Violence is often a consequence of resource scarcity, but we must look at the causes of scarcity to understand this connection.[1] As we saw in Chapter 6, however, conflicts over water—one of the most basic of human needs and often the most revered and nationalized of resources—can lead to cooperative outcomes and even institutional evolution.

Although most of the literature on eco-violence has gone the Homer-Dixon (1999) route (also referred to as the "Toronto School" in some publications), which asks "whether and why environmental scarcity, abundance, or dependence might cause militarized conflict, less research has focused on the environmental impacts of violent conflict, war, or military activities" (Khagram and Saleem, 2006:395; see also Austin and Bruch, 2000). Post-conflict analysis has certainly provided empirical evidence of the environmental costs of war; the UNEP's Post-Conflict and Disaster Management Branch has identified numerous sources of concern in the 17 states it has been charged with investigating, from depleted uranium weaponry in Iraq and Bosnia and Herzegovina to hazardous wastes in Somalia to illegal forestry in Afghanistan (see Conca and Wallace, 2009). Meanwhile, we are moving much closer to an established body of literature on the impact of the ecological costs of displacement resulting from warfare, including competition over local resources between refugees and host communities (Martin et al., 2005). These costs also include, of course, the long-term psychological damage caused by displacement from traditional lands, which "harms the ecological self and therefore creates an internal sense of alienation" (Ramanathapillai, 2008:114), further blending the line between agential and structural violence. There is also a critical take on the environment-insecurity linkage; from this perspective, conservation projects such as the establishment of "peace parks" and nature preserves are really efforts by politicians or military elites to deepen or expand territorial power (see Peluso and Watts, 2001).

Today, it is widely acknowledged that climate change will have a severe impact on national security concerns (Campbell, 2008; Webersik, 2010). Canadian defense specialists have been scrambling for decades to adjust to the consequences of retreating arctic ice; as sea levels rise, small island states have their existence, not just borders, at stake. Susan Martin suggests there are at least four developments associated with climate change that will provoke massive population movements: "the intensification of natural disasters, such as hurricanes and cyclones"; "increased warming and drought that affects agricultural production, reducing people's livelihoods and access to clean water"; "rising sea levels that render coastal areas uninhabitable"; and "competition over natural resources that may lead to conflict, which in turn precipitates displacement" (Martin, 2010:398). Sudden, large-scale population movements can provoke defensive reactions in the areas where people suddenly appear and demand survival resources. We don't need climate change to suggest this. But it is a commonly explicated concern that a causal link between climate change, population displacement, and cycles of violence will be highly visible in the coming decades, just as it is suggested that the violence in Sudan's Darfur region or Somalia has been exacerbated by desertification. Arguably, however, most people affected by such displacement will not cross national borders but will be "internally displaced," and thus, this migration in response to environmental disaster is best viewed as a human security challenge and not just a national one. I return to this theme in the concluding section of this chapter.

Moving beyond the climate security issue, this chapter will discuss the most obvious connection between the environment and militarism: the advent of *ecocide*, which we can define in either narrow (minimalist) terms or, taking a cue from those who advocate environmental justice, wider (maximalist) terms.[2] There is a longstanding causal chain that links conflict to environmental destruction and back again. This chain is an integral part of the history of imperialism, military adventurism, or civil conflicts with outside intervention. Indeed, the entire bipolar approach of the cold war era—mutually assured nuclear destruction—was premised on the ability to perpetuate the ultimate act of ecocide. A test ban treaty was inspired partially by concerns about the environmental impact of nuclear weapons and is often heralded as a partial success; another international arrangement seeks to limit the environmental damage caused by war itself. The former has been remarkably successful, guided by superpower commitment and fairly widespread legitimacy; the other is but a shell of what might evolve into a substantive instrument to curb future military actions. Finally, I return to the question of security and suggest that, though national security and military action will continue to dominate state decisions, global environmental justice and human security are the defining needs of our time, and we need to continue their pursuit.

Ecocide: The Circle of Death

When I visited Bosnia several years after the terrible civil war there had ground to a final, if tentative, halt, I was often overwhelmed with sadness at the evidence of destruction still readily viewable throughout the country: buildings scarred with bullet holes, burnt-out houses, churches, and mosques, entire walls missing from factories and restaurants, large areas still cordoned with yellow tape due to suspected land mines. And the cemeteries, including an area in Sarajevo that once hosted the Olympics, now full of the dead from the siege of that city, with so many of the gravestones dated between 1992 and 1995. But I was also struck by the beauty of the countryside, its almost defiant resilience, and the crystal-clear waters of the Una River near Bihać. Indeed, the somewhat perverse argument was often made to me that the war was good for nature because it stopped most industrial production, which, under the many years of Tito's dictatorship, had been encouraged without much thought about pollution. But the impact of war on nature is not always so obvious, and there are often unseen consequences.

There are at least three subtypes of what I refer to as deliberate eco-violence, or the purposeful infliction of harm on ecosystems: the deliberate or neglectful harm of animals, eco-sabotage, and ecocide. I will not expand on animal welfare here, as this subject falls within the category of psychopathic behavior or is a manifestation of the food industry, which, though it seems quite violent to some, is considered quite routinized and even beneficial to others (we return to this theme in our discussion of food security in Chapter 10). The animal rights literature is vast, challenging, and beyond the scope of this book (see Regan, 1983). Meanwhile, ecological sabotage refers largely to terrorist activity (conducted by individuals, states, or other actors) designed to harm or frighten human populations, but the term is also often used to refer to the actions of radical ecologists resorting to the sabotage of property to protect the natural environment itself. Examples would include ramming a whaling ship and "spiking" old-growth trees with long nails to render them inaccessible to loggers. Of course, most environmental protest movements have involved peaceful resistance, but the use of violence attracts quicker media attention.

Maximalist examples of ecocide include everything from driving SUVs, flying to academic conferences, and eating dubiously farmed salmon. Higgins (2010), for example, adopts a maximalist definition that directly links corporate irresponsibility and the concept of ecocide. I am not opposed to these wider uses of the term, but have found that the maximalist definition serves better as a heuristic device than as a legal conceptualization (Stoett, 2000a). The more helpful minimalist definition refers exclusively to the deliberate destruction of nature as part of a military strategy designed to subjugate an enemy.[3] Ecocide is classic agential violence in which ecosystems suffer, but one end result is, of course, the prolonged suffering of human populations, and thus an act of indirect collective violence is also committed. The minimalist definition is more widely accepted and, in legal terms, only it can make procedural sense because it implies intent on the behalf of the perpetrator. Though some people who drive gasoline-guzzling Hummers might be misanthropic in character, we would not generally assume that they are trying to destroy the biosphere every time they start the engine.

The scientific study of ecocide spiked during the United States war in Vietnam, which soon doubled as a justice issue. Work on the long-term impact of the US defoliation campaign, called "Operation Ranch Hand," and of the anvil-shaped bulldozers called Roman Plows used to destroy agricultural land is still emerging, and the long-term damage to local ecology and human health is still evident (see Westing, 1984a, 1984b; Zierler, 2011).[4] Photos of oil wells set on fire by Saddam Hussein's troops following the Gulf War of 1990–91 stung the public mind and led to a resurgence of concern about ecocide (see Joyner and Kirkhope, 1992; Roberts, 1993; Sands et al., 1991). Ruiz (2010) offers an interesting discussion of Saddam's destruction of the Iraqi marshes and of the homes of the Marsh Arabs; he sees it as an act not only of ecocide but also of genocide.[5]

In between the maximalist and minimalist perspectives, we have military preparation, which was an especially deleterious activity during the height of the cold war and remains a significant factor today, especially if we include such nasty incidentals as greenhouse gas emissions resulting from military production and weapons shipments, as well as leakage problems related to stored toxic wastes. Indeed, it has become a truism that the military-industrial complex is the largest pollution sector on earth, which makes inherent sense if we consider its breadth. It encompasses uncountable factories, supply routes, and military exercises; herbicide-spraying campaigns over Colombia, Afghanistan, and other drug-growing regions; and risky space-based research: the list is virtually endless and is expanded by today's emphasis on biotechnology and nanotechnology. Naval ships, some nuclear powered and some carrying nuclear weapons, patrol the oceans, posing special risks to the marine environment, and there are many other examples of how seemingly routine military actions cause ecological harm, such as the Distant Early Warning system's deleterious ecological impact in northern Canada. One of the most obvious cases of military preparation causing environmental damage, to which I now turn, was atmospheric nuclear weapons testing.

The Atmospheric Test Ban Treaty

You'll notice I ended the previous sentence in the past tense, which is probably optimistic. There could well be a series of nuclear tests in the near future as countries such as North Korea, Iran, and Pakistan further develop their nuclear programs. And small nuclear weapons testing is still ongoing as the "great" nuclear powers (the five veto holders in the Security Council) modernize their arsenals even while reducing them. For the most part, however, large-scale nuclear testing is a thing of the past. We still face serious threats from the possible use of nuclear weapons by armies and terrorists, the potential radioactive fallout from nuclear accidents such as those witnessed following the earthquake and tsunami in Japan in 2011, and the illegal dumping of radioactive waste. And underground testing has certainly spread radiation as well. But atmospheric nuclear weapons testing represented a whole different level of destructiveness, a potent combination of technological prowess, ideological fixation, and the classic security dilemma, wherein efforts to improve one's sense of security simply cause less security in one's opponent; the latter takes further preventive measures, lessening the security of the other, and a spiral of military spending, weapons development, and demonstrative weapons testing evolves to the point of absurdity.

When a nuclear bomb is detonated in open air, radiation can be carried thousands of miles from the point of explosion. It is easy to forget the extent of atmospheric nuclear testing.[6] The United States conducted well over 200 atmospheric tests, largely in the Nevada desert and the Pacific Ocean, before a test ban treaty was finally hammered out in 1963. The Soviet Union conducted nearly as many, while the United Kingdom, France, and China joined the fun as well. Results included

> ... marked increases in cancer (especially leukemia) amongst the military personnel involved in tests ... and among civilians in neighboring areas [including] residents of Utah, Nevada, and Arizona, and Pacific Islanders.... Cows ... grazed contaminated pastures, and the isotopes which concentrated in their milk were passed on to the schoolchildren of Las Vegas.... [B]omb tests of the 1950s and early 1960s added appreciable quantities of radioactive matter to the upper atmosphere, where winds distributed it globally.... Isotopes such as strontium 90 (which mimics calcium, [and is] incorporated into the skeleton) are now present in the bodies of untold numbers of people as a consequence of these tests. (Prins, 1983:251)

And their impact on human security is another under-documented aspect of contemporary history. For example, the "sea-swept islands and coral bars" of the Pacific Marshall Islands endured 67 nuclear detonations between 1946 and 1958, creating a "radioactive ecosystem" with disastrous effects on the "relocated" indigenous population (dé Ishtar 2009:121, 126). As Teclaff (1994) writes, it is difficult to conceive of international arrangements that ban weapons because they might hurt the environment, but certain forms of behavior could illicit a strong response: "where there exists a realistic threat of ecocide on a global scale, the only adequate response may be prohibition, as in the 1963 Nuclear Test Ban Treaty" (p. 951). Indeed, after protracted negotiations between the two hostile camps of cold war bipolarity, this arrangement, better (and more accurately) known as the Limited Test Ban Treaty (LTBT), prohibited atmospheric, marine, and space-based tests, while permitting underground testing to continue. The negotiations were largely bilateral, as opposed to multilateral, though the superpowers were joined by the United Kingdom, and the LTBT would go on to widespread acceptance and ratification. Hundreds of underground tests would follow until the early 1990s, when the great powers ceased weapons testing (a multilateral Comprehensive Test Ban Treaty was negotiated by the UN and passed in the General Assembly in 1996 but never achieved the ratifications necessary to move into force, despite repeated calls for this in the United States and elsewhere—see Crook, 2010; Duarte, 2009; Nagan and Slemmens, 2009).

The LTBT is often heralded as one of the first international arrangements inspired by environmental considerations. No doubt, the impact of nuclear fallout weighed heavily on the minds of successive American administrations, and Soviet nuclear testing was proving disastrous in areas adjacent to the Semipalatinsk Test Site. Newspapers in the United States covered reports of fallout-related problems with alarm, including the prospect of mothers' breast milk contaminated with iodine-131. It would have been difficult to avoid the connection between atmospheric testing and atmospheric pollution, even if the public imagination in both the United States and the Soviet Union was captured by the grandiosity of the cold war struggle. Concern with broader ecosystem destruction was certainly a motivating factor, as fears of "nuclear winter" would spur further arms control efforts in the 1980s (Richard and Sagan 1989). Nuclear testing was one of the main reasons many environmental activists first encountered the peace movement in the 1960s, and one of the reasons peace activists encountered environmentalists. Greenpeace was born of this synthesis, when protestors joined forces to take a ship to the South Pacific in 1972 to disrupt a French atmospheric test. (France would not halt atmospheric testing until 1974, long after the LTBT was implemented in 1963.) Whiteside (2006) even suggests that concerns over the impact of atmospheric testing contributed to the subsequent development of the precautionary principle (p. 145).

Most experts are circumspect, however, about just how large a role environmental and human health issues factored into the mutual decision to go ahead with a ban back in 1963. As Ivo Daalder (1987) suggests, there is no doubt that related public pressure was "instrumental"; however, the "public record provided by Senate hearings, congressional debate, and executive statements of the time ... points to the very limited role played by the fallout issue in the LTBT ratification debate.... The two crucial issues were the existing climate of relations between the United States and the USSR following the Cuban Missile Crisis in October 1962 and the treaty's potential effect on the development of an optimal ABM system" (p. 10).[7] We should add to this list the broader concern with nuclear proliferation (the vertical, as opposed to horizontal, spread of nuclear weapons capability), which resulted in the multilateral Nuclear Non-Proliferation Treaty (NPT) later that decade. The insanity of underground testing, ensconced within the broader bounded rationality of mutually assured destruction, would continue for years before it stopped, and the United States and others have yet to ratify the more demanding CTBT; the spread of nuclear weapons to Israel, India, South Africa (which renounced them), Pakistan, and other states would continue, with North Korea conducting underground tests in 2006 and 2009.[8] Decommissioning stockpiled nuclear weapons, as well as cleaning up former atomic weaponry factories, has proven very difficult and, as always when the long-term storage of nuclear waste is involved, controversial. But, given the severity of the threats these tests posed to the global biosphere and human security, we are fortunate the agreement reached between John Kennedy and Nikita

Khrushchev was respected and inspired the other nuclear powers at the time to eventually cease atmospheric testing as well.

And yet it wasn't long after this historic development that the United States embarked on a massive campaign of deliberate ecocide that would forever draw the link between war and environmental destruction, and even give rise to a multilateral arrangement seeking to limit future episodes of large-scale ecocide.

The Convention on the Prohibition of Military or Any Other Hostile Use of Environmental Modification Techniques (ENMOD)

Both the Chemical Weapons Convention and the Biological and Toxin Weapons Convention are firmly established international arrangements, and though there has been controversy about the level of compliance they command, most analysts would agree that these conventions have played a role in curbing the spread of these weapons, which are of course inherently destructive of the environment. Less progress has been made toward making war itself a greener affair, however. Indeed it is counterintuitive to even think about an environmentally friendly mode of warfare, even if environmental impact assessment has become a standard operating procedure of military preparation today. But an international arrangement aimed at reducing the environmental harm from warfare does in fact exist. It is perhaps the weakest instrument discussed in this book, but the efforts placed toward its realization are certainly noble and inspired by the quest for human security and the extension of the "just war" tradition in ethical thought (Reichberg and Syse, 2000; Wunsch, 1980.).

Opened for signature in Geneva in 1977, ENMOD entered into force in 1978. Inspired by post-Vietnam guilt, concern over Soviet biological testing, and a growing environmental movement in the United States and Europe, the treaty expressly forbids the deliberate modification of the environment for military purposes (Goldblat, 1977; Juda, 1978). There was genuine concern that cloud-seeding techniques to induce flooding or drought had been practiced by the United States Army ("Operation Popeye"), and Operation Ranch Hand was certainly an effort to scar the natural environment and agricultural land in order to achieve military purposes. Fears that mad scientists working with military contracts on either side of the cold war divide would manufacture hurricanes, tsunamis, avalanches, and other natural disasters were not so outlandish in the Cold War era. Biological weapons, which would not just kill people but would permanently harm wildlife and agriculture, were in full development (despite the existence of the loopholed 1972 Biological and Toxin Weapons Convention mentioned previously; see Miller, Engelberg, and Broad, 2001), and the Chemical Weapons Convention would not come into force until 1997. So there were some big hopes for ENMOD, pushed by the breeze of environmental activism through a window of diplomatic opportunity. And, read loosely, it is indeed a far-ranging convention. According to Chamorro and Hammond (2001), activities that could violate ENMOD include

> Triggering earthquakes
> Manipulating ozone levels
> Alteration of the ionosphere
> Deforestation
> Provoking flood or drought
> Use of herbicides
> Setting fires
> Seeding clouds
> Introduction of invasive species
> Eradication of species
> Creation of storms
> Manipulation of El Niño / La Niña
> Destruction of crops (Quoted in Smith, 2006:113)

However—writing in 2001—they go on to note that the treaty is "all but forgotten." Little has changed in the 11 years since, despite ongoing defoliation campaigns in several areas (most people would agree that large-scale weather alteration programs had been dismissed as either unfeasible or perhaps uncontrollable by the time ENMOD was signed anyway).

Indeed, ENMOD might qualify as a "phantom convention": we suspect it exists, but it is very hard to see it in action, if at all. The number of states required to ratify ENMOD was unusually low at 20, and this, in retrospect, was probably a mistake by its framers (better to have a high ratification number required, even if it risks delaying things, as the agreement will have wider legitimacy once it comes into force). But the harder aspect of ENMOD's limited effectiveness is that it simply has not proven possible, under international law, to use it in any way, despite the many military conflicts and related ecological damage seen since its inception. Most markedly, Iraq was not condemned under ENMOD despite its blatant resort to ecocide in 1991—because it was not a party to the convention.

To be fair, ENMOD does not outlaw war or even environmental damage caused by war; it merely outlaws the purposeful use of the environment as a *weapon* in war. But what is war? Most international arrangements that cover this topic are fixated on the state level of interaction, even though many armed conflicts are internal in nature or combine domestic conflict with some form of intervention. Another reminder of the state centricity of ENMOD is its reliance on the Security Council as the main mechanism for its use, which gives members with veto powers the ability to control the outcome of related accusations. This fact alone may indeed condemn ENMOD to the role of an instrument of cognitive evolution only, but even there it has not generated sufficient public attention to be considered a worthy contributor. If we can expand the role of the International Criminal Court (ICC) to include crimes against the environment (arguably, the Rome Statue covers this already, especially if such crimes are committed in times of war) then ENMOD would perhaps become more useful. But it does not have its own secretariat (it is administered by the UN Office for Disarmament Affairs), and a secretariat would seem to be a prerequisite for generating public attention, as more publicity-conscious arrangements, such as the UNCCD and the CBD, demonstrate. Nor does it offer any services to the international community, such as monitoring or expert advice. Nor does it legitimize what is considered a vital aspect of powerful states' economies, as does, for example, the NPT, which serves to limit vertical proliferation even as it explicitly advocates the development of nuclear power. And its scope is more limited than many assume, as it does not cover the use of threats of environmental modification (which would challenge the premise of nuclear deterrence) or the testing of products (e.g., biotechnology or nanotechnology) that might result in such modification.[9] And, of course, it is supposed to operate in the cloaked world of national security, with its secrecy and severe punishments for breaching that secrecy. For example, there is considerable concern, and not just among certified conspiracy theorists, that the American military is conducting experiments aimed at various measures to control the ionosphere.[10] Because experimentation is not banned by ENMOD, the agreement cannot be used to invoke greater public knowledge about, much less the cessation of, this activity.

Despite the innovations offered by the advent of the Rome Statute of the ICC toward individual responsibility in international law, we are far from an international arrangement that shines harsh light on culpability for environmental crimes, let alone for negligence of ENMOD or other conventions (Orellana, 2005). In general, arms control treaties are not designed to promote ecological harmony, human rights, gender equality, or any of the other conceptual steps we need to take toward a more humane and sustainable future. To move in those directions, we need to move toward an enhanced vision of security, in a manner that does not lose sight of the ugliness of and real potential for warfare but that emphasizes the need for sustainable life opportunities for individuals and groups other than as citizens of the contemporary, and often highly militarized, state. The establishment of transfrontier "peace parks"—protected areas on the borders between states prone to hostile relations—may be a nice step in this direction, though this initiative, too, is subject to the usual problems of control and corruption and displacement of local people (Ali, 2007; Brock, 1991; Duffy, 2001; Peluso and Watts, 2001). Education remains a key factor: the more people know about the perils of warfare, and ecological considerations are certainly vital here, the less likely they are to blindly support leaders who incite violence. In this context, ENMOD still has a cognitive role to play, but we should expect it to achieve little else.

Toward Environmental Justice and Human Security

I will return to this theme in the conclusion but stress it here because it is directly related to how we envision the nexus between security and global environmental governance. Although I personally respect the need for military action in certain circumstances, it is best seen as a last resort, and governments, diplomats, academics, and activists alike should be engaged also in seeking a more sustainable approach to conflict resolution. This goal goes far beyond minimizing the ecological footprint of military production and action, though that should be a priority—within reason, of course—for military planners and political leaders alike. Though it has largely fallen out of fashion and raises conceptual and operational dilemmas of its own, the pursuit of human security retains its significance for most people today. There are many definitions of human security, but I am partial to that offered by Barnett, Matthew, and O'Brien (2010), who define it as a "variable condition where people and communities have the capacity to manage stresses to their needs, rights, and values. When people do not have enough options to avoid or to adapt to environmental change such that their needs, rights, and values are likely to be undermined, then they can be said to be environmentally insecure" (p. 18).[11]

The link this definition draws between human rights, human security, and environmental security is an apposite one for our time. I'll take it one step further and suggest that a variety of factors make the consideration of *global environmental justice* the new ethical frontier, the nexus between ecological thought and international relations theory we need to develop and promote further to avoid the complete dissolution of global society today.[12] Significantly, global environmental justice is not merely related to the mitigation of the anthropomorphic causes of climate change, biodiversity loss, toxic pollution, or the oceans crises; it also demands that adaptation measures undertaken by states and other actors do not further marginalize already vulnerable groups and that their voices are heard in the precautionary balance sheet. I am not suggesting that extreme weather events, infectious diseases, genetic mutations, and other manifestations of environmental problems do not ultimately affect both rich and poor but rather that there will be a profoundly differentiated impact so long as the rich have adequate resources to adapt or flee and the impoverished have little but communal ties to assist them.[13] Surely the lesson of Hurricane Katrina, which, after all, affected one of the most prosperous and powerful states in the international system today, is that poverty kills. In a must-read text for anyone concerned with climate change policy, J. Timmons Roberts and Bradley Parks (2007) offer widespread evidence that this is the case on the global level as well (see also Hossay, 2006). And the advent of warfare only worsens the condition of the economically and politically disadvantaged. We've seen how some of the international arrangements described in this book contain measures to address this inequality explicitly and how some of them could significantly improve our efforts; arms control measures, however, do not even touch the topic.

It might be held that the emphasis on and fears of the conflict potential of climate change are bringing normative justice questions back to the fore after the long reaction to 9/11 begins to lose its grip on the international imagination. However, we might also suggest that environmental justice, as a theme and a movement, is in danger of extinction as "climate justice" pushes it out of public view (Klinsky and Dowlatabadi, 2009; see also Chapter 5). This eventuality would be, in my view, unfortunate, not only because of the tenuous analytic nature of links between climate change and violence (Salehyan, 2008), the inevitable "securitization" (Waever, 1995) of the climate change issue-area (Barnett, 2003; Podesta and Ogden, 2007), the perpetually inconclusive nature of efforts at global climate governance, and the debate over the scientific validity of the more distressing geophysical predictions but also because there are so many other issues (albeit interlinked) that demand attention. We should in no way diminish, however, what should be vigilant concern about and research into the links between climate change and environmental justice, from the phenomenon of environmental refugees and migrants[14] to the cultural impact of rapid changes in local ecosystems. Reuveny (2007) argues that environmentally induced migration can lead to conflict when it is coupled with competition over scarce resources, ethnic tensions between groups, distrust between migrants and host communities, and the presence of socioeconomic "fault lines" or "auxiliary conditions" such as political instability (p. 659). These are certainly, as Barnett and Adger (2007) argue, human security concerns of the first order. But they are also social and environmental justice issues because they involve vulnerability, unequal power relationships, and potential avenues toward emancipation from these conditions. As Brown, Hammill, and McLeman (2007) argue in the African context, the degree to which climate change will actually result in violent conflicts depends upon "a given area's susceptibility to conflict and the capacity of the population to adapt to changing conditions" (p. 1149).[15] Similarly,

Salehyan (2008) argues that environmental factors alone do not predict conflict; instead it is "the *interaction* between environmental and political systems [that] is critical for understanding organized armed violence" (p. 318).

Environmental justice also allows us to focus on situations and events that are not within the usual humanitarian intervention context. Most instances of what is traditionally considered eco-violence or ecocide would escape the Responsibility to Protect (R2P) doctrine, which demands actions to protect against "genocide, war crimes, ethnic cleansing and crimes against humanity"—though there is some room to maneuver within all of these categories. Humanitarian intervention is an inherently controversial concept in the interstate system, even when mass murder is taking place. But viewing environmental justice as a fundamental precondition for human development will give us a broader vision of state responsibilities and can contribute to the evolution of the R2P norm in the process. This perspective can also filter into the realm of international criminal law, though, as previously discussed, we are some way off from an International Criminal Court with a clear mandate to punish those guilty of committing environmental crimes (though the International Criminal Police Organization, or INTERPOL, is devoted to such a pursuit) and we are even further from the use of the International Court of Justice or the Security Council to punish states engaged in widespread environmental destruction.[16] Such global governance efforts need a normative backbone.

A final reason to focus on environmental (in)justice is that it provides a normative platform from which we can move on to concrete unapologetic policy prescriptions to remedy situations in which chronic inequality or sudden catastrophe has ensured ongoing harm to vulnerable populations; the 2010 earthquake in Haiti and the Indian Ocean tsunami of 2004 certainly underscore this point, whether viewed from country-specific or global lenses. Although the more traditional eco-violence literature typically leads to calls for greater state capacity to "manage" situations, environmental justice concerns lead us to advocate more fundamental shifts in power relations and access to natural resources. Though such calls can be unrealistic and even counterproductive if they challenge the entire status quo, if articulated in a measured manner, they can be quite reasonable demands based on the enlightened self-interest of all stakeholders. Of course, some of the self-anointed clergy of the more radical branches of the movement would consider this a sacrilegious concession to the rich and greedy. But as political ecology continues its evolutionary curve toward mainstream social significance, and yet capitalism continues to prove its resilience despite recurring economic crisis and technological change, it seems that the art of adaptive governance rather than the unanswered clarion call for a global revolution will effect the changes the poor continue to die waiting for.

This chapter has explored some of the many conceptual and empirical links between human security, environmental justice, and ecological degradation. Militarism is both the cause and effect of excessive stressors on the natural environment. Conflict over resources can lead to violence, though it need not do so and is as likely to lead to new cooperative arrangements. The Limited Test Ban Treaty, a milestone of cold war diplomacy with strong legal legitimacy, had an immeasurable, positive environmental impact, if it did less than we might wish to provoke serious thought about the environment as an issue. ENMOD, by contrast, has (unsurprisingly) been little more than a phantom convention and has done very little to promote cognitive evolution or democratic equality or legitimacy. At any rate, a much broader change is necessary if we are to escape the cycle of military preparation, organized violence, and ecocide: the concept of environmental justice could become a focal point for such a movement.

Of course, human security is threatened by severe environmental change as well, and one of the causes of such change can be found in the commercial activity and unsound environmental management practices that can lead to alien invasions not of the military kind but of a more natural character. We turn to this under-regulated phenomenon, often referred to in familiar securitizing form as *bioinvasion*, in the next chapter.

Notes

1. As Barnett, Matthew, and O'Brien (2010) conclude, "violent conflict is most likely where a range of motivations converge to persuade sufficiently large numbers of people that a resort to violence is justified, profitable, inevitable, or transformational. The general point for all researchers linking the environment and conflict is that environmental stress of one kind or another will figure in some, but not all, of those motivations, and hence it will be an elusive but at times significant element of the causal network that generates conflict" (p. 12). See also the discussion in Dinar (2011).

2. I treat this distinction at greater length in Stoett (2000a); see also Teclaff (1994).

3. Note the significant ecological footprint of going to war or occupying a country: according to *The Economist*, "American forces consume more than 1m [one million] gallons of fuel a day in Afghanistan, and a similar quantity in Iraq." As for the British army, calculations are "that it takes seven gallons of fuel to deliver one gallon to Afghanistan." See the article "Greenery on the March," *The Economist Technology Quarterly*, December 12, 2009, p. 3.

4. The most infamous of the herbicides employed was "Agent Orange," but many others were used, as was napalm, to burn forest cover. The campaign set a new standard for ecocide, and controversy has raged over the impact of the some 20 million tons of

defoliants that were sprayed in Southeast Asia between 1962 and 1971, over their effects on both the local population and American soldiers, who have sued for compensation.

5. He bases this assessment on the Geneva Convention's Article 2.c, which forbids "deliberately inflicting on the group conditions of life calculated to bring about its physical destruction in whole or in part." Interestingly, the International Court of Justice once ruled that, although states have the right to self-defense through deterrence, the threat of nuclear attack constituted a threat of genocide (see Bello and Bekker, 1997).

6. For an interesting visual chronological representation see the work by Isao Hashimoto, entitled "1945–1988" and found at http://www.ctbto.org/ specials/1945-1998-by-isao-hashimoto/.

7. An ABM system is an antiballistic missile defensive system, which would threaten the logic of deterrence if it were ever proven effective (thus the debate over "Star Wars" or space-based defense systems). The LTBT did not ban the development of an ABM system, but a later arms agreement would limit ABM defense deployment.

8. Note that Barak Obama has made nuclear disarmament a centerpiece of his foreign policy (and even received a rather premature Nobel Peace Prize for doing so). He called for ratification of the CTBT (Cook, 2009), but an unresponsive Senate and continued fears of vertical nuclear proliferation by Iran, North Korea, and Pakistan have rendered his call fairly mute at this stage. Meanwhile, the threat of a nuclear North Korea has led to calls for Japan to "go nuclear," which it certainly could and in short order, partly because of all the plutonium stockpiled there in a faltering plan to use MOX reactors to dispose of American and Soviet nuclear weapons material!

9. Add Chamorro and Hammond (2001), "In addition to its lack of prohibition of development and testing, ENMOD does not prohibit anyone from threatening to use hostile environmental modification. Further, damage in ENMOD must be proven. Thus, difficulty arises in reconciling ENMOD—which requires after the fact scientific assessment of damages—with the Precautionary Principle," a cornerstone of environmental law whose emphasis on avoiding environmental damage is quite different than the focus of ENMOD (p. 56).

10. This is the controversial High Frequency Active Auroral Research Program. Many websites claim potentially dangerous consequences, but the official HARP site denies this research has immediate military applications. See http://www.haarp.alaska.edu/.

11. Meanwhile the Commission on Human Security (2003) defines it as the protection of "the vital core of all human lives in ways that enhance human freedoms and human fulfillment" including "human rights, good governance, access to education and health care, [and] the freedom of future generations to inherit a healthy natural environment" (p. 4).

12. Most of this section is from a paper entitled "What Are We Really Looking For? From Eco-violence to Environmental Injustice," presented to the "Environmental Violence and Conflict: Implications for Global Security" Conference at Dalhousie University, Halifax, February 2010 and published by the Centre for Foreign Policy Studies, edited

by Matthew Schnurr and Larry Swatuk. That paper can be found online at http://centreforforeignpolicystudies.dal.ca/pdf/newissueinsecurity5/chapter3.pdf.

13. We should not underestimate the importance of those ties, however. As Michael Thompson (1999) puts it, "Environmental security ... is all about solidarities. If the appropriate solidarities are not there, and they are not interacting with one another in appropriate ways, then the pressure-cooker model will be valid" (p. 137).

14. Ironically, perhaps, efforts at conserving nature are also possible sources of environmental injustice, and there is little information on the level of displacement of both indigenous and non-indigenous persons caused by conservation projects (see Brockington, Igoe, and Schmidt-Soltau, 2006). For an historical treatment see Warner (2006).

15. Political geographers Nordas and Gleditsch (2007) make these comments: "the prospect of human-induced climate change encourages drastic neomalthusian scenarios. A number of claims about the conflict-inducing effects of climate change have surfaced in the public debate in recent years. Climate change has so many potential consequences for the physical environment that we could expect a large number of possible paths to conflict. However, the causal chains suggested in the literature have so far rarely been substantiated with reliable evidence. Given the combined uncertainties of climate and conflict research, the gaps in our knowledge about the consequences of climate change for conflict and security appear daunting" (p. 627). See Obioha (2008) for a Nigerian case study. Meanwhile, Raleigh and Urdal (2007) conclude that, while "population growth and density are associated with increased risks, the effects of land degradation and water scarcity are weak, negligible, or insignificant. The results indicate that the effects of political and economic factors far outweigh those between local level demographic/environmental factors and conflict" (p. 674).

16. INTERPOL established an Environmental Crime Committee as far back as 1992, but few are under the illusion this is a high-priority area. The links between organized crime and illegal waste dumping (see Chapter 7) and the wildlife trade (Chapter 3) are probably the biggest draw here.

CHAPTER NINE

Another Convention Needed? Invasive Alien Species

"Drought conditions and a recent heat wave are being blamed for driving some 6,000 camels into residential areas near the Docker River, where they have been competing for water with cattle—much to the dismay of the town's 350 inhabitants. So desperate for assistance, they've enlisted the help of a meat-processing company and local aborigines to thin the camel numbers—by feeding them to crocodiles."

STEPHEN MESSENGER (2010), FROM THE ONLINE NEWS REPORT
"AUSTRALIA'S INVADING CAMELS SOON TO BE CROC FOOD"

EVENTS SUCH AS THAT DESCRIBED ABOVE ARE BIZARRE, BUT SUCH DES-perate measures are increasingly common as governments struggle to cope with the fallout of a global governance gap that has endured for centuries. As mentioned in Chapter 3, most accounts posit invasive alien species (IAS) as second only to habitat destruction in terms of the overall threat posed to bio-diversity. Trade, timber, tourism, horticulture, agriculture, aquaculture: many commercial sectors are pathways for the deliberate or unintentional spread of invasive species, and they pose serious threats to economic development, extractive industries (fishing, forestry, water provision), human health, and even national security. In short, it is gradually becoming apparent that this issue is multifaceted, not one limited to biodiversity concerns, and because it is at least partly a function of international trade and involves country borders, it is certainly the stuff of global ecopolitics. As we will see, however, the real action on avoiding IAS takes place at the regional level.

Before looking at IAS, it is important to note that the vast majority of human food security is at least partly the result of introduced species; it would be irrational, and even verge on xenophobic, in my view, to consider all "non-native" species a problem (see Hettinger, 2001). However, many human actions, often subject to little or no regulation or to regulation from absurd distances, result in incidental, or accidental, infestations of IAS. The private sector is part of the problem and part of the solution; local conservation groups, taxonomists and biologists, environmental impact assessment specialists: all are vital. The virtues of multilevel governance are tested on a daily basis by this issue, and greater policy cohesion, information, and long-term thinking are necessary if we are to make serious progress in limiting the spread of IAS.[1] There is a very weak international surveillance and policy implementation structure in place, and one facing many challenges if we are to seriously consider its improvement. At this point, the development of several databases to help policy planners and practitioners indentify IAS and their most likely pathways and destinations has certainly improved the situation, and Internet communication helps propel this information sharing further.

Regardless of the general deficit in IAS control, there is a substantial amount of regional, national, and community-level policy development, though it is in need of compilation and coordination (McGeoch et al., 2010). Many countries have developed IAS policies, and, not surprisingly, these vary according to the level of perceived threat this problem poses to them. (Island states and Australia, for example, take the issue very seriously.) Meanwhile, the Global Invasive Species Programme (GISP), located at the UNEP Secretariat in Nairobi and, one might assume, at the heart of global governance efforts in IAS, was unceremoniously shut down in the spring of 2011 due to lack of funding. (Its 2001 Global Strategy on Invasive Alien Species ended at the same time.) It had neither the mandated legitimacy nor the resources to begin to respond effectively to the complex economic, ecological, and cultural threats and opportunities posed by IAS. It was a small operation (staffed by dedicated but underfunded researchers), which worked in collaboration with the CBD, CAB International, the IUCN, and several other partners. Japanese funding was key, and the tumultuous earthquake in Japan of 2011 reverberated into the world of global environmental governance as well.

In general, invasive alien species have come to be seen as the CBD's problem (with IUCN involvement); this is in itself especially problematic, not only because its COP cannot even agree to some basic "guiding principles" but also because these species are not just threats to biodiversity; this threat to biosecurity has vital climate change, human health, national security, and trade implications as well.[2] The other locus of considerable scientific investigation and data gathering is the

IUCN, which also lacks an effective policy coordination mandate. Meanwhile, the ongoing friction between the CBD and the UNEP, and the CBD and the WTO, further complicates the question (see Siebenhüner, 2009 and our discussion of the SPS Agreement in Chapter 7).

Invasive alien species pose a particular collective action problem, often labeled the "weakest link in the public goods chain" question (Sandler, 1997). As Perrings et al. (2009) write in their recent assessment of "Globalization and Bioinvasions: The International Policy Problem,"

> The benefits offered by any inspection and interception regime to all members of the community (whether national or international) are only as good as the benefits offered by the least effective provider—the weakest link in the chain … if one quarantine facility fails to contain an invasive pathogen, the fact that all others may do so is irrelevant. (P. 240)

The same problem applies to infectious disease pathology (and many criminal activities such as trade in endangered species and toxic waste, drugs and weapons, and human trafficking and pedophilia rings). I've dedicated this chapter to this topic because it demonstrates both glaring governance gaps and ongoing improvements and regional efforts to curtail a serious threat to ecology. I have been researching in this area for several years now, funded by the Social Science and Humanities Research Council of Canada. The research has provided a unique gateway to look into the work of the WTO, IUCN, FAO, CBD, and other organizations, including the unfortunately defunct GISP. It has also raised many ethical issues that I had previously found easy to ignore, such as the extent to which humans are justified in wiping out species we have, for whatever reason, labeled pests; and it has reinforced for me the centrality of the role of science—and scientists—in the contemporary age. It even raises questions about environmental justice, as the risks associated with IAS are usually borne by the poorest and most marginalized members of society. And it is a prime example of the need for adaptive governance, as the conditions that permit bioinvasion change over time and place.

Invasive Alien Species: The Problem(s)

Though bioinvasion is nothing new (see Elton, 1958 and Di Castri, 1989), invasive alien species today pose severe challenges to ecological integrity, economic security, environmental philosophy, and international modes of governance (GISP, 2001; McNeely, 2001; Perrings, Williamson, and Dalmazzone, 2000;

Stoett, 2010; Wittenberg and Cock, 2001). Purposive introductions of alien species have often proven disastrous to local ecologies (Courtenay and Moyle, 1992; Simberloff and Stiling, 1996), and the incidental spread of IAS as a result of global trade is a pervasive problem (Van Driesche and Van Driesche, 2000). One author refers to them as "pathogens of globalization" (Bright, 1998, 1999). In addition, the symbioses between globalization and climate change are increasing the likelihood of bioinvasions at both the microbial and species levels, causing shifts in pathogenic virulence (Lounibos, 2002; Price-Smith, 2002). There is evidence that warming trends will induce species migration northward and southward (away from the equatorial zone), which raises concerns about disease and threats to native species (see Hellmann et al., 2008 and Hughes, 2000). However, such "unassisted migration" will prove difficult for rare species of plants and trees, and adaptation or extinction is as likely (see Iverson, et al., 2004). Not so for insects: for example, warming patterns have vastly extended the range of the mountain pine beetle, which has ravaged Yoho National Park in British Columbia and threatened forests in the state of Washington. In the infamous case of zebra mussels, which have clogged entire swaths of the North American Great Lakes, we might see northward migration as appropriate reproduction temperatures become more common. Flooding could expand zebra mussel territory even further. It is believed that "climate change will affect the incidence of episodic recruitment events of invasive species, by altering the frequency, intensity, and duration of flooding ... [and] by allowing aggressive species to escape from local, constrained refugia" (Kolar and Lodge, 2000; Sutherst, 2000). Climate change will have numerous impacts, including the alteration of mechanisms of transportation and introduction, lowered climatic restraint, redistributions of extant invasive alien species, the modification of their impacts, and changes in the efficacy of management programs (Hellmann et al., 2008; see also Pyke et al., 2008).

Extensive research into national approaches to bioinvasion reveals a striking array of policy directions and a lack of badly needed international coordination. Although the IUCN Invasive Species Specialist Group is networked to a large, if scattered, epistemic community devoted to the issue, it carries little political weight, is chronically underfunded, and competes with several other international programs for attention. Many IAS are the result of purposeful introductions of species to control the populations of other species; perhaps the most infamous case here is that of the venomous cane toad (*Bufo marinus*) in Australia, which continues its onslaught across the country despite highly expensive eradication efforts. Native to the southern United States and Central and South America, this species of cane toads (originally from Hawaii) was released into the Australian wild in 1935 to control pest scarab beetles harming the production of sugar cane. Other high-profile cases, such as the zebra mussel invasion of the North American Great Lakes or the brown snake in Guam, have been unintentional: the former resulted from the release of ships' ballast water; the latter was a stowaway in military aircraft.

Similar to the other international environmental issues covered in this book, bioinvasion and how to respond to the ecological threats it poses raise ancillary questions about national sovereignty; how to define risk, fear, and acceptable actions; and the politicization of science. Even deeper ontological concerns arise about human-nature interaction. Invasive alien species are a conceptual challenge because the mode of their introduction varies considerably, from intentional to incidental, and they are, to some extent, a normal natural phenomenon (see Colautti and MacIsaac, 2004; Edwards, 1998; Schwartz, 1997; Theodoropoulas, 2003; Vermeij, 1996). They are a governance challenge because they cross borders and intrastate jurisdictions and often result from trade and other factors, such as the introduction of genetically modified organisms, that rely on other governance mechanisms (Ruiz and Carleton, 2003). They raise ethical challenges because the costs of dealing with them are not always shared among those who cause this risk (Beck, 1992, 1998); and environmental ethicists struggle with the initial question of paternalistic intervention (VanDeVeer, 1986). Scientific advances are being made in the quest to increase our predictive capacity for invasive outcomes (Anderson, Lew, and Peterson, 2003; Herborg, et al., 2007), as well as in our efforts to improve post-invasion responses (Carroll and Dingle, 1996; Veitch and Clout, 2002). Policy responses have been largely taken at the local level and have not always been proactive (Miller and Fabian, 2004). However, various bilateral and often voluntary measures have been instituted, for example to deal with Great Lakes ballast water (Costello, Drake, Lodge, 2007) and the sea lamprey. There are numerous multilateral agreements that touch upon IAS; the CBD maintains an active profile; and, in 1997, the GISP was founded by the IUCN, CAB International (CABI), and SCOPE. It produced the Global Strategy on IAS (GISP, 2001), which was not an international legal instrument but may emerge as the basis for future global governance efforts, albeit in conjunction with other agreements on trade, investment, and biosafety, such as the SPS Agreement covered in Chapter 7.

Another important point is that, though global governance is generally a public affair, private industry will remain central here. Indeed, one cannot implement any of the conventions discussed in this book without the cooperation of the private sector; such public-private interaction is a decisive element of any strategic plan (see Haufler, 2009). For example, preliminary research suggests that, although companies with international interests are now ready to take the plunge and adjust to new international arrangements such as the IMO's

Ballast Water Convention, shipping firms that work primarily within the North American Great Lakes were initially quite reluctant to do so (though they have released a supplemental voluntary ballast water management plan for the control of the hemorrhagic septicemia virus, which destroys the circulatory system of fish). Indeed, the shipping industry has probably been more intensively involved with IAS issues than other transport or export-oriented industries precisely because of the negative publicity associated with ballast water discharge, which indicates reason for hope as concrete actions have been taken (see Stoett and Mohammed, 2009 and Knight, 2007, for an industry perspective). Numerous industrial sectors are involved in this issue-area, from agro-forestry to tourism to military contracting (so many that it would be impractical to think of them as a monolithic block). And, although they could be expected to oppose aggressive market intervention, they may, in fact, receive an advantage from global regulations that level playing fields and effectively ostracize those firms that do not comply. Governments need to supply incentives, however, to ensure cooperation, and not just promise punishment for offenders. If we are to take this threat seriously, then, subsidies and tax breaks should not be out of the question. Finally, the companies and NGOs actually working on the eradication of IAS are engaged in potentially dangerous work and need a strong regulatory adaptive governance framework.

If there is a dearth of serious policy coordination at the international level, it is not because the issue of IAS has been ignored; on the contrary, at least 11 international agreements have a clause written in the original text or in subsequent decisions and resolutions stating that members should voluntarily prevent this form of bioinvasion. (Interestingly, several of these guidelines and voluntary measures involve the protection of the marine environment, reflecting its importance.) The IUCN's guidelines are meant to aid in the implementation of the CBD's decisions related to IAS. Several clauses are limited in scope: for example, Agenda 21 of the UNCED applies to combating deforestation, whereas OIE applies to animal diseases, and the foremost instrument to protect plants and plant products from pests is the International Plant Protection Convention, which is run out of the FAO (Clout and de Poorter, 2005). Unsurprisingly, the CBD has the most comprehensive coverage for IAS, including multiple decisions, suggested guidelines, an in-depth review of ongoing work on IAS, and clearinghouse mechanisms for cooperation and collaboration between international organizations, research institutions, and members. Following the CBD is the Ramsar Convention, which provides guidelines on the methods of control and recognizes that IAS will become more problematic with "increasing global trade, global change and changing land use patterns (Ramsar COP, 1999). CITES promotes the eradication or control of IAS and also encourages collaboration and cooperation between conventions, organizations, and members. Furthermore, the Animal Committee of CITES produces a list of actual and potential invasive alien species with management suggestions on how to deal with them. The IMO's International Convention for the Control and Management of Ships' Ballast Water and Sediments (commonly known as the Ballast Water Convention) instructs parties to "prevent, minimize and ultimately eliminate the transfer of harmful aquatic organisms and pathogens" (IMO, 2004).

Two well-known international institutions indirectly imply that preventing the introduction or spread of IAS is essential for human health and economic growth. The World Health Organization (WHO) seeks to prevent the international spread of diseases while minimizing interference in world traffic, and it presents the International Health Regulations (IHR) to this end. And the WTO's SPS Agreement addresses all sanitary and phytosanitary issues that affect, directly or indirectly, international trade. Standards, guidelines and recommendations apply to food safety and human, animal, and plant health. Many of the issues, such as pests, diseases and disease-causing organisms, relate to IAS, though the latter are never explicitly mentioned. Furthermore, several WTO member countries provide lists of quarantined pests, establishments authorized to export, press releases, and alerts. Perrings et al. (2010) believe that the most efficient global governance approach to IAS would be to carry the IHR-SPS link over to invasive species. This measure may be excellent in the short run, and I spoke with WTO bureaucrats in Geneva who were enthusiastic about this prospect, yet I would suggest that we need a much more robust, capacity-building institutionalized response in the longer scheme of things.

This flurry of activity seems rather unorganized, perhaps emblematic of the typical global environmental governance scenarios, including climate change and habitat preservation, as we have seen in previous chapters. But a transnational policy network on IAS is certainly forming, complete with public and private sector participants. Similarly, efforts at global epidemiology surveillance and prevention have been slow to evolve, despite the enormous risks to human health of inaction (see Cooper, Kirton, and Schrecker, 2007; Dodgson and Lee, 2002; and Keefe and Zacher, 2008); it took the tragedies of the HIV/AIDS and SARS pandemics to kick-start a serious global effort. A World Bank report refers to the GISP as an "informal but highly effective partnership to promote urgent and necessary action on invasives" (quoted in Young, 2006:19). Were it to be revived with commensurate support, both moral and financial, from interested governments, it could form the hub of an extensive network of international conventions and agencies that deal with IAS-related issues; and it could work with the many regional organizations that are already coordinating policy responses on related issues, some of which we will examine next.

It is important to emphasize the emerging role being played by regional actors; any new international convention would need to be highly respectful and supportive of these important actions. Indeed, efforts to develop capacity at the regional level make obvious sense in an era when trade and travel are so heavy.

For example, many agreements legally addressing IAS have been adopted in Africa, most of which are focused purely on prevention. The Protocol Concerning Protected Areas and Wild Fauna and Flora in the Eastern African Region, which is a protocol to the Convention for the Protection, Management and Development of the Marine and Coastal Environment of the Eastern African Region, prohibits the "intentional or accidental" introduction of alien species and calls on parties to "take all appropriate measures" to honor this commitment (Article VII). Likewise, subregional agreements, such as the Convention for the Establishment of the Lake Victoria Fisheries Organization (CELVFO) and the Agreement for the Preparation of a Tripartite Environmental Management Programme for Lake Victoria (APTEMPLV) both address the threats posed by IAS and delineate parties' responsibilities in honoring their obligations in the now infamous case of Lake Victoria. These include, for APTEMPLV, "biological control" of the territory under the parties' respective jurisdiction (United States Department of Agriculture National Invasive Species Information Center [USDA], 2008). The African Convention on the Conservation of Nature and Natural Resources, dating back to 1968, presents a relatively strong precedent for tackling IAS and calls for such measures as controlling invasive species and cooperation among states in the event of an ecological emergency that may spill over across borders. The African Union (AU), meanwhile, has only addressed the issue of invasive alien species insofar as they constitute "diseases, insect pests, and other enemies of plants in Africa"; these words appear in the preamble of the AU's Phyto-Sanitary Convention for Africa. Since the AU also produces pan-African economic policies, a disconnect remains between economic and environmental policy-making organs on the continent. In the Middle East, economic agreements reign over those of the environment, which are scarce in number. Economic agreements such as the Greater Arab Free Trade Agreement (GAFTA) only attempt to address environmental issues in the context of preexisting national legislation that would hinder the import of a certain good. The striking thing about the Middle East is its shortage of environmental organizations, which corresponds to a failure to establish a channel of communication between such entities and multilateral trading or policy agreements.

North America has fewer environmental policy-making bodies with regional reach than other continents have, but the ones it does have tend to possess relative influence. The Commission for Environmental Cooperation (CEC), whose objective is partly to harmonize environmental policy within the North American Free

Trade Agreement (NAFTA), focuses on the creation of risk assessment guidelines to be shared with NAFTA and other continental organizations. These guidelines are based on both species and pathways. NAFTA itself possesses a window that may lead toward the pursuit of IAS-centered policies; Article 104.2 affirms the right of parties to include "any other environmental or conservation agreement" to the list of environmental conventions to be adhered to by member states. The North American Agreement on Environmental Cooperation makes direct reference to future recommendations regarding invasive species in Article 10.2.h. In addition, there exist agreements that are species specific, such as the Convention on Great Lakes Fisheries between the United States and Canada, "whose purpose is to control and eradicate the non-native, highly invasive Atlantic sea lamprey from the Great Lakes" (United States Department of Agriculture National Invasive Species Information Center, 2008). Indeed the sea lamprey case is often cited as an example of disaster being averted thanks to aggressive (if controversial) eradication programs (in this case employing what came to be known as "lampricide" in lamprey spawning areas).

The Caribbean Community Agreement (CARICOM) allows parties "any measures" to protect their "environments and natural resources" (Article VII.ii.c). The Port of Spain Accord to the CARICOM goes further and outlines the need to develop strategies for action against the degradation of various natural resources. The environmental community of the Caribbean region is one step ahead, as demonstrated by the Protocol Concerning Specially Protected Areas and Wildlife, a protocol to the Convention for the Protection and Development of the Marine Environment of the Wider Caribbean Area. It specifically states the need to "prohibit the intentional or accidental introduction of non-indigenous" species (United States Department of Agriculture National Invasive Species Information Center, 2008). Unfortunately, Central and South America are evidently lagging behind both in the linking of trade agreements to environmental policy in general and in regulating IAS in particular. However, the Convention for the Conservation of the Biodiversity and the Protection of Wilderness Areas in Central America does call for the establishment of "all mechanisms … for the control or eradication of all exotic species which threaten ecosystems, habitats, and wild species" (Shine, Williams, and Gundling, 2000:17).

However, most environmental policies applicable to the issue of IAS involve countries of the Pacific region and Southeast Asia. For example, the Plant Protection Agreement for the South East Asia and Pacific Region calls for preventive measures to halt the spread of species that pose a threat of plant diseases and pests, including inspections, quarantine, and eradication procedures. Broader agreements include the Association of Southeast Asian Nations (ASEAN) Agreement on the Conservation of Nature and Natural Resources, which specifically outlines the obligation to regulate or prohibit the introduction of "exotic species."

The Convention on Conservation of Nature in the South Pacific declares that each party "shall carefully consider the consequences of the deliberate introduction into ecosystems of species which have not previously occurred therein." This statement does not address the *accidental* introduction of invasive species. Moreover, the ensuing Article VI provides plenty of liberty for a party to "make appropriate provision for customary use of areas and species in accordance with traditional cultural practices," enabling such considerations to trump the previous principle.

Economic entities such as the Asia-Pacific Economic Cooperation (APEC) have made limited strides toward adopting a meaningful environmental platform. APEC's Action Plan for Sustainability of the Marine Environment seeks to "reduce marine habitat degradation in order to insure the sustainability of marine resources through effective management and protection of the marine environment" (Article 11.2.c.1). Moreover, the article goes on to state several relevant performance measures, including "enhanced sustainable use and conservation of marine living resources throughout the region." In southern Asia, the South Asia Co-operative Environmental Programme and the South Asian Association for Regional Cooperation signed a memorandum of understanding in July 2004, which provides a framework for "developing mutually supportive arrangements to implement their respective Environmental Programmes and Action Plans; exchange information on the state of the global and regional environment and emerging environmental issues; collaborating in producing studies and reports on priority concerns in the field of environment; and strengthening capacity for effectively addressing global, regional and national environmental concerns" (SAARC, 2009). Unfortunately, huge swaths of Asia, including critical bodies of water (such as the Caspian Sea) have not received the same level of attention from either environmental or economic entities that wish to address IAS. Indeed, even the relatively densely regulated Pacific region has ample room for improvement.

Europe is the most integrated of economic regions, and, despite the monetary turbulence it experienced in the fall of 2011, its integration is generally seen as a political success story. There has been a proliferation of various regional and subregional environmental agreements in Europe, almost all of which provide legroom for the establishment of policies concerning IAS. The Protocol for the Implementation of the Alpine Convention in the Field of Nature Protection and Landscape Conservation as well as the Danube Convention and the Commission for the Protection of the Rhine (see Chapter 6) urge states to engage in conservation, species protection, or, in the case of the Danube Convention, sound commercial practices that have implications for the ecosystems of fisheries. Yet many agreements go much further while focusing on narrower geographic terrains. The Protocol Concerning Specially Protected Areas and Biological Diversity in the Mediterranean, the Convention for the Establishment of the European and Mediterranean Plant Protection Organization, the Bern Convention, the Protocol Concerning Mediterranean Special Protected Areas, to name but a few, all directly address invasive alien species and seek to prevent their introduction to varying degrees.

Even in the furthest reaches of the world, IAS avoidance has become part of regional environmental governance efforts. The South Pacific Regional Environmental Programme Convention makes no specific mention of IAS, but its articles on specially protected areas and impact assessment emphasize the need to preserve and promote ecosystems as well as to coordinate strategies in combating environmental problems. Likewise, the Protocol on Environmental Protection to the Antarctic Treaty effectively bans any change to the aquatic, marine, glacial, or terrestrial environment of Antarctica. (Interestingly, given its mention of the glacial environment, the obligations under the protocol can be more directly linked to activities that perpetuate climate change than is the case under many other agreements.) The Protocol for the Conservation and Management of Protected Marine and Coastal Areas of the South East Pacific goes further and calls specifically for parties to "prevent, reduce, and control environmental deterioration in marine protected areas ... [from] exotic species of flora and fauna" (USDA National Invasive Species Information Center, 2008).

Clearly, there is a wealth of realized and potential actions on IAS at the regional level. What is needed, however, is an effective international institution that can help coordinate this work and build further capacity for having an impact on the ground. We might continue to struggle without such a body, but the weight of the threat posed by IAS on human livelihoods and biodiversity suggests we should at least explore the opportunity this problem presents.

Toward an International Convention on IAS?

We have seen, then, that an adaptive multilevel governance approach is certainly necessary to deal with this issue. Indeed, one does exist, but it is still very loose and uncoordinated, glaring gaps persist (most notably, effective management of potential pathways), and replication is an ongoing concern (Shine, 2007).[3] Arguments for a convention are, in my view, quite strong. In its absence, we have a hodge-podge quilt of loosely threaded parts, most of which are woefully underfunded and lacking in any sustainable legitimacy. For example, by all accounts, the CBD has a very important role to play, especially if we frame IAS primarily as a threat to natural biodiversity, as we so often do (though I argue elsewhere this is a tactical error—see Stoett, 2010). But the CBD has, literally, only two full-time employees on the task and is hard-pressed to host a few regional capacity building workshops each year. (Another problem is the unfortunate but infamous tension between the UNEP and the CBD.) The IUCN, without the status of an intergovernmental convention, does the bulk of the work on IAS from a global perspective. If invasive alien species are not just a biodiversity issue, we need to take solutions to another level, one as free from the territorialism inherent in global environmental governance as possible. Similarly, the SPS Agreement described in Chapter 7 can and should be used to get around the trade dilemma, but it is, after all, an agreement designed to protect trade—not local ecologies.

Current international environmental law—as far as it can—holds states responsible for the deliberate spread with intent to harm of various invasive alien species (bioterrorism is also covered under other legal frameworks, including ENMOD), but it has limited power to force states to develop careful IAS export or import strategies. A soft law approach developed by the CBD (Guiding Principles for the Prevention, Introduction and Mitigation of Alien Species that Threaten Ecosystems, Habitats or Species) does not suggest liability or account for the often substantial "lag time" between introduction and invasion (see Riley, 2009), though the Cartagena Protocol on Biosafety forces states to produce transboundary risk assessments related to living modified organisms. Indeed, one of the many accomplishments of the CBD at the recent COP 10 in Nagoya was to establish yet another ad hoc technical expert group (AHTEG).[4] Nor does the SPS Agreement of the WTO specify the prevention of transboundary harm resulting from invasive alien species (Riley, 2009). Only a new convention could give IAS regulation the type of prioritization it so obviously deserves; and it would open the possibility of the development of relevant protocols. Thus, a protocol on aquarium ornamental species trade could be fashioned within the context of a broader understanding of states' and industries' rights and responsibilities (Padilla and Williams, 2004); a protocol on tourism as a pathway would be an obvious step as well.[5] (One can hold little reasonable optimism that movement toward a solution would occur in the context of military transport, however.)

Another advantage of a convention would be its ability to target the question of environmental justice, which is rarely applied to the IAS question despite the fact that the most pernicious of bioinvasions, such as the comb jellyfish in the Caspian Sea, typically harm low-income workers (in this case, fishermen) with high dependency on ecosystem services and that the strong links between cultural identity and nature can be severed with the advent of serious bioinvasions (see Knights, 2008). A distinct IAS convention would create space for GEF-related discussions about a serious adaptation fund, similar to that evolving in the climate change portfolio. This initiative would have particular resonance with small island states, where climate change and bioinvasion are national and cultural existential threats.[6] Some of the regional arrangements discussed here involve limited funding mechanisms, but such funding mechanisms are exceptions. We need funding that can ameliorate the impact of IAS on the lowest income groups affected, help build national and especially regional capacity, and further educate the public about the costs of bioinvasion. The fund would, of course, derive from convention membership, and there would be differentiated contributions according to means. Again, the GEF could play the role of a central funding mechanism here: preventing invasive alien species would certainly fall within its mandate.

It is not with any triteness that I mention the educative role of a potential secretariat. Despite its necessarily modest efforts, the CBD is not able to convey the significance of this threat to the public. In states such as Australia or Tanzania or in the North American Great Lakes Basin area or Texas, people are, of course, aware of the drain on resources that coping with an established invasion represents. But, for the most part, I would suggest that these bioinvasions are unknown territory; when biodiversity is considered in the public imagination, it is as a concern with endangered and beautiful wildlife rather than as something being threatened by alien species such as the cane toad, feral camels, the Nile carp, zebra mussels, water hyacinth, or crazy raspberry ants. Indeed, few people in the environmental movement itself have ever read the (apparently defunct) GISP *Newsletter*, though it was a well-crafted and accessible journal. Because the private sector must be involved in any prevention or eradication campaign, the educational component is even more important. Investors are less likely to accept restrictions of their behavior if they are not convinced the public is well aware of the problem demanding such restrictions in the first place. The science of bioinvasion is proceeding, and the databases mentioned previously are available; there would be no need, beyond the low costs of some coordination work, for the secretariat to fund the science directly.[7] However, it would have a primary responsibility for getting the word out.

Those opposed to the idea of an ICIAS make several very reasonable arguments (and this is gleaned from my survey of specialists working on the topic, as—to my knowledge—the argument has not been expressed in scholarly venues). They suggest that we already have an extant network, including scientists and policy makers engaged with the SPS Agreement, which works on the issue. I would suggest this network operates at such a disjointed and even dysfunctional level that it is not nearly sufficient for the immense task at hand. They suggest that the considerable time and effort that would need to be expended on the development of a convention would be wasted, either because it is diplomatically impossible or would not be much more effective than the current architecture. Regarding the question of feasibility, I think it is certainly unlikely that such a convention, especially if it were to have any teeth in the political sense, would be an easy sell. That is no reason for abandoning the prospect, however. The time spent on this by diplomats in an open context shedding light on the issue would arguably be valuable in itself. And it is difficult to see how the global community could not witness an improvement over the present situation. Nonetheless, it is clear that *convention fatigue* has set in, especially if significant costs are entailed, and this exhaustion would present a constant challenge for those advocating such a convention.

And that is the heart of the feasibility problem: there are no avowed champions for such a thing, especially among governments. This situation could well change, however, as the cumulative costs of invasive alien species are realized. We are learning more and more about how the shaping of norms affects the development of international institutions, and vice versa (Nagtzaam, 2009). The IAS case may reinforce a larger, still embryonic norm making its way toward the surface: precaution. Regardless, an ICIAS would need to establish a secretariat with sufficient autonomy to make its own advances and mistakes. (A revived GISP could certainly serve this function if it were given adequate resources.) The development of an updated global strategy would be a first priority, as would the establishment of permanent regional secretariats. The need to coordinate the work of all the international bodies involved in IAS work is palpable, but this could be done only if there were legitimate buy-ins from the IUCN, UNEP, CBD, IPCC, CITES, OIE, WTO, IMO, ICAO, CABI, and others. Of course, we would first need the agreement of states that such a convention, and one with some teeth, was necessary. Part of the job of any international secretariat is the constant reminding of state members of the importance of their cooperation and financial obligations.

Perrings et al. (2010) remind us that the 2005 International Health Regulations (IHR) under the WHO are fairly strong in nature:

> the IHR ... both imposes reporting obligations on countries, and requires that they develop the capacity to detect, assess, notify, and report disease events within 5 years (Article 5(1). At the same time, however, it imposes an obligation on the WHO to support this. (P. 205)

Although the SPS Agreement could, arguably, be strengthened to take on such functions, this would not tackle the other issues plaguing the global governance of invasive species management, and signatories might, indeed, seek to capitalize on regime overlaps based on diverging norms, as Rosendal (2001) found with the CBD and TRIPS. Of course, a new ICIAS secretariat would need to work closely with the WTO, as well as with the UNFCCC, the IPCC, and other bodies monitoring the impact of climate change. This collaboration is vital because many of the efforts at the biological management of IAS, which depends on the introduction or reintroduction of predatory species to eliminate the invasive species, will fail if climatic conditions change (Hellmann et al., 2008). And, of course, national focal points would play a vital role in providing policy coordination and education.

In short, any international convention on invasive alien species would need to

a) Establish a well-funded secretariat with the necessary autonomy to direct its own affairs, inside or, preferably, outside of the UNEP framework, and to play a major educational role in the public eye.

b) Work closely with the myriad of other international conventions and organizations dealing with some aspect of the IAS profile.

c) Establish regional offices so as to aid the coordination of protection policies already in place and developing within regional arrangements.

d) Take advantage of the serious scientific data collection and dissemination of organizations such as the IUCN and the Intergovernmental Platform on Biodiversity and Ecosystem Services (IPBES).

e) Include a mechanism whereby states are held responsible if there is flagrant disregard for the golden rule of precaution in the export of species or lack of attention to transport corridors, tourism, military operations, etc.; this could include the application of sanctions.

f) Hold tri-annual conferences of the parties where major decisions could be made and regional reports made public, drawing public attention to the issue.

g) Play a role in distributing compensation to those who have suffered economically as a result of IAS or IAS eradication strategies, and encourage sustainable strategies for using IAS for biofuel, food, or other initiatives.

Obviously, we are quite some way from such a development, and only time will tell if we get closer. The emphasis on multilevel governance, especially the support of regional arrangements, may be the long-term key to a more robust, effective political architecture designed to counter the contemporary threat of bioinvasion. The bizarre scenario referred to in the opening quotation—where a conscious effort to feed invasive camels to crocodiles is being hatched out of sheer desperation—is being mirrored in many areas. The explosion of Asian carp in the Mississippi and the spread of exotic snakes in Florida are serving to awaken the American imagination on this issue. The huge jumping carp have knocked people out of boats; the snakes are making tourist spots frightening for worried parents. But, in many parts of the world, invasive alien species are a matter of economic and cultural life and death, and, though we will never completely halt this natural process, we can and must do more to curb it. An international arrangement would be a welcome step, but—as always—only local enforcement and vigilance will prove decisive.

Notes

1. As for the intentional spread of IAS, this falls within the purview of those concerned with bioterrorism, mentioned briefly in the previous chapter. Suffice to say at this stage that the slow nature of IAS contamination would effectively preclude the deliberate spread of most IAS by terrorists or ecocidal governments; however, the deliberate spread of microbial diseases, which are themselves IAS by most definitions, is another matter altogether.

2. Reference is made to the 2002 COP 6 Decision VI/23 taken at The Hague, Netherlands (CBDCOP, 2002).

3. As Perrings et al. (2010) report, the CBD "has identified a number of gaps and areas of inconsistency induced by overlapping responsibility at the international level including, for example, animals that are not plant pests (pets, aquarium species, live bait, live food), marine biofouling, tourism, emergency aid and development assistance, military activities and interbasin water transfers and canals, marine aquaculture, and civil air transport.... OIE's focus on diseases related to livestock and other commercially valuable species neglects both interactions between species, and the wider and longer-term effects of species dispersal" (p. 203).

4. The group is to "suggest ways and means ... on the possible development of standards by appropriate bodies that can be used at an international level to avoid spread of invasive alien species [sic] that current international standards do not cover [particularly] the introduction of invasive alien species as pets, aquarium and terrarium species, as live bait and live food...." See UNEP/CBD/COP/10/L.35, A(2).

5. For a recent discussion of the tropical ornamental fish trade and the Marine Aquarium Council, see Auld et al., (2009). Most of the focus of the MAC is on the destructive pattern of fishing with cyanide (stunning fish, not killing them) in coral reef areas in the Philippines and Indonesia.

6. Note also that, as Perrings et al. (2009) point out, "Where invasive species have effectively displaced functionally similar native species, the people who have come to depend on the invasive species will not generally support its eradication. Indeed, it is not always obvious that eradication or control is the optimal strategy in such cases" (p. 246).

7. This point was stressed by Dr. Stas Burgiel, then the policy director for the GISP (and presently employed as Assistant Director for Prevention and Budgetary Coordination at the US National Invasive Species Council), in an interview conducted November 11, 2009.

CHAPTER TEN

Governance Gaps and Green Goals

"Once there were brook trout in the streams in the mountains. You could see them standing in the amber current where the white edges of their fins wimpled softly in the flow. They smelled of moss in your hand. Polished and muscular and torsional. On their backs were vermiculate patterns that were maps of the world in its becoming. Maps and mazes. Of a thing which could not be put back. Not made right again. In the deep glens where they lived all things were older than man and they hummed of mystery."

CORMAC MCCARTHY (2006:286–87)

MCCARTHY'S POSTAPOCALYPTIC BOOK, *THE ROAD*, AND THE MOVIE IT inspired hit a nerve with many. We are never told what cataclysmic event puts his father and son characters on the road past our collective ruin toward the promise of their own, minuscule, salvation. But we don't need to stretch our imaginations very far. If it's not nuclear holocaust after a senseless war, it's the ravages of unstoppable industrialization. Or it's the ecocidal butterfly effect, the climate tipping point, unraveling the web of life that ecosystem support services have provided, free of charge, for so many years; or the breakdown of civility when we face sudden scarcity, peak oil and peak soil, and the end of plentiful water. It matters less to McCarthy how it happened than how we deal with it, and he does a beautiful job reminding us of the centrality of love and hope in the human psyche, and the endless dance between fragility and courage.

But international diplomats, environmental activists, educators, business managers, and all the other people who have agential significance in the evolution of global ecopolitics must care, and care a great deal, about how we are getting there. And perhaps we are on the wrong road. There are certainly glaring gaps in our collective efforts to avoid losing the things we cherish most. It is not without reason that we are exhausted by the continuous drone of negative information, that the disaffected turn to apathy for comfort, that the more immediate fears of physical danger and economic ruin so often overshadow necessary long-term thinking. But we can turn ourselves around, in adaptive fashion, if we train our vision on the goal of sustainability. Many of our case studies demonstrate remarkable progress in constructing effective and even fair international arrangements—especially given the context of international relations today. Every arrangement can use improvement, wider legitimacy, and a more democratic inclusive approach that favors human security and environmental justice. Yet the very existence of these arrangements and our ongoing efforts to improve them provide evidence that we are not walking autonomously, automatically to certain ruin.

This concluding chapter has two main goals: to present additional areas showing serious gaps in global governance capacity and to present some observations readdressing the central question animating the book. I will look briefly at four areas of inadequate coordination at the global level, focusing specifically on the use of new, largely unregulated nanotechnology in production processes; the impact of global tourism; the need for global governance in the pursuit of food security; and the lack of a global energy strategy. I am not suggesting that any of these ecopolitical challenges will soon be subject to effective global governance but rather that the possibilities need to be discussed among an educated public. Then I turn to a brief concluding section, revisiting the question of collective survival. Though we have seen much evidence of inadequate efforts, there is much to be pleased with, and great room for hope. Translating that into sustained, concrete, adaptive policy action will not be easy, but it is not impossible.

Nanotechnology

Every economic era has a dominant technology, be it stone or brass implements, the steam or combustion engine, the radio or Internet. Arguably, we have quietly moved into another era where a serious threat to environmental health has met with surprisingly little regulatory zeal: nanotechnology, a new form of molecular engineering which is fast becoming a rapid growth area (Roco and Bainbridge, 2001; Shelley, 2006).[1] The applications are widespread, from textiles to information technology to medicine to water filtration services to military equipment. Though it may have many "green" forms of application, we are less sure about the ultimate environmental impact of nanotechnology, including that of related waste products being released into ecosystems; it has even been suggested that the self-replicating quality of nanotechnology could result in an out-of-control scenario (see Preston, 2005; this is the so-called green goo effect, where runaway self-replicating biotech products created with nanotechnology become the ultimate invasive species). This worry mirrors similar—and closely related—concerns about the impact of biotechnology, genetics, and artificial intelligence, which hold great potential for advancing planetary survival and human well-being but also need regulatory multilevel governance frameworks if safe and ethical implementation is to follow.

The OECD has been somewhat active in monitoring these developments (for example, its Chemical Committee hosted a Special Session on the Potential Implications of Manufactured Nanomaterials for Human Health and Environmental Safety in 2005). The WTO, by virtue of the SPS Agreement (described in Chapter 7), the Technical Barriers to Trade Agreement, and the Trade-Related Aspects of Intellectual Property Rights (TRIPS) Agreement, will certainly be involved, though without better foreknowledge of the impact of nanotechnology, it is hard, under a neoliberal framework that pays uneven respect to the precautionary principle, to justify intervention in trade. Bowman and Hodge (2007) refer to a "regulatory fissure" in our control of nanotechnologies:

> In countries such as the United Kingdom, Australia, Japan and
> the United States, regulation of nanotechnologies continues to
> rely primarily on the trigger of "new chemicals" being identified.
> Critically though, existing chemicals now being produced at the
> nanoscale are not considered to be "new" for purposes of these
> regulatory frameworks, despite the unpredictability and novelty
> of manufactured nanoparticles. (P. 36)

International standard-setting bodies have dominated the policy and regulatory work so far, but the authors conclude, "nanotechnology is likely to fall between the regulatory cracks of ad hoc, incomplete and decentralised regulatory regimes" (p. 36). The UN Industrial Development Organization (UNIDO) has begun a north-south dialogue on nanotechnology but is, arguably, more interested in promoting than regulating new inventions; the WTO TRIPS arrangement is more interested in protecting patents.

And this does not even begin to touch upon the potential military applications of nanotechnology, which range from bioterror to potentially harmful "nanobots" to advances in space-based weaponry.[2] (Some of these applications would presumably fall under the auspices of ENMOD, but as we saw in Chapter 8, it has very limited efficacy.) Sensor technology poses deeper threats to civil liberties in the name of national or corporate security. Indeed, such concerns are driving what Rob DeLeo (2010) refers to as "anticipatory-conjectural policy problems" that demand speculative risk assessment without proper scientific understanding of the potential problems—making adaptive governance even more difficult to sustain without firm grounding in the precautionary principle. And Shelley (2006) warns of the "danger that promises of environmental remediation through nano-technology might foster a view of the environment as a commodity that could be fixed when it breaks" (p. 129). As with other major technological advents, we will struggle to arrive at common approaches to both understanding and regulating nanotechnology; the sooner we begin in earnest the better.

Global Tourism

We are accustomed to thinking of tourism as one of the drivers of globalization today. But it is less common to address explicitly the environmental costs of this multibillion-dollar global industry. Tourists can help support conservation projects and sustainable development, but they also trample precious foliage and coastal reefs, bring invasive species and diseases with them, disperse litter, and leave a large transportation carbon footprint. Indeed, air travel is a major contributor to greenhouse gas emissions, and many have suggested that flying might need to be curtailed almost entirely if we are serious about addressing climate change. (Luckily for the tourism industry, so far we have not been serious about addressing it!) The Protocol on Environmental Protection to the Antarctic Treaty (see Chapter 6) limits and manages tourist operations in the hostile yet relatively fragile environment of Antarctica (believe it or not, this region has become an increasingly popular tourist destination, though it is certainly not in immediate danger of being colonized by cheap hotels and golf courses). But, despite rhetorical exhortations by the UN World Tourism Organization, there is no set of international regulations covering the rest of the earth.[3] The chief emphasis has been placed on raising tourist awareness and promoting ecotourism, both laudable goals but perhaps inadequate tools to address the size of the problem.

Studies have suggested that public awareness campaigns have limited impact. In spontaneous interviews with participants from different age groups and professional backgrounds as late as 2010, Hares et al. (2010) found that climate change seemed to be the last thing on their minds when they made travel plans. Interviewees said, "I don't think about it at all ... to be honest I never care" and "I don't find that important for a holiday ... I think with the flights they've made them so cheap now that would just override any climate change things." Some even expressed the belief that they should travel more now, "before travel is possibly restricted or made more difficult in the future due to climate change concerns" (Hares, Dickinson, and Wilkes, 2010:469). Carbon offset purchases, which in true entrepreneurial spirit have emerged as a cottage industry, will match but a fraction of the carbon released from tourist travel, assuming they are in fact implemented in the first place. Still, I would strongly support the idea of a person voluntarily planting a tree each time he or she flies!

And yet we love to travel, and so should we, as it provides discovery, relaxation, economic growth opportunities, and truly educational experiences for our children and ourselves. The global nature of tourism today is self-evident, and we need to ensure that ecological footprints are minimized. So much activity is being directed toward ecotourist opportunities, marine protected areas, consumption reduction campaigns, and carbon offset programs that there is hope here. But we will have to curtail air travel markedly and move beyond largely industry-promoting tourist organizations to reduce the footprint size of this activity. Even ecotourism can present problems for local people and the environment (see Duffy, 2002). Is there a role for global environmental governance here? Beyond the complex web of arrangements that overlap with tourist activity, we could still use a stronger set of global standards of conduct and better capacity-building mechanisms for tourist destination states than those offered by the UNWTO. The International Civil Aviation Organization (ICAO), with its secretariat located across the street from the CBD here in Montreal, should play a leading role, but it has a vested interest in supporting the airline industry as well as in pursuing sustainable development.[4] We need a broader approach and personal responsibility at the same time. As enticing as it sounds, do we really need to see the Galapagos Islands in person?

Food Security

The authors of *Our Common Future*, the landmark report of the Brundtland Commission issued in 1987, were sure to include a chapter on food security (Brundtland et al., 1987:118–46). Though it is often lambasted as a neoliberal blueprint for slightly adjusted business as usual, even the WCED explicitly labeled land reform a "basic requirement" where "land is very unequally distributed" (p. 141). Following on a severe food shortage in 2008, food prices soared in 2011 as demand rose and oil prices stabilized at high levels. The price of weekly groceries, then, has become an added hardship on the heels of the global recession, even for the middle class in developed countries, but those without land and farming rights in highly populated southern states are particularly hard pressed to make ends meet, adding further distance between us and the realization of the Millennium Goal of halving world hunger between 1990 and 2015. Though various instruments exist to distribute food aid, these are short-term solutions that offer few sustainable prospects.

Desertification, deforestation, and the collapse of fisheries will only contribute to this global problem. The demand for biofuel displaces food crops; the use of oil byproducts in the nitrogen cycle ties food and volatile oil prices; the use of vegetation to feed high-end farm animals to produce beef and pork increases costs as well. Pesticides, herbicides, animal waste: all these forms of agricultural runoff are the result of an unsustainable global food production system. There is no global environmental governance mechanism to redesign that system, but organizations such as the FAO have a mandate to avoid food insecurity even as they also promote agribusiness. GMOs are often touted as possible technological solutions, but they are politically contested and promote further our shortsighted acceptance of mono-cropping as the "modern" mode of agriculture. The EU has decided that "the process of genetic modification is in itself a potential hazard which presents unique risks that must be regulated, which has been further underpinned by the adoption and strict interpretation of the precautionary principle" (Bowman and Hodge, 2006:12).

Here is a no-brainer for most of us: farmers are the key. They have the greatest stake in sustainable agriculture. They feed us and even clothe us, yet they are taken for granted and subjected to product-pushing schemes to sell them the latest chemical savior. A nonbinding International Treaty on Plant Genetic Resources for Food and Agriculture negotiated by the FAO in 1983 was revamped in the early 2000s to reflect the Cartagena Protocol of the CBD (see Chapter 3). It aims to help farmers and small breeders have access to seeds and genetic material as well as to the benefits of sharing information. This arrangement "has the potential to make an important contribution to global food security and sustainable agriculture" (Cooper, 2002:1). Yet most farmers around the world are beleaguered by big agribusiness, dependent on corporations for materials and banks for short-term financing. The World Bank and other international financial institutions take food security and the role of farmers seriously, but we need to do more to help farmers cope with climate change and aggressive global agribusiness.

Of course, food security is a function of political context as well, and violent conflict and inequity are obvious impediments. As discussed in Chapter 8, war often overrides all other considerations, and avoiding it must be the first priority of global governance. But we ignore food security and farmers' rights at our obvious peril. Biotechnology will not overcome the need for food and organic farming, urban agriculture, and the humane treatment of the animals we have designated as sources of protein. And devoting land to fuel automobiles is a shameful waste of precious soil, which leads to our next topic: energy production.

A Global Energy Strategy?

Because it is so heavily ensconced in national security and the political economy of daily survival, the production and distribution of energy is hard to visualize as a global phenomenon. Yet it is seen by many as the holy grail of a concerted international arrangement to guide our collective future.

Obviously, the marketplace is the main focal point of energy production at the international level; here we see the use of pricing, often reflecting political developments, to "control" the distribution of oil and gasoline, and trade in natural resources for energy production has at least partially defined the economies of resource-rich states such as Saudi Arabia or Canada. Canada's Conservative government has even openly declared its desire to be the next "energy superpower" and is developing the tar/oil sands in Alberta and lobbying to build continental and Asia-bound pipelines in the process.[5] However, it is not radical to surmise that we will run out of affordable oil within our grandchildren's lifetimes (indeed it would be optimistic to think we wouldn't). We are not prepared for this, and global governance without a social conscience will only worsen the situation.

I became fascinated by the international energy question in the early 1990s, when it was apparent that energy sources were highly politicized, the precautionary principle was in its formal normative infancy, and the Iraqi invasion of Kuwait invited such a determined Western response to defend that tiny, oil-soaked kingdom (see Stoett, 1994a). Over several campfire night conversations, a dear and brilliant friend, Shane Mulligan, convinced me further that peak oil is near (Mulligan, 2010). Global oil discovery peaked in the early 1960s, and most giant oil fields were found decades ago (Homer-Dixon, 2006:90–91; see also Bardi, 2009). We are going to extraordinary lengths to find and process more oil and natural gas, risking environmental hazards and human life in the process. The international arrangements on energy production include cartels, such as OPEC; IFIs such as the World Bank; consumer organizations such as the OECD's International Energy Agency; and promotional and regulatory organizations such as the International Atomic Energy Agency, which has one mandate to avoid the misuse of nuclear energy but another to promote it. Some predict a financial catastrophe will accompany the fall of oil, but this prediction is usually tempered with exhortations to seek adaptive technologies and consumption habits (see Leggett, 2005). Widespread subsidies to fossil fuel producers are the "antithesis of the polluter pays principle, and it is clear that these subsidies need to be abolished altogether" (Lesage, Van de Graaf, and Westphal, 2010:47). Shifting the billions of dollars wasted on subsidies would be a good start, and international institutions such as the GEF might be a palatable, if still contestable, repository for such funding. Giving petro-tyrannies the need to actually earn their political legitimacy would not be such a bad thing either, though civil unrest in the OPEC world has already emerged as one of the defining characteristics of this century. And though nuclear power has a future (if not in Germany, which in the wake of Japan's winter 2011 disaster has sworn off it), it will always be a contentious power source.[6] Alternative energy sources, from solar and geothermal to wind and wave, need our utmost devotion today. Coal may be abundant (though this is the subject of some debate: see Goodell, 2006), but burning it contributes to climate change.

Since the reality of limited oil reserves is so difficult to publicly conceptualize, any possible global energy strategy will probably carry greater legitimacy if it is premised on collective action on climate change. But I am convinced that biofuels, although they are certainly tried and tested in many local contexts, are not the solution to the global problem of energy supply. Indeed, a debate over biofuels is raging today, as it should be.[7] Demand for palm oil is so high (and rising, especially from China) that palm plantations have become a major source of deforestation (see Chapter 4). Relatively successful biodiesel projects, such as Brazil's use of sugarcane ethanol, were based on limited national markets not on inexorably rising demands from other economic juggernauts or from those seeking high profit margins.[8] And though it is certainly "cleaner" than gasoline or oil, there are serious debates about the net benefits of ethanol as an alternative fuel (Böhm and Saldiva, 1998; Molina and Molina, 2004). While millions live in chronic hunger and the benefits of mass transit are overwhelmingly clear, the demands of car culture should take a second seat until we have technological answers. There is no getting around the basic imperatives here: the reduction of energy demand in the north, the development of affordable and transferable alternative technologies, and the equitable sharing of the earth's resources.

And yet we are very far indeed from an effective global energy governance system. There is no coordinating body, and, as energy is so tightly wrapped in the fold of national security, except for the climate change and development links, there have been few concrete initiatives at the UN level. Lesage, Van de Graaf, and Westphal (2010) believe the G8 has played a default leadership role: "Although the G8 has never openly claimed to be the 'world's steering committee' for energy governance ... much in the behavior of the G8 hints at such an aspiration" (p. 147). However, The "G8 clearly goes after the 'low hanging fruit': fostering international cooperation on energy efficiency and cleaner energy on a completely voluntary basis" (p. 173–74). For example, the energy ministers of the G8, China, India, and South Korea announced the creation of the International Partnership for Energy Efficiency Cooperation (IPEEC) at their meeting in Aomori, Japan, in June 2008; its secretariat is located at the IEA in Paris. But, as many of our case studies have demonstrated, there is a well-established friction between an elite club of largely northern states and those southern states where global governance is often perceived as a means to maintain the status quo. Local action, not international institutions or global oil conglomerates, will have the most beneficial impact as communities pursue ecological self-sufficiency within the context of the evolving world economy.

It is hard to disagree with Homer-Dixon (2006): "...when it comes to energy, and particularly when it comes to conventional oil, we're constrained on every side: our appetite for energy is enormous and quickly growing; we're deeply dependent on oil to satisfy that appetite, yet oil's supply is tightening quickly; some alternatives to oil endanger national and international security, while others are technically or economically unfeasible" (p. 100). This may be too gloomy a picture, however. Adaptive multilevel governance with the twin goals of decreasing reliance on fossil fuels while promoting human equality and security must pave the way for an energy revolution. Indeed, this radical change is a long-term project, and perhaps only our grandchildren's children will see it to fruition. But it would be premature and self-defeating to slip into despair. The sheer breadth of people working hard to resolve these issues, from scientists to human rights and climate justice advocates to dedicated citizens, is an overwhelmingly positive factor. And if we need to move toward a Marshall Plan for renewable energy, Norway is paving the way with a multibillion-dollar investment in technological development for southern states that it calls "Energy +"; the initiative is accompanied by a billion-dollar forest conservation deal with Indonesia (see Chapter 4).[9] It is hard to think of a more constructive way for Norway to spend its wealth, accumulated from years of oil extraction, than on reforestation and renewable energy development.

From Angst to Resolve

Back at the riverside, I reflect again on the flow of water and our liquid state of being. Water fills the bloodstream of all living things, and your heart would be dry without it. Though some deep ecologists and animal welfarists remain critical of the anthropocentrism of international human rights law (see Redgwell, 1998), it is fairly widely accepted that the right to a safe environment is a fundamental human right. As Dinah Shelton (2003) suggests, a human rights approach to environmental protection seeks "to ensure that the natural world does not deteriorate to the point where international guaranteed rights such as the rights to life, health, property, a family, a private life, culture, and safe drinking water are seriously impaired. Environmental protection is thus instrumental, not an end in itself" (p. 1). However, one can position this in opposite terms, suggesting the "legal protection of human rights is an effective means to achieving the ends of conservation and environmental protection" (M.R. Anderson, 1998:3). Water is, of course, a prime example. Access to clean water is often recognized as a human right of the first order. Its denial, whether through occupation, usurpation, or privatization, is at the root of an increasingly visible if politically limited water justice movement, which has given rise to calls for an international arrangement that explicitly guarantees water as a universal human right to reduce looming water-related conflicts (see Davidson-Harden et al., 2007 and Chapter 8).

The failure to pursue environmental justice at an international level can only lead us further on the troubled road toward a world defined by *bioapartheid*; a systemic physical separation of the people who have suffered the deleterious impacts of the health threats related to climate change and infectious diseases (and the malnourishment resultant from absolute poverty) from the people with the means to escape these threats to human security and who are free to roam wherever their transnational capital can take them. Bioapartheid may or may not involve the application of military power to maintain such separation; it may or may not overlap with religious war; it may or may not assume a visibly racial character. The central theme of bioapartheid is the enforced separation of humans based on markedly divergent levels of access to health services, disease control, education, and natural resources; any serious consideration of environmental justice would need to dismiss this as a long-term option (see Aginam, 2005; Hossay, 2006).

When viewing the impact of our own highly invasive species upon the planet, we can easily slide into misanthropic fatalism, which furnishes statements such as this one: "...the decay of Congo's Belgian-built roads, which in 1960 ran to over 100,000 km, must rank as one of the greatest boons to forests since the Black Death" (Astill, 2010:5). Let's keep this in perspective: estimates are that the earth's population should hit 9 billion by 2050, and, though it is never easy to predict these things, the population clock keeps ticking. Recall our discussion in Chapter 3 on the services provided by nature that will sustain this population: provision services (such as food, water, and timber), regulating services (such as wetland water filtration and forest air purification), cultural services (such as recreation and spiritual fulfillment), and supporting services (such as photosynthesis, nutrient cycling, and soil formation). Working against this web of sustainability becomes less rational with each net gain in the human population. A safe bet: people will continue to seek the fulfillment of creating and nurturing children, so we need to give *our* fullest support to these natural supportive networks. Global environmental governance will play a key role here. But it is only one factor, and local and national initiatives, tied to global partnerships, are the only true route to a multilevel adaptive governance approach that respects unique ecosystem properties and community differences and identities and that addresses historic inequalities.

This is why I am not a strong advocate of the "World Environment Organization" approach, or of the suggestion that it would be best to create a global institution that can put the environment on the global governance map, up there with trade and international finance and war and peace. Although it seems a logical extension of a global governance approach, it would invariably lack widespread legitimacy and stand accused of usurping power from local authorities. In my view, beyond the tremendous diplomatic energy that would probably be wasted in such a grandiose initiative, this idea runs counter to the multilevel adaptive governance architecture that is slowly, painfully emerging from the wilderness of global ecopolitics. Although some issue-areas may well demand a new international arrangement (I've mentioned invasive alien species, nanotechnology, global tourism, food security, and energy), such arrangements need to be multilayered and integrated with other, traditionally non-environmental sectors. A nuanced view of ecological systems, including human activity and political structures, suggests that separating environmental "problems" from others can be a misleading effort to grab headlines. Similarly, those impatient with the "softness" of international law are certainly warranted to be so, but more coercive approaches will only reflect the interests of structural power and discourage the pursuit of initiatives reflecting self-enlightened interest. As Bodansky (2010) suggests,

> [an] alternative approach to international environmental law is less ambitious but more realistic. It views international environmental law as a process to encourage and enable, rather than require, international co-operation [and] attempts to help states achieve mutually beneficial outcomes ... by building scientific and normative consensus and by addressing barriers to compliance, such as mistrust between states and lack of domestic capacity. (p. 16)

As the tumultuous events of the winter and spring of 2011 in the Middle East reminded us, predicting political change is a hazardous occupation at best. Few scholars foresaw the end of the cold war either. It is equally difficult to predict where environmental change will lead us in the political sense. After the rush of diplomatic activity in the 1970s slowed its pace in the 1980s, most observers would not have predicted the grand scale on which the UN Conference on Environment and Development took place in 1992. Now, after decades of global ecopolitics, awareness campaigns, and the continued manifestation of problems, the question may well be whether environmental issues can retain any sort of mainstream prominence when there are so many other questions—though they are of course ecological questions as well—fighting for attention on the world stage. But they must if we are to move forward in a collective manner. Happily, cognitive evolution is occurring. The first "Earth Day" took place in 1970—a grassroots campaign in the United States harnessed by Senator Gaylord Nelson, who learnt from the anti-Vietnam demonstrations that were sweeping the country how grassroots protests can push an issue onto the political agenda.[10] Today Earth Day is celebrated around the world on April 22.

Grassroots campaigns and celebrations alone will not be enough, of course. But, as mammals, we do not lack the urge to survive. With apologies to deep ecologists and others critical of reflexive anthropomorphism, I assume that our primary concern is with human security. It is impossible, without sustainable environmental conditions, to achieve true human security for any but a small group of people with such disproportionate means that they can literally buy their security—on a temporary basis. Our future may be cloudy and our thoughts troubled by shades of angst, but our dogged love of life will persevere. You need only to enjoy a child's smiling eyes to feel this, if only for a happy moment. Regardless of our religious background, ethnic heritage, or station in life, each one of us should be grateful for the life-support systems the earth has offered not only our generation but countless preceding generations. In my view, we have a moral obligation as individuals living in multilayered communities and working for responsible corporations to reduce our ecological footprint. Linking human rights with environmental protection demands that we take the impact of both deleterious behavior and efforts to curb it into account. It demands that we take environmental justice seriously as a long-term goal for all of humanity, not just for those in pockets of relative affluence. And it insists that we avoid the temptation to permit climate change, disease, and resource scarcity to become excuses for the rise of neo-authoritarianism and state violence.

There is no definitive answer to the questions I raised in the introduction to this book. But I remain convinced that we can win this race against time, provided a critical mass of human intellect and genuine care is generated and makes itself present in the daily stuff of global ecopolitics. We need to combine passion, sacrifice, and determination; we must pursue the adaptive capacity for which humanity is rightly known. From my own professional perspective, academics need to infuse scholarship with a critical yet optimistic spirit. As Elizabeth DeSombre (2011) suggests, "critical scholars view the world's effort to address environmental issues not as progress but as perpetuation of the underlying dynamics that created the problems in the first place" (p. 134). Breaking from this cycle without resorting to fatalistic pessimism is the task ahead of those who believe adaptive governance is not an empty shell, a cynical ploy to avoid the hard work of taking the next step toward sustainability, a false step. International arrangements are, obviously, the result of power relations and constructed realties, and they can prove ineffective or, worse, counterproductive. But they are also tangible evidence of our concern, of our ingenuity, of our resolve to make things better. We need to harness them and make them work for the collective good.

We can do this.

1. Nanotechnology can be understood as "a range of products, research paths and processes that have in common the deliberate manipulation or employment of materials in order to harness particular qualities exhibited at the nanoscale. That is to say one-billionth of a metre.... Those properties might be electrical conductivity, reactivity to light, enhanced catalytic qualities, strength combined with light weight, or ability to attract or repel other materials" (Shelley, 2006:131).

2. Some people may argue that any form of nonhuman soldier, be it large or small, is an improvement over using real human beings to fight wars. In a fantasyland where robots could swing it out against each other on a world stage, this argument might make some sense, but the reality is already quite different, as the debate over the use of drone planes by the United States demonstrates. Reducing the human element in warfare could have the perverse effect of dehumanizing its human victims, including the actual soldiers who eventually end up on the ground; and, in an era of the privatization of security forces, there are additional questions about the role of private firms in the design, research, and deployment of advanced technology.

3. The 154-member UNWTO has a Department of Sustainable Development and has produced a "Global Code of Ethics" for tourism adopted by the UN General Assembly (A/RES/56/212–2001); it is not only very soft law but also sparse on environmental policy suggestions.

4. See Gossling and Upham (2009) for a broad discussion of the scientific and policy links between climate change and aviation.

5. I will not enter the endless debate about whether to call the Albertan oil boon the result of exploiting "tar sands" or "oil sands"; either way, their ecological footprint is undeniable.

6. While nuclear power enjoyed a bit of a resurgence because of its claim to lower carbon emissions, safety concerns, including radiation leaks, waste disposal issues, and possible nuclear weapons development, persist. See Stoett (2003) for a discussion.

7. For balanced treatments, see Heintzman and Solomon (2009) and Rosillo-Calle and Johnson (2010).

8. In 2006, Brazil produced approximately 16 billion liters of ethanol a year, requiring approximately 3 hectares of land and not detracting substantially from land available for food production—sugarcane occupies only 10 per cent of total cultivated land in Brazil and 1 per cent of land available for agriculture (Goldemberg, 2007:808).

9. On the promises and barriers (in both the north and south) of technology transfers for renewable energy, see Wilkins (2002).

10. Nelson's enlightened perspective was that "the economy is a wholly owned subsidiary of the environment"; for this quotation and others, see the Gaylord Nelson and Earth Day website (http://www.nelsonearthday.net/).

Afterword: What Can You Do?

THERE ARE FAR TOO MANY POSITIVE STEPS INDIVIDUALS CAN TAKE TO lessen their ecological footprint, carbon and otherwise, to list here, but I cannot resist the urge to name a few. Take seriously the words attributed to Mahatma Gandhi, that sacrifice is a call to "live simply so others can live" (Wapner 2010:35). Think hard before you purchase any disposable product, and also consider whether the packaging of any product is necessary. The oceans are full of plastic because of human carelessness. Fast food has its obvious advantages, but it will benefit your health and the biosphere if you limit your intake; and be careful not to eat food from threatened species or ecosystems. Vote with your wallet. If you are purchasing an automobile, go as green as possible. We drive two hybrids at home, and they are both excellent, durable, low maintenance cars; I look forward to purchasing an all-electric vehicle next. Drive sparingly; fly even less. Recycle when possible, and start a compost heap; if you have the space, grow your own vegetables. Visit a farm and thank a farmer. Practice green tourism when traveling, especially in areas with fragile ecosystems such as islands, the Arctic, or rainforests. Lobby politicians to keep promises and commitments to international arrangements, to contribute to the shift toward renewable power, and to think seriously about adaptation to climate change around the globe. Demand corporate responsibility from business leaders, and push management at work or school toward completing an environmental audit and pursuing sustainability initiatives. Engage your children, parents, siblings, and friends in discussions about the future of the environment. Follow environmental diplomacy through newspapers and websites, including alternative media; try to stay on top of things, and know how your own country's government (national and local) stands on major issues. (Don't feel obliged to agree with this stance.) Learn more about the science and policy issues discussed in this book and other texts. Join an NGO or other form of advocacy group with which you agree. Watch out for greenwashing, disinformation, and empty promises. Take time to enjoy the warmth and beauty of natural settings; they will recharge you, enrich you, and teach you more than you could ever learn in a book like this one.

References

Adeel, Z., U. Safriel, D. Niemeijer, and R. White. 2008. *Ecosystems and Human Well-Being: Desertification Synthesis*. Millennium Ecosystems Assessment. Washington: World Resources Institute.

Adger, W.N., J. Paavola, S. Huq, and M.J. Mace. 2006. *Fairness in Adaptation to Climate Change*. Cambridge, MA: MIT Press.

Aginam, O. 2005. *Global Health Governance: International Law and Public Health in a Divided World*. Toronto: University of Toronto Press.

Agius, E. 2006. "Environmental Ethics: Towards an Intergenerational Perspective." In *Environmental Ethics and International Policy*, ed. H.A.M.J. ten Have, 89–115. Paris: UNESCO.

Agriculture and Agri-Food Canada. Economic and Policy Analysis Directorate. 2000. *The Relevance and Potential Impact of Kyoto Protocol Mechanisms for the Canadian Agriculture and Agri-Food Sector*. Ottawa: EPAD.

Aldy, J., and R. Stavins. 2010a. "Lessons for the International Policy Community." In *Post-Kyoto International Climate Policy: Implementing Architectures for Agreement*, ed. J. Aldy and R. Stavins, 899–929. New York: Cambridge University Press.

Aldy, J., and R. Stavins. 2010b. *Post-Kyoto International Climate Policy: Implementing Architectures for Agreement*. New York: Cambridge University Press.

Ali, S.H., ed. 2007. *Peace Parks: Conservation and Conflict Resolution*. Cambridge, MA.: MIT Press.

Ali, S.H. 2008. "Water Politics in South Asia: Technocratic Cooperation and Lasting Security in the Indus Basin and Beyond." *Journal of International Affairs* 61 (2): 167–82.

Allan, J.B. 2008. "People and Pandas in Southwest China." *Journal of International Wildlife Law and Policy* 11 (2-3): 156–88. http://dx.doi.org/10.1080/13880290802470174.

Allen, R. 2010. *International Management of Tuna Fisheries: Arrangements, Challenges and a Way Forward*. Rome: FAO Fisheries and Aquaculture Technical Paper.

Altinbilek, D. 2004. "Development and Management of the Euphrates-Tigris Basin." *Water Resources Development* 20 (1): 15–33. http://dx.doi.org/10.1080/07900620310001635584.

Amer, S.E.D., Y. Arsano, A. El-Battahani, O.E.T. Hamad, M.A.E.M. Hefny, I. Tamrat, and Simon A. Mason. 2005. "Sustainable Development and International Cooperation in the Eastern Nile Basin." *Aquatic Sciences* 67 (1): 3–14. http://dx.doi.org/10.1007/s00027-004-0764-z.

Anderson, D.H. 1994. "Further Efforts to Ensure Universal Participation in the United Nations Convention on the Law of the Sea." *International and Comparative Law Quarterly* 43 (4): 886–93. http://dx.doi.org/10.1093/iclqaj/43.4.886.

Anderson, D.H. 1995. "Legal Implications of the Entry into Force of the UN Convention on the Law of the Sea." *International and Comparative Law Quarterly* 44 (2): 313–26. http://dx.doi.org/10.1093/iclqaj/44.2.313.

Anderson, D.H. 1996. "The Straddling Stocks Agreement of 1995: An Initial Assessment." *International and Comparative Law Quarterly* 45 (2): 463–75.

Anderson, M.R. 1996. "Human Rights Approaches to Environmental Protection: An Overview." In *Human Rights Approaches to Environmental Protection*, ed. A. Boyle and M. Anderson, 2–10. Oxford: Clarendon Press.

Anderson, R., D. Lew, and A. Peterson. 2003. "Evaluating Predictive Models of Species' Distributions: Criteria for Selecting Optimal Models." *Ecological Modelling* 162 (3): 211–32. http://dx.doi.org/10.1016/S0304-3800(02)00349-6.

Angus, I. ed. 2010. *The Global Fight for Climate Justice*. Winnipeg: Fernwood.

Aoki, C. 2008. "ITTO's Holistic Approach to Forestry and Environmental Education." In *New Perspectives in Forestry Education*, ed. A.B. Temu, S.A.O. Chamshama, J. Kung'u, J. Kaboggoza, B. Chikamai, and A. Kiwia, 26–46. Nairobi: World Agroforestry Centre (ICRAF).

Arrhenius, S. 1896. "On the Influence of Carbonic Acid in the Air upon the Temperature of the Ground." *Philosophical Magazine and Journal of Science* 5 (41): 237–76.

Association of Southeast Asian Nations (ASEAN). 2010. Update on the ASEAN Agreement on Transboundary Haze Pollution. Paper presented at the 2009 Pan Asia Forest Fire Consultation, Busan, Korea. Retrieved April 8, 2009. http://www.fire.uni-freiburg.de/GlobalNetworks/Northeast-Asia/ICS Symposium/ICS-03-ASEAN-1.pdf.

Astill, J. 2010. "Seeing the Wood." *The Economist*, September 23.

Athanasiou, T., and P. Baer. 2002. *Dead Heat: Global Justice and Global Warming*. New York: Seven Stories Books.

Atkinson, R.W., B. Barratt, B. Armstrong, H.R. Anderson, S.D. Beevers, I.S. Mudway, D. Green, R.G. Derwent, P. Wilkinson, C. Tonne et al. 2009. "The Impact of the Congestion Charging Scheme on Ambient Air Pollution Concentrations in London." *Atmospheric Environment* 43 (34): 5493–500. http://dx.doi.org/10.1016/j.atmosenv.2009.07.023.

Auld, G., C. Balboa, S. Bernstein, and B. Cashore. 2009. "The Emergence of Non-state Market Driven (NSMD) Global Environmental Governance: A Cross-Sectoral Assessment." In *Governing the Environment: Interdisciplinary Perspectives*, ed. M. Delmas and O. Young, 183–218. Cambridge: Cambridge University Press.

Austin, J., and C.E. Bruch, eds. 2000. *The Environmental Consequences of War: Legal, Economic, and Scientific Perspectives*. Cambridge: Cambridge University Press. http://dx.doi.org/10.1017/CBO9780511522321.

Bache, I., and M. Flinders, eds. 2005. *Multi-level Governance*. Oxford: Oxford University Press.

Baggs, J. 2009. "International Trade in Hazardous Waste." *Review of International Economics* 17 (1): 1–16. http://dx.doi.org/10.1111/j.1467-9396.2008.00778.x.

Bailey, J.L. 1996. "Hot Fish and (Bargaining) Chips." *Journal of Peace Research* 33 (3): 257–62. http://dx.doi.org/10.1177/0022343396033003001.

Baker, C.S. 2008. "A Truer Measure of the Market: The Molecular Ecology of Fisheries and Wildlife Trade." *Molecular Ecology* 17 (18): 3985–98. http://dx.doi.org/10.1111/j.1365-294X.2008.03867.x. Medline:18643915.

Bardi, U. 2009. "Peak Oil: The Four Stages of a New Idea." *Energy* 34 (3): 323–26. http://dx.doi.org/10.1016/j.energy.2008.08.015.

Barker, D.R. 2002. "Biodiversity Conservation in the Wider Caribbean Region." *Reciel* 11 (1): 74–83.

Barkin, S.J. 2004. "Time Horizons and Multilateral Enforcement in International Cooperation." *International Studies Quarterly* 48 (2): 363–82. http://dx.doi.org/10.1111/j.0020-8833.2004.00305.x.

Barnett, J. 2003. "Security and Climate Change." *Global Environmental Change* 13 (1): 7–17.

Barnett, J., and W.N. Adger. 2007. "Climate Change, Human Security, and Violent Conflict." *Political Geography* 26: 639–55.

Barnett, J., R. Matthew, and K. O'Brien. 2010. "Global Environmental Change and Human Security: An Introduction." In *Global Environmental Change and Human Security*, ed. R. Matthew, J. Barnett, B. McDonald, and K. O'Brien, 3–32. Cambridge, MA: MIT Press.

Barton, J. 2008. "Canada-Wide Standards and Innovative Transboundary Air Quality Initiatives." *Journal of Toxicology and Environmental Health, Part A: Current Issues* 71 (1): 74–80. http://dx.doi.org/10.1080/15287390701558022. Medline:18080897.

Basel Action Network (BAN). 2010. Welcome to the Basel Action Network—BAN. Retrieved May 5, 2010. http://www.ban.org.

Basel Action Network (BAN). 2011. About the Basel Ban: A Chronology of the Basel Ban. Retrieved December 11, 2011. http://www.ban.org/about_basel_ban/chronology.html.

Batterbury, S.P.J., and A. Warren. 2001. "Desertification." In *International Encyclopedia of the Social and Behavioral Sciences*, ed. N. Smelser and P. Baltes, 3526–29. Amsterdam: Elsevier Press. http://dx.doi.org/10.1016/B0-08-043076-7/04172-3.

Bauer, S. 2006. "Does Bureaucracy Really Matter? The Authority of Intergovernmental Treaty Secretariats in Global Environmental Politics." *Global Environmental Politics* 6 (1): 23–49. http://dx.doi.org/10.1162/glep.2006.6.1.23.

Bauer, S. 2009. "The Desertification Secretariat: A Castle Made of Sand." In *Mangers of Global Change: The Influence of International Environmental Bureaucracies*, ed. F. Biermann and B. Siebenhuner, 293–318. Cambridge, MA: MIT Press.

Bauer, S., and L. Stringer. 2009. "The Role of Science in the Global Governance of Desertification." *Journal of Environment & Development* 18 (3): 248–67. http://dx.doi.org/10.1177/1070496509338405.

Beck, U. 1992. *The Risk Society: Towards a New Modernity*. Trans. M. Ritter. London: Sage Productions.

Beck, U. 1998. "Politics of Risk Society." In *The Politics of Risk Society*, ed. J. Franklin, 9–22. Cambridge: Polity.

Bello, J.H., and P.H.F. Bekker. 1997. "Legality of the Threat or Use of Nuclear Weapons." *American Journal of International Law* 91 (1): 126–33. http://dx.doi.org/10.2307/2954150.

Benedict, R. 1991. *Ozone Diplomacy: New Directions in Safeguarding the Planet*. Cambridge, MA: Harvard University Press.

Bernauer, T., and P. Moser. 1996. "Reducing Pollution of the River Rhine: The Influence of International Cooperation." *Journal of Environment & Development* 5 (4): 389–415. http://dx.doi.org/10.1177/107049659600500402.

Bernstein, S. 2002. "International Institutions and the Framing of Domestic Policies: The Kyoto Protocol and Canada's Response to Climate Change." *Policy Sciences* 35: 203–36.

Bernstein, S. 2005. "Legitimacy in Global Environmental Governance." *Journal of International law and International Relations* 1 (1): 139–66.

Bestor, T.C. 2001. "Supply-Side Sushi: Commodity, Market, and the Global City." *American Anthropologist* 103 (1): 76–95. http://dx.doi.org/10.1525/aa.2001.103.1.76.

Betsill, M., and H. Bulkeley. 2004. "Transnational Networks and Global Environmental Governance: The Cities for Climate Protection Program." *International Studies Quarterly* 48 (2): 471–93. http://dx.doi.org/10.1111/j.0020-8833.2004.00310.x.

Biermann, F., et al. 2009. *Earth System Governance: People, Places, and the Planet. Science and Implementation Plan of the Earth System Governance Project. Earth System Governance Report 1, IHDP Report 20*. Bonn: Earth System Governance Project.

Biermann, F., and B. Siebenhuner, eds. 2009. *Managers of Global Change: The Influence of International Environmental Bureaucracies*. Cambridge, MA: MIT Press.

Bilcke, C. 2002. "The Stockholm Convention on Persistent Organic Pollutants." *Review of European Community and International Environmental Law* 11 (3): 328–42.

Birnie, P., A. Boyle, and C. Redgwell. 2009. *International Law and the Environment*. 3rd ed. Oxford: Oxford University Press.

Björkbom, L. 1999. "Negotiations over Transboundary Air Pollution: The Case of Europe." *International Negotiation* 4 (3): 389–411. http://dx.doi.org/10.1163/15718069920848543.

Blamford, A., A. Brunder, P. Cooper, et al. 2004. Economic Reasons for Conserving Wild Nature. Paper presented at The Hague Conference on Environment, Security and Sustainable Development, The Hague, The Netherlands, May 9–12. Retrieved December 1, 2011. http://www.envirosecurity.org/conference/working/ReasonsConservWildNature.pdf.

Bodansky, D. 2010. *The Art and Craft of International Environmental Law*. Cambridge, MA: Harvard University Press.

Böhm, G.M., and P.H.N. Saldiva. 1998. "Science as a Promoter of Environmental and Human Health: The Experience of São Paulo's Air Pollution." *Ecosystem Health* 4 (4): 196–98. http://dx.doi.org/10.1046/j.1526-0992.1998.98094.x.

Bohm, S., and S. Dabhi, eds. 2009. *Upsetting the Offset: The Political Economy of Carbon Markets*. London: Mayfly Books.

Borgerhoff Mulder, M., and P. Coppolillo. 2005. *Conservation: Linking Ecology, Economics and Culture*. Princeton: Princeton University Press.

Borgerson, S.G. 2009. *The National Interest and the Law of the Sea*. New York. Council on Foreign Relations.

Boucher, D. 1998. *Political Theories of International Relations: From Thucydides to the Present*. Oxford: Oxford University Press.

Bowman, D., and G. Hodge. 2007. "A Small Matter of Regulation: An International Review of Nanotechnology Regulation." *The Columbia Science and Technology Law Review* 8: 1–36.

Boyle, A.E.J. 1997. "Dispute Settlement and the Law of the Sea Convention: Problems of Fragmentation and Jurisdiction." *International and Comparative Law Quarterly* 46 (1): 37–54. http://dx.doi.org/10.1017/S0020589300060103.

Boyle, A.E.J. 2007. "The Environmental Jurisprudence of the International Tribunal for the Law of the Sea." *International Journal of Marine and Coastal Law* 22 (3): 368–83.

Boyle, A., and M. Anderson. 1998. *Human Rights Approaches to Environmental Protection*. London: Clarendon Press.

Bright, C. 1998. *Life Out of Bounds: Bioinvasion in a Borderless World*. New York: Norton.

Bright, C. 1999. "Invasive Species: Pathogens of Globalization." *Foreign Policy* 119: 51–64.

Brock, L. 1991. "Peace through Parks: The Environment on the Peace Research Agenda." *Journal of Peace Research* 28 (4): 407–23. http://dx.doi.org/10.1177/0022343391028004006.

Brockington, D., J. Igoe, and K. Schmidt-Soltau. 2006. "Conservation, Human Rights, and Poverty Reduction." *Conservation Biology* 20 (1): 250–52.

Broder, J.M. 2010. "China and India Join Climate Accord." *The New York Times*, March 9, 2010. Retrieved December 6, 2011. http://www.nytimes.com/2010/03/10/world/10climate.html.

Brooks, D.B. 1997. "Between the Great Rivers: Water in the Heart of the Middle East." *Water Resources Development* 13 (3): 291–310. http://dx.doi.org/10.1080/07900629749700.

Brown, O., A. Hammill, and R. McLeman. 2007. "Climate Change as the 'New' Security Threat: Implications for Africa." *International Affairs* 83 (6): 1141–54.

Brown, P. 2007. *Global Warning: The Last Chance for Change*. Pleasantville, NY: Reader's Digest.

Brown, P., and G. Garver. 2009. *Right Relationship: Building a Whole Earth Economy*. San Francisco: Berrett-Koehler.

Brundtland, G.H., et al. 1987. *Our Common Future: Report of the World Commission on Environment and Development*. Oxford: Oxford University Press.

Bruyninckx, H. 2004. "The Convention to Combat Desertification and the Role of Innovative Policy-Making Discourses: The Case of Burkina Faso." *Global Environmental Politics* 4 (3): 107–27. http://dx.doi.org/10.1162/1526380041748010.

Bruyninckx, H. 2005. "Sustainable Development: The Institutionalization of a Contested Policy Concept." In *International Environmental Politics*, ed. M.M. Betsill, K. Hochstetler, and D. Stevis, 265–98. Basingstoke: Palgrave Macmillan.

Bull, H. 1977. *The Anarchical Society: A Study of Order in World Politics*. London: Macmillan Press.

Bull, K., M. Johansson, and M. Krzyzanowski. 2008. "Impacts of the Convention on Long-Range Transboundary Air Pollution on Air Quality in Europe." *Journal of Toxicology and Environmental Health, Part A: Current Issues* 71 (1): 51–55. http://dx.doi.org/10.1080/15287390701557883. Medline:18080894.

Burgiel, S. 2002. "The Cartegena Protocol on Biosafety: Taking the Steps from Negotiation to Implementation." *Reciel* 11 (1): 53–61.

Burns, W., ed. 2006. "Special Issue on the Precautionary Principle and its Operationalisation in International Environmental Regimes and Domestic Policymaking." *International Journal of Global Environmental Issues* 5: 1–2.

Burns, W., and G. Wandesforde-Smith. 2002. "The International Whaling Commission and the Future of Cetaceans in a Changing World." *Review of European Community & International Environmental Law* 11 (2): 199–210. http://dx.doi.org/10.1111/1467-9388.t01-1-00317.

Campbell, Kurt, ed. 2008. *Climate Cataclysm: The Foreign Policy and National Security Implications of Climate Change.* Washington: Brookings Institution Press.

Cardwell, M. 2010. "Public Participation in the Regulation of Genetically Modified Organisms: A Matter of Substance or Form?" *Environmental Law Review* 12 (1): 12–25.

Carr, E.H. 1939. *The Twenty Year's Crisis, 1919–1939: An Introduction to the Study of International Relations.* London: Harper Perennial.

Carr, J., and M. Gianni. 1993. "High Seas Fisheries, Large-Scale Drift Nets, and the Law of the Sea." In *Freedom for the Seas in the 21st Century: Ocean Governance and Environmental Harmony*, ed. J. Van Dyke, D. Zaelke, and G. Hewison, 272–91. Washington: Island Press.

Carroll, S., and H. Dingle. 1996. "The Biology of Post-Invasion Events." *Biological Conservation* 78 (1-2): 207–14. http://dx.doi.org/10.1016/0006-3207(96)00029-8.

Chamorro, S.P., and E. Hammond. 2001. *Addressing Environmental Modification in Post-Cold War Conflict: The Convention on the Prohibition of Military or Any Other Hostile Use of Environmental Modification Techniques (ENMOD) and Related Agreements.* Edmonds, WA: Edmonds Institute.

Chase, B.J. 1993. "Tropical Forests and Trade Policy: The Legality of Unilateral Attempts to Promote Sustainable Development under the GATT." *Third World Quarterly* 14 (4): 749–74. http://dx.doi.org/10.1080/01436599308420355.

Chasek, P. 1997. "The Convention to Combat Desertification: Lessons Learned for Sustainable Development." *Journal of Environment & Development* 6 (2): 147–69. http://dx.doi.org/10.1177/107049659700600204.

Chayes, A., and A. Chayes. 1995. *The New Sovereignty: Compliance with International Regulatory Agreements.* Cambridge, MA.: Harvard University Press.

Chivian, E., and A. Bernstein, eds. 2008. *Sustaining Life: How Human Health Depends on Biodiversity.* Oxford: Oxford University Press.

Choksi, S. 2001. "The Basel Convention on the Control of Transboundary Movements of Hazardous Wastes and Their Disposal: 1999 Protocol on Liability and Compensation." *Ecology Law Quarterly* 28: 509–39.

Chow, J., J.G. Watson, J.J. Shah, C.S. Kiang, C. Loh, M. Lev-On, J.M. Lents, M.J. Molina, and L.T. Molina. 2004. "Megacities and Atmospheric Pollution." *Journal of the Air & Waste Management Association* 54 (10): 1226–35. Medline:15540575.

Clapp, J. 1994. "The Toxic Waste Trade with Less-Industrialised Countries: Economic Linkages and Political Alliances." *Third World Quarterly* 15 (3): 505–18. http://dx.doi.org/10.1080/01436599408420393.

Clapp, J., and P. Dauvergne. 2008. *Paths to a Green World: The Political Economy of the Global Environment.* 2nd ed. Cambridge, MA: MIT Press.

Clout, N., and M. de Poorter. 2005. "International Initiatives against 'Invasive' Alien Species." *Weed Technology* 19 (3): 523–27. http://dx.doi.org/10.1614/WT-04-126.1.

Cohen, M. 1997. "Risk Society and Ecological Modernisation: Alternative Visions for Post-Industrial Nations." *Futures* 29 (2): 225–47. http://dx.doi.org/10.1016/S0016-3287(96)00071-7.

Colautti, R., and H. MacIsaac. 2004. "A Neutral Terminology to Define 'Invasive' Species." *Diversity & Distributions* 10 (2): 135–41. http://dx.doi.org/10.1111/j.1366-9516.2004.00061.x.

Coleman, W., and M. Gabler. 2002. "Agricultural Biotechnology and Regime Formation: A Constructivist Assessment of the Prospects." *International Studies Quarterly* 46 (4): 481–506. http://dx.doi.org/10.1111/1468-2478.00242.

Commission for Environmental Cooperation. 2008. *Operational Plan of the CEC, 2007–2009.* Retrieved July 24, 2010. http://www.cec.org/Page.asp?PageID=1180&SiteNodeID=333.

Commission on Human Security. 2003. *Human Security Now.* New York: Commission on Human Security.

Conca, K. 2005. *Governing Water: Contentious Transnational Politics and Global Institution Building.* Cambridge, MA: MIT Press.

Conca, K., and J. Wallace. 2009. "Environment and Peacebuilding in War-Torn Societies: Lessons from the UN Environment Programme's Experience with Postconflict Assessment." *Global Governance* 15 (4): 485–505.

Conliffe, A. 2011. "Combating Ineffectiveness: Climate Change Bandwagoning and the UN Convention to Combat Desertification." Paper presented at the annual meeting of the International Studies Association Annual Conference "Global Governance: Political Authority in Transition," Montreal, Quebec, March 16.

Convention on Biological Diversity (CBD). 2002. *Bonn Guidelines of Access to Genetic Resource and Fair and Equitable Sharing of the Benefits Arising out of Their Utilization.* Montreal: Secretariat of the Convention on Biological Diversity.

CBD. 2004. *The Convention on Biological Diversity: From Conception to Implementation; historical perspectives on the occasion of the 10th Anniversary of the entry into force of the CBD.* Montreal: Secretariat of the Convention on Biological Diversity.

CBD. 2005. *Handbook of the Convention on Biological Diversity Including its Cartagena Protocol on Biosafety.* 3rd ed. Montreal: Secretariat of the Convention on Biological Diversity.

CBD. 2006a. *Gincana: Supplement.* Montreal: Secretariat of the Convention on Biological Diversity.

CBD. 2006b. *International Day for Biological Diversity—22 May 2006: Achieving the 2010 Biodiversity Target.* Montreal: Secretariat of the Convention on Biological Diversity. Retrieved November 30, 2011. https://www.cbd.int/doc/bioday/2006/ibd-2006-report-en.pdf.

CBD. 2010a. *Global Biodiversity Outlook 3.* Montreal: Secretariat of the Convention on Biological Diversity.

CBD. 2010b. "2010 International Day for Biodiversity Celebrations around the World." Accessed June 24, 2011. http://www.cbd.int/idb/2010/celebrations/.

CBD. 2011a. Cartagena Protocol on Biosafety. Retrieved April 17, 2011. http://bch.cbd.int/protocol/.

CBD. 2011b. "National Biodiversity and Strategy and Action Plans (NBSAPs)." Retrieved December 1, 2011. http://www.cbd.int/nbsap/.

Convention on Biological Diversity Conference of the Parties (CBDCOP). 2002. *COP 6 Decision VI/23 Alien Species that Threaten Ecosystems, Habitats or Species.* Retrieved December 12, 2011. http://www.cbd.int/decision/cop/?id=7197.

Convention on International Trade in Endangered Species (CITES). 2011a. "CITES National Export Quotas for 2011 (excluding quotas for Acipenseriformes)." Retrieved May 16, 2011. http://www.cites.org/common/quotas/2011/ExportQuotas2011.pdf.

CITES. 2011b. What is CITES? Retrieved May 9, 2011. http://www.cites.org/eng/disc/what.php.

Convention on the Conservation of Antarctic Marine Living Resources (CCAMLR). 1982. Text of the Convention on the Conservation of Antarctic Marine Living Resources. Retrieved December 7, 2011. http://www.ccamlr.org/pu/e/e_pubs/bd/pt1.pdf.

Cook, J.R. 2009. "President Obama Calls for Nuclear-Weapons-Free World, New Strategic Arms Reduction Treaty, Senate Approval of CTBT, and Strengthened Anti-Proliferation Efforts." *American Journal of International Law* 103 (3): 600–2.

Cooper, A., J. Kirton, and T. Schrecker. 2007. *Governing Global Health: Challenge, Response, Innovation.* Aldershot: Ashgate.

Cooper, D. 2002. "The International Treaty on Plant Genetic Resources for Food and Agriculture." *Reciel* 11 (1): 1–16.

Corell, E. 1999. "Non-state Actor Influence in the Negotiation of the Convention to Combat Desertification." *International Negotiation* 4 (2): 197–223. http://dx.doi.org/10.1163/15718069920848453.

Costello, C., J.M. Drake, and D.M. Lodge. 2007. "Evaluating an Invasive Species Policy: Ballast Water Exchange in the Great Lakes." *Ecological Applications* 17 (3): 655–62. http://dx.doi.org/10.1890/06-0190. Medline:17494386.

Courtenay, W., and P. Moyle. 1992. "Crimes against Biodiversity: The Lasting Legacy of Fish Introductions." *Transactions of the North American Wildlife and Natural Resources Conference* 56: 365–72.

Cox, R. 2008. "The Point is not Just to Explain the World but to Change It." In *The Oxford Handbook of International Relations*, ed. C. Reus-Smit and D. Snidal, 84–94. Oxford: Oxford University Press. http://dx.doi.org/10.1093/oxfordhb/9780199219322.003.0004.

Crook, J. 2010. "Vice President Addresses U.S. Nuclear Weapons Policy, Calls for CTBT Ratification." *American Journal of International Law* 104 (2): 297–99.

CTV News. 2007. "Conservatives Abandon Kyoto for Own Climate Plan." *CTV News*, April 26. Retrieved December 6, 2011. http://www.ctv.ca/CTVNews/TopStories/20070425/tories_climate_070426/.

Currie, D.E.J., and K. Wowk. 2009. "Climate Change and CO$_2$ in the Oceans and Global Oceans Governance." *Carbon & Climate Review* 387–404.

Da Rosa, J.E. 1983. "Economics, Politics, and Hydroelectric Power: The Paraná River Basin." *Latin American Research Review* 18 (3): 77–107.

Daalder, I. 1987. "The Limited Test Ban Treaty." In *Superpower Arms Control: Setting the Record Straight*, ed. A. Carneslae and R. Haass, 9–40. Cambridge, MA.: Ballinger.

Dalby, S. 2006. "Environmental Security: Ecology or International Relations?" In *International Ecopolitical Theory: Critical Approaches*, ed. E. Lafferiére and P. Stoett, 17–33. Vancouver: UBC Press.

Dauvergne, P., and J. Lister. 2011. "Governing Timber Consumption." In *Timber*, 137–63. Madison: Polity.

Davidson-Harden, A., A. Naidoo, and A. Harden. 2007. "The Geopolitics of the Water Justice Movement." *Peace, Conflict, and Development* 11: 1–34.

dé Ishtar, Z. 2009. "Nuclearised Bodies and Militarised Space: The US in the Marshall Islands." In *Eco-sufficiency and Global Justice: Women Write Political Ecology*, ed. A. Salleh, 121–39. New York: Pluto Press.

De Las Carreras, A. 1987. "International River Boundaries in the Argentine Republic." *International Relations* 9 (1): 56–63. http://dx.doi.org/10.1177/004711788700900105.

DeLeo, R. 2010. "Anticipatory–Conjectural Policy Problems: A Case Study of Avian Influenza." *Risk, Hazards & Crisis in Public Policy* 1 (1): 147–84. http://dx.doi.org/10.2202/1944-4079.1002.

Delmas, M.A., and O.R. Young, eds. 2009. *Governance for the Environment: New Perspectives.* Cambridge: Cambridge University Press.

Der Derian, J., ed. 1995. *International Theory: Critical Investigations.* New York: New York University Press.

DeSombre, E.R. 2005. "The Evolution of International Environmental Cooperation." *Journal of International Law and International Relations* 1 (1): 75–87.

DeSombre, E.R. 2006. *Global Environmental Institutions.* London: Routledge.

DeSombre, E.R. 2011. "Studying and Protecting the Global Environment: Protecting the Trees but Sometimes Missing the Forest." *International Studies Review* 13 (1): 133–43. http://dx.doi.org/10.1111/j.1468-2486.2010.01004.x.

Dessai, S., N. Lacasta, and K. Vincent. 2003. "International Political History of the Kyoto Protocol: From The Hague to Marrakech and Beyond." *International Review for Environmental Strategies* 4 (2): 183–205.

Dewailly, E., A. Nantel, J.P. Weber, and F. Meyer. 1989. "High Levels of PCBs in Breast Milk of Inuit Women from Arctic Quebec." *Bulletin of Environmental Contamination and Toxicology* 43 (5): 641–46. http://dx.doi.org/10.1007/BF01701981. Medline:2508801.

Di Castri, F. 1989. "History of Biological Invasions with Special Emphasis on the Old World." In *Biological Invasions: A Global Perspective*, ed. J. Drake and H.A. Mooney, 1–30. Scientific Committee on Problems of the Environment (SCOPE) Report, 37. New York: John Wiley.

Dickson, B. 2008. "CITES and the Livelihoods of the Poor." *Oryx* 42 (4): 548–53. http://dx.doi.org/10.1017/S0030605307999786,

Diehl, P., and B. Frederking, eds. 2010. *The Politics of Global Governance: International Organizations in an Interdependent World*. 4th ed. Boulder: Lynne Rienner.

Dinar, S., ed. 2011. *Beyond Resource Wars: Scarcity, Environmental Degradation, and International Cooperation*. Cambridge, MA: MIT Press.

Djelic, M.-L., and K. Sahlin-Andersson, eds. 2006. *Transnational Governance: Institutional Dynamics of Regulation*. Cambridge: Cambridge University Press. http://dx.doi.org/10.1017/CBO9780511488665.

Dobson, A. 2003. *Citizenship and the Environment*. Oxford: Oxford University Press.

Dodgson, R., and K. Lee. 2002. "Global Health Governance: A Conceptual Review." In *Global Governance: Critical Perspectives*, ed. R. Wilkinson and S. Hughes, 92–110. London: Routledge. http://dx.doi.org/10.4324/9780203302804_chapter_6.

Dougherty, J., and R. Pfaltzgraff. 2000. *Contending Theories of International Relations: A Comprehensive Survey*. 5th ed. New York: Harper & Row.

Doukakis, P., E.C.M. Parsons, W.C.G. Burns, A.K. Salomon, E. Hines, and J.A. Cigliano. 2009. "Gaining Traction: Retreading the Wheels of Marine Conservation." *Conservation Biology* 23 (4): 841–46. http://dx.doi.org/10.1111/j.1523-1739.2009.01281.x. Medline:19627316.

Doyle, M. 1997. *Ways of War and Peace: Realism, Liberalism, and Socialism*. New York: W.W. Norton.

Draper, S.E., and J.E. Kundell. 2007. "Impact of Climate Change on Transboundary Water Sharing." *Journal of Water Resources Planning and Management* 133 (5): 405–15.

Dreher, K., and S. Pulver. 2008. "Environment as 'High Politics'? Explaining Divergence in US and EU Hazardous Waste Export Policies." *Reciel* 17 (3): 308–20.

Dryzek, J. 1997. *The Politics of the Earth: Environmental Discourse*. Oxford: Oxford University Press.

Dryzek, J., and D. Schlosberg, eds. 2005. *Debating the Earth: The Environmental Politics Reader*. Oxford: Oxford University Press.

Duarte, S. 2009. "The Future of the Comprehensive Nuclear-Test-Ban Treaty." *UN Chronicle* 46 (1/2): 30–35.

Duffy, R. 2001. "Peace Parks: The Paradox of Globalisation." *Geopolitics* 6 (2): 1–26. http://dx.doi.org/10.1080/14650040108407715.

Duffy, R. 2002. *A Trip Too Far: Ecotourism, Politics and Exploitation*. London: Earthscan.

Early, G. 2008. "Australia's National Environmental Legislation and Human/Wildlife Interactions." *Journal of International Wildlife Law and Policy* 11 (2-3): 101–55. http://dx.doi.org/10.1080/13880290802470141.

Eckersley, R. 2004. *The Green State: Rethinking Democracy and Sovereignty*. Cambridge, MA: MIT Press.

Economic Commission for Europe (ECE). 2007. *Strategies and Policies for Air Pollution Abatement*. New York, Geneva: United Nations.

ECE. 2010. Convention on Long-Range Transboundary Air Pollution. Retrieved April 8, 2010. http://www.unece.org/env/lrtap/.

Edwards, K. 1998. "A Critique of the General Approach to Invasive Plant Species." In *Plant Invasions: Ecological Mechanisms and Human Responses*, ed. U. Starfinger, K. Edwards, I. Kowarik, and M. Williamsom, 85–94. Leiden: Backhuys.

Ehresman, T., and D. Stevis. 2011. "International Environmental and Ecological Justice." In *Global Environmental Politics: Concepts, Theories, and Case Studies*, ed. Gabriela Kutting, 87–104. London: Routledge.

Elton, C. 1958. *The Ecology of Invasions by Animals and Plants.* London: Methuen.

Environment Canada. 2010a. Air Pollution. Retrieved April 8, 2010. http://www.ec.gc.ca.

Environment Canada. 2010b. Backgrounder: Persistent Organic Pollutants. Retrieved December 4, 2011. http://www.ec.gc.ca/lcpe-cepa/default.asp?lang=En&n=135D347F-1.

Environment Canada. 2010c. International Environmental Agreements. Retrieved January 10, 2012. http://www.ec.gc.ca/international/default.asp?lang=En&n=0E5CED79-1.

Environment Canada. 2011. Pollutants. Retrieved December 4, 2011. http://www.ec.gc.ca.

Environment News Service. 2006. "World Health Experts Warn Air Pollution Kills Two Million a Year." *ENS*, October 6, 2006. Retrieved December 12, 2011. http://www.ens-newswire.com/ens/oct2006/2006-10-06-01.html.

Epstein, C. 2006. "The Making of Global Environmental Norms: Endangered Species Protection." *Global Environmental Politics* 6 (2): 32–54. http://dx.doi.org/10.1162/glep.2006.6.2.32.

European Commission. 2007. "Co-benefits of the Montreal Protocol." *Science for Environment Policy: DB Environment News Alert*, September 6. Retrieved January 12, 2012. http://ec.europa.eu/environment/integration/research/newsalert/pdf/76na3.pdf.

European Commission. 2010. Environment—Persistent Organic Pollutants. Retrieved April 8, 2010. http://ec.europa.eu/environment/pops/index_en.htm.

Falloux, F., S. Tressler, and K. Mayrand. 2006. "The Global Mechanism and UNCCD Financing: Constraints and Opportunities." In *Governing Global Desertification: Linking Environmental Degradation, Poverty and Participation*, ed. P.-M. Johnson, K. Mayrand, and M. Paquin, 131–45. Alderhsot: Ashgate.

Flejzor, L. 2005. "Reforming the International Tropical Timber Agreement." *Review of European Community & International Environmental Law* 14 (1): 19–27. http://dx.doi.org/10.1111/j.1467-9388.2005.00420.x.

Florano, E.R. 2003. "Assessment of the 'Strengths' of the New ASEAN Agreement on Transboundary Haze Pollution." *International Review for Environmental Strategies* 4 (1): 127–47.

Ford, J., T. Pearce, F. Duerden, C. Furgal, and B. Smit. 2010. "Climate Change Policy Responses for Canada's Inuit Population: The Importance of and Opportunities for Adaptation." *Global Environmental Change* 20 (1): 177–91. http://dx.doi.org/10.1016/j.gloenvcha.2009.10.008.

Foster, C.E. 2008. "Public Opinion and the Interpretation of the World Trade Organization's Agreement on Sanitary and Phytosanitary Measures." *Journal of International Economic Law* 11 (2): 427–58. http://dx.doi.org/10.1093/jiel/jgno11.

Foster, C.E. 2009. "Precaution, Scientific Development and Scientific Uncertainty under the WTO Agreement on Sanitary and Phytosanitary Measures." *Review of European Community & International Environmental Law* 18 (1): 50–58. http://dx.doi.org/10.1111/j.1467-9388.2009.00617.x.

Freeman, K. 2001. "Water Wars? Inequalities in the Tigris-Euphrates River Basin." *Geopolitics* 6 (2): 127–40. http://dx.doi.org/10.1080/14650040108407720.

Frijters, I.D. and J. Leentvaar. 2003. *Rhine Case Study.* Technical Documents in Hydrology, 17. New York: UNESCO.

Garrett, B., and B. Glaser. 1995–96. "Chinese Perspectives on Nuclear Arms Control." *International Security* 20 (3): 43–78. http://www.jstor.org/stable/2539139.

Geist, H. 2005. *The Causes and Progression of Desertification.* Burlington: Ashgate.

Gensler, D., R. Oad, and K.D. Kinzli. 2009. "Irrigation System Modernization: Case Study of the Middle Rio Grande Valley." *Journal of Irrigation and Drainage Engineering* 135 (2): 169–76. http://dx.doi.org/10.1061/(ASCE)0733-9437(2009)135:2(169).

Global Invasive Species Programme (GISP). 2001. *Global Strategy on Invasive Alien Species.* Cambridge: IUCN.

Goldblat, J. 1977. "The Environmental Warfare Convention: How Meaningful Is It?" *Ambio* 6 (4): 216–21.

Goldemberg, J. 2007. "Ethanol for a Sustainable Energy Future." *Science* 315 (5813): 808–10. http://dx.doi.org/10.1126/science.1137013. Medline:17289989.

Goodell, J. 2006. *Big Coal: The Dirty Secret behind America's Energy Future*. Boston: Houghton Mifflin Harcourt.

Gore, C. 2010. Are Cities Willing Agents? North American Cities and Climate Governance. Paper presented at the annual conference for the Canadian Political Science Association, Montreal, Quebec, June 1–3.

Gossling, S., and P. Upham. 2009. *Climate Change and Aviation: Issues, Challenges, and Solutions*. Washington, DC: Earthscan.

Government of Canada. 2002. *A Discussion Paper on Canada's Contribution to Addressing Climate Change*. Ottawa: Government of Canada.

Government of Canada. 2006. *Canada's National Implementation Plan under the Stockholm Convention on Persistent Organic Pollutants*. Ottawa: Environment Canada.

Grainger, Allan. 2005. "Environmental Globalization and Tropical Forests." *Globalizations* 2 (3): 335–48. http://dx.doi.org/10.1080/14747730500367942.

Grubb, M. 2003. "The Economics of the Kyoto Protocol." *World Economics* 4 (3): 143–89.

Grundmann, R. 2001. *Transnational Environmental Policy: Reconstructing Ozone*. London: Routledge. http://dx.doi.org/10.4324/9780203464731.

Gupta, A., and R. Falkner. 2006. "The Influence of the Cartagena Protocol on Biosafety: Comparing Mexico, China, and South Africa." *Global Environmental Politics* 6 (4): 23–55. http://dx.doi.org/10.1162/glep.2006.6.4.23.

Hardin, G. 1968. "The Tragedy of the Commons." *Science* 162 (3859): 1243–48. http://dx.doi.org/10.1126/science.162.3859.1243.

Hares, A., J. Dickinson, and K. Wilkes. 2010. "Climate Change and the Air Travel Decisions of UK Tourists." *Journal of Transport Geography* 18: 466–73.

Harris, P. 2011. "Climate Change." In *Global Environmental Politics: Concepts, Theories, and Case Studies*, ed. Gabriela Kutting, 107–18. London: Routledge.

Haufler, V. 2009. "Transnational Actors and Global Environmental Governance." In *Governance for the Environment: New Perspectives*, ed. M.A. Delmas and O.R. Young, 119–43. Cambridge: Cambridge University Press.

Heintzman, A., and E. Solomon, eds. 2009. *Food and Fuel: Solutions for the Future*. Toronto: Anansi.

Hellmann, J.J., J.E. Byers, B.G. Bierwagen, and J.S. Dukes. 2008. "Five Potential Consequences of Climate Change for Invasive Species." *Conservation Biology* 22 (3): 534–43. http://dx.doi.org/10.1111/j.1523-1739.2008.00951.x. Medline:18577082.

Hensengerth, O. 2009. "Transboundary River Cooperation and the Regional Public Good: The Case of the Mekong River." *Contemporary Southeast Asia* 31 (2): 326–49. http://dx.doi.org/10.1355/cs31-2f.

Herber, B. 1991. "The Common Heritage Principle: Antarctica and the Developing Nations." *American Journal of Economics and Sociology* 50 (4): 391–406. http://dx.doi.org/10.1111/j.1536-7150.1991.tb03335.x.

Herborg, L.M., C.L. Jerde, D.M. Lodge, G.M. Ruiz, and H.J. MacIsaac. 2007. "Predicting Invasion Risk Using Measures of Introduction Effort and Environmental Niche Models." *Ecological Applications* 17 (3): 663–74. http://dx.doi.org/10.1890/06-0239. Medline:17494387.

Herkenrath, P. 2002. "The Implementation of the Convention on Biological Diversity—A Non-Government Perspective Ten Years On." *Reciel* 11 (1): 29–37.

Herkenrath, P., and J. Harrison. 2011. "The 10th Meeting of the Conference of the Parties to the Convention on Biological Diversity—A Breakthrough for Biodiversity?" *Oryx* 45 (1): 1–2. http://dx.doi.org/10.1017/S0030605310001663.

Hettinger, N. 2001. "Exotic Species, Naturalization, and Biological Nativism." *Environmental Values* 10 (2): 193–224. http://dx.doi.org/10.3197/096327101129340804.

Higgins, P. 2010. *Eradicating Ecocide: Laws and Governance to Prevent the Destruction of Our Planet*. London: Shepheard-Walwyn.

Hilz, C. 1992. *The International Toxic Waste Trade*. New York: Van Nostrand Reinhold.

Holland, T., G.D. Peterson, and A. Gonzalez. 2009. "A Cross-National Analysis of How Economic Inequality Predicts Biodiversity Loss." *Conservation Biology* 23 (5): 1304–13. http://dx.doi.org/10.1111/j.1523-1739.2009.01207.x. Medline:19765041.

Homer-Dixon, T. 1999. *Environment, Scarcity, and Violence*. Princeton: Princeton University Press.

Homer-Dixon, T. 2006. *The Upside of Down: Catastrophe, Creativity, and the Renewal of Civilization*. Toronto: Alfred Knopf Canada.

Homer-Dixon, T., and J. Blitt. 1998. *Eco-violence: Links among Environment, Population, and Security*. Lanham, MD: Rowman and Littlefield.

Hornsby, D.J., A.J.S. Summerlee, and K.B. Woodside. 2007. "NAFTA's Shadow Hangs over Kyoto Implementation." *Canadian Public Policy/Analyse de Politques* 33 (3): 285–98.

Hossay, P. 2006. *Unsustainable: A Primer for Global Environmental and Social Justice*. London: Zed Books.

Hough, P. 2011. "Persistent Organic Pollutants and Pesticides." In *Global Environmental Politics: Concepts, Theories and Case Studies*, ed. G. Kutting, 179–91. London: Routledge.

Howes, M. 2005. *Politics and the Environment: Risk and the Role of Government and Industry*. London: Earthscan.

Hughes, I. 2000. "Biological Consequences of Global Warming: Is the Signal Already Apparent?" *Trends in Ecology & Evolution* 15 (2): 56–61. http://dx.doi.org/10.1016/S0169-5347(99)01764-4. Medline:10652556.

Huisman, P., J. de Jong, and K. Wieriks. 2000. "Transboundary Cooperation in Shared River Basins: Experiences from the Rhine, Meuse, and North Sea." *Water Policy* 2 (1-2): 83–97. http://dx.doi.org/10.1016/S1366-7017(99)00023-9.

Humphreys, D. 2004. "Redefining the Issues: NGO Influence on International Forest Negotiations." *Global Environmental Politics* 4 (2): 51–74. http://dx.doi.org/10.1162/152638004323074192.

Humphreys, D. 2011. "International Forest Politics." In *Global Environmental Politics: Concepts, Theories, and Case Studies*, ed. G. Kutting, 135–50. London: Routledge.

Hurd, I. 2008. "Myths of Membership: The Politics of Legitimation in UN Security Council Reform." *Global Governance* 14 (2): 199–217.

Hutchinson, C.F., and S.M. Herrmann. 2008. *The Future of Arid Lands—Revisited: A Review of 50 Years of Drylands Research*. Paris and Dordrecht: Springer and United Nations Educational, Scientific and Cultural Organization (UNESCO).

Intergovernmental Panel on Climate Change (IPCC). 2008. *Climate Change 2007: Synthesis Report*. Geneva: IPCC. Retrieved December 5, 2011. http://www.ipcc.ch/publications_and_data/publications_ipcc_fourth_assessment_report_synthesis_report.htm.

International Law Association (ILA). 2004. *Report of the Seventy-First Conference of the International Law Association*. London: ILA.

International Maritime Organization (IMO). 2004. International Convention for the Control and Management of Ships' Ballast Water and Sediments. Retrieved December 14, 2011. http://www.imo.org/about/conventions/listofconventions/pages/international-convention-for-the-control-and-management-of-ships%27-ballast-water-and-sediments-%28bwm%29.aspx.

International Tropical Timber Organization (ITTO). 1994. *International Tropical Timber Agreement—1994*. United Nations Conference on Trade and Development TD/TIMBER.2/16. Geneva: International Tropical Timber Organization. Retrieved January 7, 2012. http://www.itto.int/itta/.

ITTO. 2006. *International Tropical Timber Agreement, February 1, 2006*. United Nations Conference on Trade and Development TD/TIMBER.3/12. Yokohama: International Tropical Timber Organization. Retrieved December 4, 2011. http://www.itto.int/itta/.

ITTO. 2008. *ITTO Action Plan 2008-2011*. Yokohama: International Tropical Timber Agreement Secretariat.

ITTO. 2009. *Sustaining Tropical Forests: Annual Report 2009*. Yokohama: International Tropical Timber Organization. Retrieved December 4, 2011. http://www.itto.int/annual_report/.

Iverson, L., M.W. Schwartz, and A.M. Prasad. 2004. "How Fast and Far Might Tree Species Migrate in the Eastern United States Due to Climate Change?" *Global Ecology and Biogeography* 13 (3): 209–19. http://dx.doi.org/10.1111/j.1466-822X.2004.00093.x.

Jackson, R., and G. Sorensen. 2007. *Introduction to IR: Theories and Approaches.* Oxford: Oxford University Press.

Jeffers, J. 2010. "Climate Change and the Arctic: Adapting to Changes in Fisheries Stocks and Governance Regimes." *Ecology Law Quarterly* 37 (3): 917–76.

Joas, M., K. Kern, and S. Sandberg. 2007. "Actors and Arenas in Hybrid Networks: Implications for Environmental Policymaking in the Baltic Sea Region." *Ambio* 36 (2): 237–42. http://dx.doi.org/10.1579/0044-7447(2007)36[237:AAAIHN]2.0.CO;2. Medline:17520939.

Johnson, B. 1985. "Chimera or Opportunity? An Environmental Appraisal of the International Tropical Timber Agreement." *Ambio* 14: 42–44.

Jordan, A., D. Huitema, H. van Asselt, T. Rayner, and F. Berkhout, eds. 2010. *Climate Change Policy in the European Union.* Cambridge: Cambridge University Press.

Joyner, C.C., and J.T. Kirkhope. 1992. "The Persian Gulf War Oil Spill: Reassessing the Law of Environmental Protection and the Law of Armed Conflict." *Case Western Reserve Journal of International Law* 24 (1): 29–62.

Juda, L. 1978. "Negotiating a Treaty on Environmental Modification Warfare: The Convention on Environmental Warfare and its Impact on the Arms Control Negotiations." *International Organization* 32 (4): 975–91. http://dx.doi.org/10.1017/S0020818300032057.

Jurdi, M. 2002. "Transboundary Movement of Hazardous Wastes into Lebanon: Part 1. The Silent Trade." *Journal of Environmental Health* 64 (6): 9–14. Medline:11826629.

Kagwanja, P. 2007. "Calming the Waters: The East African Community and Conflict over the Nile Resources." *Journal of Eastern African Studies* 1 (3): 321–37. http://dx.doi.org/10.1080/17531050701625565.

Kamuk, B., and J.A. Hansen. 2007. "Global Recycling—Waste Trafficking in Disguise?" *Waste Management & Research* 25 (6): 487–88. http://dx.doi.org/10.1177/0734242X07025006120. Medline:18229742.

Kaufman, L. 1993. "Why the Ark is Sinking." In *The Last Extinction.* 2nd ed., ed. K. Mallory, 1–46. Cambridge, MA: MIT Press.

Kaul, I., I. Grunberg, and M. Stern, eds. 1999. *Global Public Goods: International Cooperation in the 21st Century.* Oxford: Oxford University Press.

Keck, M., and K. Sikkink. 1998. *Activists beyond Borders: Advocacy Networks in International Politics.* Ithaca: Cornell University Press.

Keefe, T., and M. Zacher. 2008. *The Politics of Global Health Governance: United by Contagion.* New York: Palgrave. http://dx.doi.org/10.1057/9780230611955.

Kennedy, M. 2011. "Canada to Formally Exit from Kyoto Accord." *The Montreal Gazette,* December 13, 2011, A12. Retrieved December 14, 2011. http://www.montrealgazette.com/business/business/5849635/story.html.

Khagram, S., and S. Ali. 2006. "Environmental and Security" *Annual Review of Environment and Resources* 31: 395–411.

Kim, I. 2007. "Environmental Cooperation of Northeast Asia: Transboundary Air Pollution." *International Relations of the Asia-Pacific* 7 (3): 439–62. http://dx.doi.org/10.1093/irap/lcmoo8.

Kinchy, A.J., D.L. Kleinman, and R. Autry. 2008. "Against Free Markets, Against Science? Regulating the Socio-Economic Effects of Biotechnology." *Rural Sociology* 73 (2): 147–79.

Klein, N. 2010. "Paying Our Climate Debt." In *Climate Change: Who's Carrying the Burden? The Chilly Climates of the Global Environmental Dilemma,* ed. L. Anders Sandberg and T. Sandberg, 55–70. Ottawa: Canadian Centre for Policy Alternatives.

Kleinman, D.L., A.J. Kinchy, and R. Autry. 2009. "Local Variation or Global Convergence in Agricultural Biotechnology Policy? A Comparative Analysis." *Science and Public Policy* 36 (5): 361–71. http://dx.doi.org/10.3152/030234209X442043.

Klinsky, S., and H. Dowlatabadi. 2009. "Conceptualizations of Justice in Climate Policy." *Climate Policy* 9: 88–108.

Knight, R. 2007. "Alien Invasion." *The BP Magazine* 4: 47–57.

Knights, P. 2008. "Native Species, Human Communities, and Cultural Relationships." *Environmental Values* 17 (3): 353–73. http://dx.doi.org/10.3197/096327108X343121.

Koester, V. 2002. "The Five Global Biodiversity-Related Conventions: A Stocktaking." *Reciel* 11 (1): 96–103.

Kolar, C., and D. Lodge. 2000. "Freshwater Nonindigenous Species: Interactions with Other Global Changes." In *Invasive Species in a Changing World*, ed. H. Mooney and R. Hobbs, 3–30. Washington DC: Island Press.

Koswanage, N., and M. Taylor. 2011, May 25. "Analysis: Land Banks Buffer Indonesian Palm Oil from Forest Ban" *Reuters News*. Retrieved December 4, 2011. http://www.reuters.com/article/2011/05/25/us-indonesia-palmoil-forests-idUSTRE74O2LA20110525.

Krueger, J. 1998. "Prior Informed Consent and the Basel Convention: The Hazards of What Isn't Known." *Journal of Environment & Development* 7 (2): 115–37. http://dx.doi.org/10.1177/107049659800700203.

Krueger, J. 1999. "What's to Become of Trade in Hazardous Wastes? The Basel Convention One Decade Later." *Environment* 41 (9): 10–21. http://dx.doi.org/10.1080/00139159909605534.

Kummer, K. 1998. "The Basel Convention: Ten Years On." *Reciel* 7 (3): 227–36.

Kummer, K. 1999. "Prior Informed Consent for Chemicals in International Trade: The 1998 Rotterdam Convention." *Reciel* 8(3): 323–30.

Laferrière, E., and P. Stoett. 1999. *International Relations Theory and Ecological Thought: Towards Synthesis*. London: Routledge. http://dx.doi.org/10.4324/9780203169407.

Laszlo, E. 1991. "Cooperative Governance." *World Futures* 31 (2): 215–21. http://dx.doi.org/10.1080/02604027.1991.9972240.

Leggett, J. 2005. *The Empty Tank: Oil, Gas, Hot Air, and the Coming Global Financial Catastrophe*. New York: Random House.

Leous, J.P., and N.B. Parry. 2005. "Who is Responsible for Marine Debris? The International Politics of Cleaning Our Oceans." *Journal of International Affairs* 59 (1): 257–69.

LePrestre, P., ed. 2002. *Governing Global Biodiversity: The Evolution and Implementation of the Convention on Biological Diversity*. London: Ashgate.

LePrestre, P., and P. Stoett, eds. 2006. *Bilateral Ecopolitics: Canadian-American Environmental Relations*. London: Ashgate.

Lesage, D., T. Van de Graaf, and K. Westphal. 2010. *Global Energy Governance in a Multipolar World*. London: Ashgate.

Levy, M. 1984. "Oil Pollution in the World's Oceans." *Ambio* 13 (4): 226–35.

Lidskog, R., and G. Sundqvist. 2004. "From Consensus to Credibility: New Challenges for Policy-Relevant Science." *Innovation (Abingdon)* 17 (3): 205–26. http://dx.doi.org/10.1080/1351161042000241144.

Lindseth, G. 2004. "The Cities for Climate Protection Campaign and the Framing of Local Climate Policy." *Local Environment* 9 (4): 325–36. http://dx.doi.org/10.1080/1354983042000246252.

Lipman, Z. 2002. "A Dirty Dilemma: The Hazardous Waste Trade." *Harvard International Review* 23 (4): 67–71.

Lipman, Z. 2010. "Trade in Hazardous Waste: Environmental Justice versus Economic Growth: Environmental Justice and Legal Process." Basal Action Network (BAN) website. Retrieved May 5, 2010. http://www.ban.org/library/lipman.html.

Litfin, K. 1994. *Ozone Discourses: Science and Politics in Global Environmental Cooperation*. New York: Columbia University Press.

Litfin, K. 2003. "Towards an Integral Perspective on World Politics: Secularism, Sovereignty, and the Challenge of Global Ecology." *Millennium: Journal of International Studies* 32 (1): 29–56. http://dx.doi.org/10.1177/03058298030320010201.

Litfin, K. 2010. "The Sacred and the Profane in the Ecological Politics of Sacrifice." In *The Environmental Politics of Sacrifice*, ed. M. Maniates and J. Meyer, 117–44. Cambridge, MA.: MIT Press.

Lodge, M.W. 2006. "The International Seabed Authority and Article 82 of the UN Convention on the Law of the Sea." *International Journal of Marine and Coastal Law* 21 (3): 323–33. http://dx.doi.org/10.1163/157180806778884723.

Lounibos, L.P. 2002. "Invasions by Insect Vectors of Human Disease." *Annual Review of Entomology* 47 (1): 233–66. http://dx.doi.org/10.1146/annurev.ento.47.091201.145206. Medline:11729075.

Lovelock, J. 2006. *The Revenge of Gaia: Why the Earth is Fighting Back—And How We Will Save Humanity*. New York: Basic.

Mace, M.J. 2006. "Adaptation under the UUFCC: The International Legal Framework." In *Fairness in Adaption to Climate Change*, ed. N. Adger, J. Paavola, S. Huq, and M.J. Mace, 53–76. Cambridge, MA: MIT Press.

Majumdar, S. 1990. "Institutions for International Co-operation: An Analysis of the United Nations Law of the Sea Conference and Convention." *Economic and Political Weekly* 25 (48/49): 2681–85.

Manu A.T. Thurow, A.S.R. Juo, and I. Zanguina. 2000. "Agroecological Impacts of 5 Years of Practical Program for Restoration of a Degraded Sahelian Watershed." In *Integrated Watershed Management in the Global Ecosystem*, ed. R. Lai, 145–63. Boca Raton: CRC Press.

Martello, M.L. 2004. "Expert Advice and Desertification Policy: Past Experience and Current Challenges." *Global Environmental Politics* 4 (3): 85–106. http://dx.doi.org/10.1162/1526380041748074.

Martin, S.F. 2010. "Climate Change, Migration, and Governance." *Global Governance* 16: 397–414.

Martin, S.F., P.W. Fagen, K. Jorgensen, L. Mann-Bondat, and N. Schoenholtz. 2005. *The Uprooted: Improving Humanitarian Responses to Forced Migration*. Lanham, MD: Lexington Books.

Mathur, A. 2009. "CITES and Livelihood: Converting Words Into Action." *Journal of Environment & Development* 18 (3): 291–305. http://dx.doi.org/10.1177/1070496509337788.

Mayeda, G. 2004. "Developing Disharmony? The SPS and TBT Agreements and the Impact of Harmonization on Developing Countries." *Journal of International Economic Law* 7 (4): 737–64. http://dx.doi.org/10.1093/jiel/7.4.737.

McCarthy, C. 2006. *The Road*. New York: Vintage International.

McGeoch, M., S. Butchart, D. Spear, E. Marais, E. Kleynhans, A. Symes, J. Chanson, and M. Hoffmann. 2010. "Global Indicators of Biological Invasion: Species Numbers, Biodiversity Impact and Policy Responses." *Diversity & Distributions* 16 (1): 95–108. http://dx.doi.org/10.1111/j.1472-4642.2009.00633.x.

McGraw, D. 2002. "The CBD—Key Characteristics and Implications for Implementation." *Reciel* 11 (1): 17–28. http://dx.doi.org/10.1111/1467-9388.00299.

Mckinley, G., M. Zuk, M. Höjer, M. Avalos, I. González, R. Iniestra, I. Laguna, M.A. Martínez, P. Osnaya, L.M. Reynales, et al. 2005. "Quantification of Local and Global Benefits from Air Pollution Control in Mexico City." *Environmental Science & Technology* 39 (7): 1954–61. http://dx.doi.org/10.1021/es035183e. Medline:15871223.

McNeely, J., ed. 2001. *The Great Reshuffling: Human Dimensions of Invasive Alien Species*. Gland: IUCN.

Metawie, A.F. 2004. "History of Co-operation in the Nile River." *Water Resources Development* 20 (1): 47–63. http://dx.doi.org/10.1080/07900620310001635601.

Mikesell, R. 1992. *Economic Development and the Environment: A Comparison of Sustainable Development with Conventional Development Economics*. London: Mansell.

Milgrom, P., D. North, and B. Weingast. 1990. "The Role of Institutions in the Revival of Trade: The Law Merchant, Private Judges, and the Champagne Fairs." *Economics and Politics* 1: 1–23. http://dx.doi.org/10.1111/j.1468-0343.1990.tb00020.x.

Millennium Ecosystem Assessment (MEA). 2005a. *Ecosystem and Human Well-being: Biodiversity Synthesis*. Washington, DC: World Resources Institute.

MEA. 2005b. *Ecosystems and Human Well-being: Desertification Synthesis.* Washington, DC: World Resources Institute.

MEA. 2005c. *Ecosystem and Human Well-being: Synthesis.* Washington, DC: World Resources Institute.

Miller, J., S. Engelberg, and W. Broad. 2001. *Germs: Biological Weapons and America's Secret War.* New York: Simon and Schuster.

Miller, M., and R. Fabian. 2004. *Harmful Invasive Species: Legal Responses.* Washington, DC: Environmental Law Institute.

Messenger, S. 2010. "Australia's Invading Camels Soon to be Croc Food." *Treehugger,* February 11. Retrieved December 13, 2011. http://www.treehugger.com/natural-sciences/australias-invading-camels-soon-to-be-croc-food.html.

Molina, M.J., and L.T. Molina. 2004. "Megacities and Atmospheric Pollution." *Journal of the Air & Waste Management Association* 54 (6): 644–80. Medline:15242147.

Molina, M.J., and F.S. Rowland. 1974. "Stratospheric Sink for Chlorofluoromethanes: Chlorine Atom Catalyzed Destruction of Ozone." *Nature* 249 (5460): 810–12. http://dx.doi.org/10.1038/249810a0.

Monbiot, G. 2008. *Bring on the Apocalypse: Essays on Self-Destruction.* Toronto: Anchor.

Montgomery, M.A. 1995. "Reassessing the Waste Trade Crisis: What Do We Really Know?" *Journal of Environment & Development* 4 (1): 1–28. http://dx.doi.org/10.1177/107049659500400102.

Morgenthau, Henry. 1948. *Politics amongst Nations.* New York: Knopf.

Mortimore, M. 1998. *Roots in the African Dust: Sustaining the Sub-Saharan Drylands.* Cambridge: Cambridge University Press. http://dx.doi.org/10.1017/CBO9780511560064.

Mostert, E. 2009. "International Co-Operation on Rhine Water Quality 1945–2008: An Example to Follow?" *Physics and Chemistry of the Earth* 34 (3): 142–49. http://dx.doi.org/10.1016/j.pce.2008.06.007.

Moyle, B. 2000. "The Ecology of Trade." *Journal of Bioeconomics* 2 (2): 139–52. http://dx.doi.org/10.1023/A:1011414717756.

Mulligan, S. 1999. "For Whose Benefit? Limits to Sharing in the Bioprospecting 'Regime'." *Environmental Politics* 8 (4): 35–65. http://dx.doi.org/10.1080/09644019908414493.

Mulligan, S. 2010. "Heads in the Sand? Or, Why Don't Governments Talk about Peak Oil?" *The Oil Drum,* January 5. http://www.theoildrum.com/node/6100.

Munro, M. 2011. "Gaping Hole Opened in Arctic Ozone Layer." *Montreal Gazette,* October 3, A3.

Murphy, I.L., and E. Sabadell. 1986. "International River Basins: A Policy Model for Conflict Resolution." *Resources Policy* 12 (2): 133–44. http://dx.doi.org/10.1016/0301-4207(86)90017-6.

Nagan, W.P., and E.K. Slemmens. 2009. "National Security Policy and the Ratification of the Comprehensive Test Ban Treaty." *Houston Journal of International Law* 32 (1): 1–96.

Nagtzaam, G. 2009. *The Making of International Treaties: Neoliberal and Constructivist Analyses of Normative Evolution.* Northampton: Edward Elgar.

Najam, A. 2004. "Dynamics of the Southern Collective: Developing Countries in Desertification Negotiations." *Global Environmental Politics* 4 (3): 128–54. http://dx.doi.org/10.1162/1526380041748100.

Nicol, A. 2003. *The Nile: Moving beyond Cooperation.* Technical Documents in Hydrology, PC-CP Series, 16. New York: UNESCO.

Nordas, R., and N. Gleditsch. 2007. "Climate Change and Conflict." *Political Geography* 26 (6): 627–38.

Oad, R., and R. Kullman. 2006. "Managing Irrigation for Better River Ecosystems—A Case Study of the Middle Rio Grande." *Journal of Irrigation and Drainage Engineering* 132 (6): 579–86. http://dx.doi.org/10.1061/(ASCE)0733-9437(2006)132:6(579).

Obioha, E. 2008. "Climate Change, Population Drift, and Violent Conflict Over Land Resource in Northeastern Nigeria." *Journal of Human Ecology* 23 (4): 311–24.

Olsen, M. 1971. *The Logic of Collective Action: Public Goods and the Theory of Groups.* Cambridge, MA: Harvard University Press.

O'Neill, K. 2000. *Waste Trading among Rich Nations: Building a New Theory of Environmental Regulation.* Cambridge, MA: MIT Press.

Ophuls, W. 1977. *Ecology and the Politics of Scarcity.* San Francisco: W.H. Freeman.

Orellana, M. 2005. "Criminal Punishment for Environmental Damage: Individual and State Responsibility at a Crossroad." *Georgetown International Environmental Law Review* 17: 673.

O'Riordan, T., and A. Jordan. 1995. "The Precautionary Principle in Contemporary Environmental Politics." *Environmental Values* 4: 191–212.

Ortiz, E.F., and G. Tang. 2005. *Review of the Management, Administration and Activities of the Secretariat of the United Nations Convention to Combat Desertification (UNCCD).* JIU/REP/2005/5. Geneva: United Nations, Joint Inspection Unit.

Ostrom, E. 1990. *Governing the Commons: The Evolution of Institutions for Collective Action.* Cambridge: Cambridge University Press.

Osuoka, I. 2010. "Operation Climate Change: Between Community Resource Control and Carbon Capitalism in the Niger Delta." In *Climate Change—Who's Carrying the Burden? The Chilly Climates of the Global Environmental Dilemma,* ed. A. Sandberg and T. Sandberg, 161–72. Ottawa: The Canadian Centre for Policy Alternatives.

Outhwaite, O. 2010. "The International Legal Framework for Biosecurity and the Challenges Ahead." *Review of European Community & International Environmental Law* 19 (2): 207–26. http://dx.doi.org/10.1111/j.1467-9388.2010.00678.x.

Padilla, D., and S. Williams. 2004. "Beyond Ballast Water: Aquarium and Ornamental Trades as Sources of Invasive Species in Aquatic Ecosystems." *Frontiers in Ecology and the Environment* 2 (3): 131–38. http://dx.doi.org/10.1890/1540-9295(2004)002[0131:BBWAAO]2.0.CO;2.

Paehlke, R. 2005. "Democracy and Environmentalism: Opening a Door to the Administrative State?" In *Managing Leviathan: Environmental Politics and the Administrative State,* ed. R. Paehlke and D. Torgerson, 25–45. Toronto: University of Toronto Press.

Paehlke, R. 2008. *Some Like It Cold: The Politics of Climate Change in Canada.* Toronto: Between the Lines.

Page, E. 2006. *Climate Change, Justice, and Future Generations.* Cheltenham: Edward Elgar.

Parris, T.M. 2005. "Engaging with Africa." *Environment: Science and Policy for Sustainable Development* 47 (1): 3. http://dx.doi.org/10.3200/ENVT.47.1.3.

Parrish, D.D., and T. Zhu. 2009. "Climate Change. Clean Air for Megacities." *Science* 326 (5953): 674–75. http://dx.doi.org/10.1126/science.1176064. Medline:19900921.

Parsons, M.L. 1995. *Global Warming: The Truth Behind the Myth.* New York: Plenum Press.

Paterson, M., and J. Stripple. 2007. "Singing Climate Change into Existence: On the Territorialization of Climate Policymaking." In *The Social Construction of Climate Change: Power, Knowledge, Norms, Discourses,* ed. M. Pettenger, 149–72. London: Ashgate.

Patiño-Gomez, C., D.C. McKinney, and D.R. Maidment. 2007. "Sharing Water Resources Data in the Binational Rio Grande/Bravo Basin." *Journal of Water Resources Planning and Management* 133 (5): 416–26. http://dx.doi.org/10.1061/(ASCE)0733-9496(2007)133:5(416).

Peel, J. 2006. "A GMO by any Other Name . . . Might be an SPS Risk!: Implications of Expanding the Scope of the Sanitary and Phytosanitary Measures Agreement." *European Journal of International Law* 17 (5): 1009–31. http://dx.doi.org/10.1093/ejil/chl033.

Peluso, N.L., and M. Watts, eds. 2001. *Violent Environments.* Ithaca: Cornell University Press.

Perrings, C., S. Burgiel, M. Lonsdale, H. Mooney, and M. Williamson. 2009. "Globalization and Bioinvasions: The International Policy Problem." In *Bioinvasions and Globalization, Ecology, Economics, Management, and Policy,* ed. B.C. Perrings, H. Mooney, and M. Williamson, 235–50. Oxford: Oxford University Press. http://dx.doi.org/10.1093/acprof:oso/9780199560158.003.0016.

Perrings, C., S. Burgiel, M. Lonsdale, H. Mooney, and M. Williamson. May 2010. "International Cooperation in the Solution to Trade-Related Invasive Species Risks." *Annals of the New York Academy of Sciences* 1195 (1): 198–212. http://dx.doi.org/10.1111/j.1749-6632.2010.05453.x. Medline:20536824.

Perrings, C., M. Williamson, and S. Dalmazzone, eds. 2000. *The Economics of Biological Invasions*. Cheltenham: Edward Elgar.

Peterson, M., and J. Winter. 1992. "Whalers, Cetologists, Environmentalists, and the International Management of Whaling." *International Organization* 46 (1): 147–86. http://dx.doi.org/10.1017/S0020818300001478.

Peterson, S. 1980. "The Common Heritage of Mankind? Regulating the Uses of the Oceans." *Environment* 22 (1): 6–11. http://dx.doi.org/10.1080/00139157.1980.9929731.

Phillips, D.J.H., S. Attili, S. McCaffrey, and J.S. Murray. 2007. "The Jordan River Basin: Potential Future Allocations to the Co-riparians." *International Water Resources Association, Water International* 32 (1): 39–62. http://dx.doi.org/10.1080/02508060708691964.

Pirages, D. 1978. *The New Context for International Relations: Global Ecopolitics*. Belmont, CA: Duxbury.

Pirages, D., and T.M. DeGeest. 2004. *Ecological Security: An Evolutionary Perspective on Globalization and Environment*. Lanham, MD: Rowman and Littlefield.

Plass, G. 1956. "Carbon Dioxide and the Climate." *American Scientist* 44: 302–16.

Podesta, J., and P. Ogden. 2007. "The Security Implications of Climate Change." *The Washington Quarterly* 31 (1): 115–38.

Pontecorvo, G. 1986a. "Division of the Spoils: Hydrocarbons and Living Resources." In *The New Order of the Oceans: The Advent of a Managed Environment*, ed. G. Pontecorvo, 15–28. New York: Columbia University Press.

Pontecorvo, G. 1986b. "Opportunity, Abundance, Scarcity: An Overview." In *The New Order of the Oceans: The Advent of a Managed Environment*, ed. G. Pontecorvo, 1–14. New York: Columbia University Press.

Poore, D. 2003. *Changing Landscapes: The Development of the International Tropical Timber Organization and its Influence on Tropical Forest Management*. London: Earthscan.

Preston, C. 2005. "The Promise and Threat of Nanotechnology: Can Environmental Ethics Guide Us?" *International Journal for Philosophy of Chemistry* 11 (1): 19–44.

Price-Smith, A. 2002. *The Health of Nations: Infectious Disease, Environmental Change, and Their Effects on National Security and Development*. Cambridge, MA: MIT Press.

Prins, G., ed. 1983. *Defended to Death: A Study of the Nuclear Arms Race*. New York: Penguin.

Puckett, J. 1997. The Basel Ban: A Triumph Over Business-As-Usual. Retrieved December 11, 2011. http://www.ban.org/about_basel_ban/jims_article.html.

Puckett, J. 2000. The Basel Treaty's Ban on Hazardous Waste Exports: An Unfinished Success Story. Retrieved December 11, 2011. http://www.ban.org/library/ierarticle.html.

Puckett, J., and C. Fogel. 1994. A Victory for Environment and Justice: The Basel Ban and How It Happened. http://www.ban.org/about_basel_ban/a_victory.html.

Putnam, R. 1988. "Diplomacy and Domestic Politics: The Logic of Two-Level Games." *International Organization* 42 (3): 427–60. http://dx.doi.org/10.1017/S0020818300027697.

Pyke, C.R., R. Thomas, R.D. Porter, J.J. Hellmann, J.S. Dukes, D.M. Lodge, and G. Chavarria. 2008. "Current Practices and Future Opportunities for Policy on Climate Change and Invasive Species." *Conservation Biology* 22 (3): 585–92. http://dx.doi.org/10.1111/j.1523-1739.2008.00956.x. Medline:18577088.

Rajan, S.C. 2010. "Parental Sacrifice as Atonement for Future Climate Change." In *The Environmental Politics of Sacrifice*, ed. M. Maniates and J. Meyer, 165–84. Cambridge, MA: MIT Press.

Raleigh, C., and H. Urdal. 2007. "Climate Change, Environmental Degradation, and Armed Conflict." *Political Geography* 26 (6): 674–94.

Ramanathapillai, R. 2008. "Modern Warfare and the Spiritual Disconnection from Land." *Peace Review* 20 (1): 113–20.

Ramsar Conference of the Parties (Ramsar COP). 1999. *Invasive Species and Wetlands*. COP 7, Document 24. Retrieved December 14, 2011. http://www.ramsar.org/cda/en/ramsar-documents-cops-cop7-ramsar-cop7-doc-24/main/ramsar/1-31-58-83^18617_4000_0__.

Raustiala, K., and D. Victor. 1996. "Biodiversity Since Rio: The Future of the Convention on Biological Diversity." *Environment* 38 (4): 16–20, 37–45. http://dx.doi.org/10.1080/00139157.1996.9929252.

Redgwell, C. 1998. "Life, the Universe, and Everything: A Critique of Anthropocentric Rights." In *Human Rights Approaches to Environmental Protection*, ed. A. Boyle and M. Anderson, 71–87. Oxford: Clarendon Press.

Reeve, R. 2006. "Wildlife Trade, Sanctions and Compliance: Lessons from the CITES Regime." *International Affairs* 82 (5): 881–97. http://dx.doi.org/10.1111/j.1468-2346.2006.00576.x.

Regan, T. 1983. *The Case for Animal Rights*. Berkeley. University of California Press.

Reichberg, G., and H. Syse. 2000. "Protecting the Natural Environment in Wartime: Ethical Considerations from the Just War Tradition." *Journal of Peace Research* 37 (4): 449–68. http://dx.doi.org/10.1177/0022343300037004003.

Reuveny, R. 2007. "Climate Change-Induced Migration and Violent Conflict." *Political Geography* 26 (6): 656–73.

Rieser, A. 2009. "Whales, Whaling, and the Warming Oceans." *Boston College Environmental Affairs Law Review* 36 (2): 401–29.

Riley, S. 2009. "Preventing Harm from Transboundary Invasive Alien Species." *Review of European Community & International Environmental Law* 18 (2): 198–210.

Rittel, H., and M. Webber. 1973. "Dilemmas in a General Theory of Planning." *Policy Sciences* 4 (2): 155–69. http://dx.doi.org/10.1007/BF01405730.

Roberts, A. 1993. "The Laws of War in the 1990–91 Gulf Conflict." *International Security* 18 (3): 134–81. http://dx.doi.org/10.2307/2539208.

Roberts, D. 1998. *Implementation of the WTO Agreement on the Application of Sanitary and Phytosanitary Measures* WTO/WRS-98-44. Washington, DC: Economic Research Service, United States Department of Agriculture.

Roberts, J.T., and B. Parks. 2007. *A Climate of Injustice: Global Inequality, North-South Politics, and Climate Policy*. Cambridge, MA: MIT Press.

Roco, M.C., and W.S. Bainbridge, eds. 2001. *Societal Implications of Nanoscience and Nanotechnology*. New York: Springer.

Rosenau, J., and E.O. Czempiel, eds. 1992. *Governance without Government*. Cambridge: Cambridge University Press. http://dx.doi.org/10.1017/CBO9780511521775.

Rosendal, G.K. 2001. "Impacts of Overlapping International Regimes: The Case of Biodiversity." *Global Governance* 7 (1): 95–117.

Rosillo-Calle, F., and F. Johnson, eds. 2010. *Food versus Fuel: An Informed Introduction to Biofuels*. London: Zed.

Roszak, T. 1973. *Where the Wasteland Ends: Politics and Transcendence in Postindustrial Society*. Garden City: Anchor.

Ruiz, D. 2010. "Ecocide in the Iraqi Marshes." *Freedom from Fear Magazine* 6 Retrieved May 25, 2010. http://www.freedomfromfearmagazine.org/index.php?option=com_content&view=article&id=228: ecocide-in-the-iraqi-.

Ruiz, G., and J. Carleton, eds. 2003. *Invasive Species and Management Strategies*. Washington, DC: Island Press.

Salehyan, I. 2008. "From Climate Change to Conflict? No Consensus Yet." *Journal of Peace Research* 45 (3): 315–26.

Sánchez, R. 1994. "International Trade in Hazardous Wastes: A Global Problem with Uneven Consequences for the Third World." *Journal of Environment & Development* 3 (1): 139–52. http://dx.doi.org/10.1177/107049659400300110.

Sand, P. 1999. *Transnational Environmental Law: Lessons in Global Change*. London: Kluwer.

Sandberg, L.A., and T. Sandberg, eds. 2010. *Climate Change: Who's Carrying the Burden? The Chilly Climates of the Global Environmental Dilemma*. Ottawa: Canadian Centre for Policy Alternatives.

Sandler, T. 1997. *Global Challenges*. Cambridge: Cambridge University Press.

Sandler, T. 2004. *Global Collective Action*. Cambridge: Cambridge University Press. http://dx.doi.org/10.1017/CBO9780511617119.

Sands, P. 2003. *Principles of International Environmental Law*. 2nd ed. Cambridge, MA: Cambridge University Press.

Sands, P., P. Szasz, S. Hawkins, and G. Greiveldinger. 1991. "The Gulf War: Environment as a Weapon." *Proceedings of the 85th Annual Meeting of the American Society of International Law* 85: 214–29.

Schmidt, C.W. 2006. "Unfair Trade: E-Waste in Africa." *Environmental Health Perspectives* 114 (4): A232–35. http://dx.doi.org/10.1289/ehp.114-a232. Medline:16581530.

Schneider, S., and J. Lane. 2006. "Dangers and Thresholds in Climate Change and the Implications for Justice." In *Fairness in Adaption to Climate Change*, ed. N. Adger, J. Paavola, S. Huq, and M.J. Mace, 23–51. Cambridge, MA: MIT Press.

Schreuder, Y. 2009. *The Corporate Greenhouse: Climate Change Policy in a Globalizing World*. London: Zed.

Schroeder, D., and T. Pogge. 2009. "Justice and the Convention on Biological Diversity." *Ethics & International Affairs* 23 (3): 267–80.

Schrope, Mark. 2002. "Ocean Policy: Troubled Waters." *Nature* 418: 718–20. http://dx.doi.org/10.1038/418718a.

Schwartz, M.S. 1997. "Defining Indigenous Species: An Introduction." In *Assessment and Management of Plant Invasions*, ed. J. Luken and J. Thierst, 7–17. New York: Springer-Verley. http://dx.doi.org/10.1007/978-1-4612-1926-2_2.

Selby, J. 2003. "Dressing up Domination as 'Cooperation': The Case of Israeli-Palestinian Water Relations." *Review of International Studies* 29 (01): 121–38. http://dx.doi.org/10.1017/S026021050300007X.

Selin, H., and S. VanDeveer. 2009. *Changing Climates in North American Politics: Institutions, Policymaking, and Multilevel Governance*. Cambridge, MA: MIT Press.

Sen, A. 1981. *Poverty and Famines: An Essay on Entitlement and Deprivation*. Oxford: Clarendon Press.

Sen, A. 1999. *Development as Freedom*. New York: Oxford University Press.

Sens, A., and P. Stoett. 2010. *Global Politics: Origins, Currents, Directions*. Toronto: ITP Nelson.

Shelley, T. 2006. *Nanotechnology: New Promises, New Dangers*. London: Zed.

Shelton, D. 2003. "The Environmental Implications of International Human Rights Tribunals." In *Linking Human Rights and the Environment*, ed. R. Picolotto and J. Taillant, 1–30. Tucson: University of Arizona Press.

Shibata, A. 2003. "The Basel Compliance Mechanism." *Reciel* 12 (2): 183–98.

Shine, C. 2007. "Invasive Species in an International Context: IPPC, CBD, European Strategy on IAS and Other Legal Instruments." *Bulletin OEPP/EPPO Bulletin: A Journal of Regulatory Plant Protection* 37: 103–13.

Shine, C., N. Williams, and L. Gundling. 2000. *A Guide to Designing Legal and Institutional Frameworks on Alien Invasive Species*. Gland: IUCN.

Siebenhüner, B. 2009. "The Biodiversity Secretariat: Lean Shark in Troubled Waters." In *Managers of Global Change: The Influence of International Environmental Bureaucracies*, ed. F. Biermann and B. Siebenhüner, 265–92. Cambridge, MA: MIT Press.

Siegal, C.D. 1975. "Proposals for a True Comprehensive Nuclear Test Ban Treaty." *Stanford Law Review* 27 (2): 387–418. http://dx.doi.org/10.2307/1228270.

Simberloff, D., and P. Stiling. 1996. "Risks of Species Introduced for Biological Control." *Biological Conservation* 78 (1–2): 185–92. http://dx.doi.org/10.1016/0006-3207(96)00027-4.

Singer, J.D. 1961. "The Level of Analysis Problem in International Relations." *World Politics* 14 (1): 77–92. http://dx.doi.org/10.2307/2009557.

Sliggers J., and W. Kakebeeke, eds. 2004. *Clearing the Air: 25 Years of the Convention on Long-Range Transboundary Air Pollution*. New York: United Nations Economic Commission for Europe (ECE).

Smit, B., and J. Wandel. 2006. "Adaptation, Adaptive Capacity, and Vulnerability." *Global Environmental Change* 16 (3): 282–92. http://dx.doi.org/10.1016/j.gloenvcha.2006.03.008.

Smith, J.E. 2006. *Weather Warfare*. Kempton, IL: Adventures Unlimited Press.

Somanathan, E. 2010. "What Do We Expect From an International Climate Agreement? A Perspective from a Low-Income Country." In *International Climate Policy: Implementing Architectures for Agreement Post-Kyoto*, ed. J. Aldy and R. Stavins, 599–617. Cambridge: Cambridge University Press.

South Asian Association for Regional Cooperation (SAARC). 2009. SAARC Information. Retrieved December 14, 2011. http://www.saarc-sec.org.

Stabinsky, D. 2000. "Bringing Social Analysis into a Multilateral Environmental Agreement: Social Impact Assessment and the Biosafety Protocol." *Journal of Environment & Development* 9 (3): 260–83. http://dx.doi.org/10.1177/1070496500009003004

Sterling-Folker, J., ed. 2005. *Making Sense of IR Theory*. Boulder: Lynne Rienner.

Stern, N. 2007. *The Economics of Climate Change*. Cambridge: Cambridge University Press.

Steurer, P. 2003. "The US's Retreat from the Kyoto Protocol: An Account of a Policy Change and its Implications for Future Climate Policy." *European Environment* 13 (6): 344–60.

Stoett, P. 1994a. "Global Environmental Security, Energy Resources, and Planning: A Framework and Application." *Futures* 26 (7): 741–58. http://dx.doi.org/10.1016/0016-3287(94)90042-6.

Stoett, P. 1994b. "Redefining 'Environmental Refugees': Canada and the UNHCR." *Canadian Foreign Policy* 2 (3): 29–45. http://dx.doi.org/10.1080/11926422.1994.9673040.

Stoett, P. 1997. *The International Politics of Whaling*. Vancouver: UBC Press.

Stoett, P. 2000a. *Human and Global Security: An Exploration of Terms*. Toronto: University of Toronto Press.

Stoett, P. 2000b. "Mission Diplomacy or Arctic Haze? Canadian Foreign Policy and the Arctic Council." In *Worthwhile Initiatives? Canadian Mission-Oriented Diplomacy*, ed. A. Cooper and G. Hayes, 90–102. Toronto: Irwin Press.

Stoett, P. 2001. "Fishing for Norms: Foreign Policy and the Turbot Dispute of 1995." In *Ethics and Security in Canadian Foreign Policy*, ed. R. Irwin, 249–68. Vancouver: UBC Press.

Stoett, P. 2002. "The International Regulation of Trade in Wildlife: Institutional and Normative Considerations." *International Environmental Agreement: Politics, Law and Economics* 2 (2): 195–210. http://dx.doi.org/10.1023/A:1020942110468.

Stoett, P. 2003. "Toward Renewed Legitimacy? Nuclear Power, Global Warming and Security." *Global Environmental Politics* 3 (1): 99–116.

Stoett, P. 2004. "Wildlife Conservation: Institutional and Normative Considerations." In *International Law and Sustainable Development: Principles and Practice*, ed. N. Schrijver and F. Weiss, 501–18. Leiden, Netherlands: Martinus Nijhoff.

Stoett, P. 2005. "Mekong River Politics and Environmental Security." In *Confronting Environmental Change in East and Southeast Asia: Ecopolitics, Foreign Policy, and Sustainable Development*, ed. P.G. Harris, 167–82. London: United Nations University Press.

Stoett, P. 2006. "Canada, Kyoto, and the Conservatives: Thinking/Moving Ahead." In *Climate Change Politics in North America: The State of Play*, ed. H. Selin and S.D. VanDeveer, 7–16. Washington, DC: Woodrow Wilson International Center for Scholars.

Stoett, P. 2007. "Counter-Bioinvasion: Conceptual and Governance Challenges." *Environmental Politics* 16 (3): 433–52. http://dx.doi.org/10.1080/09644010701251672.

Stoett, P. 2010. "Framing Bioinvasion: Biodiversity, Climate Change, Security, Trade, and Global Governance." *Global Governance* 16 (1): 103–20.

Stoett, P., and L. Mohammed. 2009. "Industry and Bioinvasion: Costs and Responsibilities." *Business 2010: A Magazine on Business and Biodiversity*, 4 (1): 24–25.

Stoett, P., and S. Mulligan. 2000. "A Global Bioprospecting Regime: Partnership or Piracy?" *International Journal* 56 (2): 224–46.

Strauss, A. 2009. "Climate Change Litigation: Opening the Door to the International Court of Justice." In *Adjudicating Climate Change: State, National, and International Approaches*, ed. W. Burns and H. Osofsky, 334–56. Cambridge: Cambridge University Press. http://dx.doi.org/10.1017/CBO9780511596766.017.

Stringer, L.C. 2008. "Reviewing the International Year of Deserts and Desertification 2006: What Contribution towards Combating Global Desertification and Implementing the United Nations Convention to Combat Desertification?" *Journal of Arid Environments* 72 (11): 2065–74. http://dx.doi.org/10.1016/j.jaridenv.2008.06.010.

Su, Y.Z., W.Z. Zhao, P.X. Su, Z.H. Zhang, T. Wang, and R. Ram. 2007. "Ecological Effects of Desertification Control and Desertified Land Reclamation in an Oasis-Desert Ecozone in an Arid Region: A Case Study in Hexi Corridor, Northwest China." *Ecological Engineering* 29 (2): 117–24. http://dx.doi.org/10.1016/j.ecoleng.2005.10.015.

Sutherst, R. 2000. "Climate Change and Invasive Species: A Conceptual Framework." In *Invasive Species in a Changing World*, ed. A. Mooney and R. Hobbs, 211–40. Washington, DC: Island Press.

Tanno D., and T. Hamazaki. 2000. "Is American Opposition to Whaling Anti-Japanese?" *Asian Affairs* 27 (2): 81–92. http://dx.doi.org/10.1080/00927670009598832.

Teclaff, L.A. 1994. "Beyond Restoration: The Case of Ecocide." *Natural Resources Journal* 34: 933–56.

Temple Swing, J. 2003. "What Future for the Oceans?" *Foreign Affairs (Council on Foreign Relations)* 82 (5): 139–52. http://dx.doi.org/10.2307/20033689.

Theodoropoulas, D. 2003. *Invasion Biology: Critique of a Pseudoscience*. Blythe, CA: Avvar Books.

Thomas, D.S.G., and N.J. Middleton. 1994. *Desertification: Exploding the Myth*. Chichester: John Wiley & Sons.

Thompson, M. 1999. "Security and Solidarity: An Anti-Reductionist Analysis of Environmental Policy." In *Living with Nature: Environmental Politics as Cultural Discourse*, ed. F. Fischer and M.A. Hajer, 135–50. Oxford: Oxford University Press.

Tibbetts, J. 1996. "Ocean Commotion." *Environmental Health Perspectives* 104 (4): 380–5. http://dx.doi.org/10.1289/ehp.96104380. Medline:8732946.

Tickner, J.A. 2002. "Feminist Perspectives on International Relations." In *Handbook of International Relations*, ed. W. Carlsnaes, T. Risse, and B.A. Simmons, 275–91. London: Sage.

Tsimplis, M.M. 2001. "Liability and Compensation in the International Transport of Hazardous Wastes by Sea: The 1999 Protocol to the Basel Convention plus Appendix 'Basel Protocol on Liability and Compensation for Damage Resulting from Transboundary Movements of Hazardous Wastes and Their Disposal'." *International Journal of Marine and Coastal Law* 16 (2): 295–346. http://dx.doi.org/10.1163/15718080120493038.

Tucker, L. 2009. "New Dog, Old Tricks: Has Australia's Overhaul of the Wildlife Export Regime Met Its International Environmental Obligations?" *Journal of International Wildlife Law and Policy* 11 (4): 334–72. http://dx.doi.org/10.1080/13880290902870117.

Turco, R., and C. Sagan. 1989. "Policy Implications of Nuclear Winter." *Ambio* 18 (7): 372–76.

United Nations. 1992. *Convention on Biological Diversity*. New York: United Nations. Retrieved December 1, 2011. http://www.cbd.int/convention/text/.

United Nations. 1994. *United Nations Convention to Combat Desertification in those Countries Experiencing Serious Drought and/or Desertification, Particularly in Africa, 12 September 1994*. A/AC.241/27. Bonn: UNCCD Secretariat. Retrieved December 4, 2011. http://www.unccd.int/convention/text/pdf/conv-eng.pdf.

United Nations. 2011. "International Years." United Nations Observances. Retrieved September 29, 2011. http://www.un.org/en/events/observances/years.shtml.

United Nations Association in Canada (UNA-Canada). 2011. UN Days, Weeks and Years: International Years. Retrieved November 30, 2011. http://www.unac.ca/en/news_events/un_days/international_years.asp.

United Nations Environment Programme (UNEP). 1995. *Evaluation of the Effectiveness of the Basel Convention*. UNEP/CHW.3/Inf.7. New York: United Nations.

United Nations Environment Programme (UNEP). 2002. *Success Stories in the Struggle against Desertification: A Holistic and Integrated Approach to Environmental Conservation and Sustainable Livelihoods*. Nairobi: UNEP.

United Nations Framework Convention on Climate Change (UNFCCC). 2007. *Climate Change: Impacts, Vulnerabilities and Adaptation in Developing Countries*. Bonn: UNFCCC Climate Change Secretariat.

United Nations Framework Convention on Climate Change (UNFCCC). 2009. "Kyoto Protocol's Joint Implementation Mechanism Passes Milestone with Accreditation of First Project Verifier." *UNFCCC Press Release*, February 18. Retrieved December 6, 2011. http://unfccc.int/files/press/news_room/press_releases_and_advisories/application/pdf/20091902_pr_jisc_milestone.pdf.

United Nations Framework Convention on Climate Change (UNFCCC). 2011. Adaptation Fund. Retrieved December 6, 2011, http://unfccc.int/cooperation and support/financial_mechanism/adaptation_fund/items/3659.php.

United States Department of Agriculture National Invasive Species Information Center (USDA). 2008. *International Laws and Regulations*. Beltsville, MD: USDA National Agricultural Library. Retrieved December 14, 2011. http://www.invasivespeciesinfo.gov/laws/intl.shtml.

United States Environmental Protection Agency (US EPA). 1998. International Trade in Hazardous Waste: An Overview. http://www.epa.gov/compliance/resources/policies/civil/rcra/intnltrahazwas-rpt.pdf.

United States Environmental Protection Agency (US EPA). 2011. Persistent Organic Pollutants: A Global Issue, A Global Response. Retrieved December 4, 2011. http://www.epa.gov/international/toxics/pop.htm#stockholm.

Vail, B. 2008. "Illegal Transnational Shipment of Waste in the EU: Culprits and Collaborators in Germany and the Czech Republic." *Environmental Politics* 17 (5): 828–34. http://dx.doi.org/10.1080/09644010802422685.

Van DeVeer, D. 1986. *Paternalistic Intervention*. Princeton: Princeton University Press.

Van Driesche, J., and R. Van Driesche. 2000. *Nature Out of Place: Biological Invasions in the Global Age*. Washington, DC: Island Press.

van Kooten, G.C. "Smoke and Mirrors: The Kyoto Protocol and Beyond." *Canadian Public Policy / Analyse de Politiques* 29 (4): 397–415.

Vanderheiden, S. 2008. *Atmospheric Justice: A Political Theory of Climate Change*. Oxford: Oxford University Press.

Veitch, C., and M. Clout, eds. 2002. *Turning the Tide: The Eradication of Invasive Species*. Gland: IUCN.

Velders, G.J.M., S.O. Andersen, J.S. Daniel, D.W. Fahey, and M. McFarland. 2007. "The Importance of the Montreal Protocol in Protecting Climate." *Proceedings of the National Academy of Science* 104 (12): 4814–19.

Vermeij, G.J. 1996. "An Agenda for Invasion Biology." *Biological Conservation* 78: 3–9.

Victor, D.G., K. Raustiala, and E.B. Skolnikoff, eds. 1998. *The Implementation and Effectiveness of International Environmental Commitments: Theory and Practice*. Cambridge, MA: MIT Press.

Vicuna, F.O. 2007. "The International Tribunal for the Law of the Sea and Provisional Measures: Settled Issues and Pending Problems." *International Journal of Marine and Coastal Law* 22 (3): 450–63.

von Stein, J. 2008. "The International Law and Politics of Climate Change: Ratification of the United Nations Framework Convention and the Kyoto Protocol." *Journal of Conflict Resolution* 52 (2): 243–68. http://dx.doi.org/10.1177/0022002707313692.

Waever, O. 1995. "Securitization and Desecuritization." In *On Security*, ed. R. Lipschutz, 46–86. New York: Columbia University Press.

Waltz, K. 1959. *Man, the State, and War: A Theoretical Analysis*. New York: Columbia University Press.

Wapner, P. 1995. "Politics Beyond the State: Environmental Activism and World Civic Politics." *World Politics* 47 (03): 311–40. http://dx.doi.org/10.1017/S0043887100016415.

Wapner, P. 2010. "Sacrifice in an Age of Comfort." In *The Environmental Politics of Sacrifice*, ed. Michael Maniates and John Meyer, 33–60. Cambridge, MA.: MIT Press.

Warner, R. 2006. "The Place of History in International Relations and Ecology: Discourses of Environmentalism in the Colonial Era." In *International Ecopolitical Theory: Critical Approaches*, ed. E. Laferrierre and P. Stoett, 34–51. Vancouver: UBC Press.

Weber, C. 2005. *IR Theory: A Critical Introduction*. 2nd ed. London: Routledge.

Webersik, C. 2010. *Climate Change and Security: A Gathering Storm of Global Challenges*. Santa Barbara: Praeger.

Webster, D.G. 2009. *Adaptive Governance: The Dynamics of Atlantic Fisheries Management*. Cambridge, MA: MIT Press.

Weiss, E.B. 1989. *Fairness to Future Generations: International Law, Common Patrimony, and Intergenerational Equity*. Dobbs Ferry, NY: Transnational.

Weiss, E.B., ed. 1992. *Environmental Change and International Law*. Tokyo: United Nations University Press.

Westing, A.H., ed. 1984a. *Environmental Warfare: A Technical, Legal and Policy Appraisal*. New York: Taylor & Francis.

Westing, A.H. 1984b. *Herbicides in War: The Long-Term Ecological and Human Consequences*. New York: Taylor & Francis.

Whiteside, K. 2006. *Precautionary Politics: Principle and Practice in Confronting Environmental Risk*. Cambridge, MA: MIT Press.

Wijnstekers, W. 2005. *The Evolution of CITES: Version 1.0*. Geneva: Secretariat of the Convention on International Trade in Endangered Species of Wild Fauna and Flora. http://www.cites.org/common/docs/Evolution1_01.exe.

Wilkins, G. 2002. *Technology Transfer for Renewable Energy: Overcoming Barriers in Developing Countries*. London: Earthscan.

Wilkinson, C. 2006. "Status of Coral Reefs of the World: Summary of Threats and Remedial Action." *Coral Reef Conservation* 13: 3–39.

Williams, M. 2001. "Trade and Environment in the World Trading System: A Decade of Stalemate?" *Global Environmental Politics* 1 (4): 1–9. http://dx.doi.org/10.1162/152638001317146336.

Williams, M. 2011. "Agriculture and the Environment." In *Global Environmental Politics: Concepts, Theories and Case Studies*, ed. G. Kutting, 164–78. London: Routledge.

Wilson, E.O. 1984. *Biophilia: The Human Bond with Other Species*. Cambridge, MA: Harvard University Press.

Winham, G.R. 2009. "The GMO Panel: Applications of WTO Law to Trade in Agricultural Biotech Products." *Journal of European Integration* 31 (3): 409–29. http://dx.doi.org/10.1080/07036330902782261.

Winickoff, D., S. Jasanoff, L. Busch, R. Grove-White, and B. Wynne. 2005. "Adjudicating the GM Food Wars: Science, Risk, and Democracy in World Trade Law." *Yale Journal of International Law* 30: 81–123.

Wittenberg, R., and M. Cock, eds. 2001. *Invasive Alien Species: A Toolkit of Best Prevention and Management Practices*. Oxon: GISP. http://dx.doi.org/10.1079/9780851995694.0000.

Wolf, A., A. Kramer, A. Carius, and G. Dabelko. 2005. *State of the World 2005 Global Security Brief #5: Water Can Be a Pathway to Peace, Not War*. Washington, DC: Worldwatch Institute. Retrieved November 23, 2011. http://www.worldwatch.org/node/79.

World Trade Organization (WTO). 1994. *Agreement on the Application of Sanitary and Phytosanitary Measurements*. Geneva: WTO. Retrieved January 9, 2012. http://www.wto.org/english/docs_e/legal_e/legal_e.htm#sanitary.

WTO. 2010. *Review of the Operation and Implementation of the SPS Agreement*. G/SPS/53. Geneva: WTO Committee on Sanitary and Phytosanitary Measures. Retrieved January 9, 2012. http://docsonline.wto.org/imrd/directdoc.asp?DDFDocuments/t/G/SPS/53.doc.

Wunsch, C. 1980. "The Environmental Modification Treaty." *American Society of International Law Journal* 4 (91): 117.

Yanagida, J.A. 1987. "The Pacific Salmon Treaty." *American Journal of International Law* 81 (3): 577–92. http://dx.doi.org/10.2307/2202013.

Young, O., ed. 1997. *Global Governance: Drawing Insights from the Environmental Experience*. Cambridge, MA: MIT Press.

Young, O. 1999. *The Effectiveness of International Environmental Regimes: Causal Connections and Behavioural Mechanisms*. Cambridge, MA: MIT Press.

Young, O. 2006. *National and Regional Legislation for Promotion and Support to the Prevention, Control, and Eradication of Invasive Species*. Washington, DC: World Bank.

Young, O. 2010. "Governance for Sustainable Development in a World of Rising Interdependencies." In *Governance for the Environment: New Perspectives*, ed. M.A. Delmas and O.R. Young, 12–40. Cambridge: Cambridge University Press. http://dx.doi.org/10.1017/CBO9780511627170.003

Zahran, S., E. Kim, X. Chen, and M. Lubell. 2007. "Ecological Development and Global Climate Change: A Cross-National Study of Kyoto Protocol Ratification." *Society & Natural Resources* 20 (1): 37–55. http://dx.doi.org/10.1080/08941920600981355.

Ze Meka, E., and S. Johnson. 2008. "Putting Sustainability into Practice." *Environmental Policy and Law* 38: 261–66.

Zierler, D. 2011. *The Invention of Ecocide: Agent Orange, Vietnam, and the Scientists Who Changed The Way We Think about the Environment*. Athens: University of Georgia Press.

Index

New Zealand, 135

newspapers. *See* media

NGOS, 12, 23, 49, 56, 67, 71–72, 77, 94
  acknowledged by Berne Convention, 121
  advocacy and scientific roles, 30
  ENGOS, 109
  observer status, 72
  presence at CITES COPS, 58
  working on IAS, 170

Nicaragua, 101, 120

nickel, 115

Nigeria, 26, 132

Nile Basin Initiative (NBI), 122

Nile carp, 177

Nile River, 121–22

NIMBY ("Not In My Backyard") politics, 23

nitrogen oxides (NO), 87, 89, 95

noise pollution, 117

non-excludability, 7

nongovernmental groups, 55

nongovernmental organizations (NGOS), 7

"Non-Legally Binding Instrument on All Types
  of Forests," 29, 69

"nonrivalry," 7

North America
  agreements addressing IAS, 172

North American Agreement on Environmental
  Cooperation, 173

North American Free Trade Agreement
  (NAFTA), 26, 172–73
  side agreement on environment, 130

North Atlantic Marine Mammal
  Commission, 117

North Korea, 12
  nuclear weapons, 152, 154

North Sea, 121

North Sea Fisheries Convention, 48

North Sea Fisheries Convention (1882), 112

Northern Contaminants Program (1991), 90

northern investment in sustainable
  development initiatives in the south, 11

northern states
  energy demand, 188
  funds for R & D on non-carbon energy
    sources, 102
  willingness to pay into a technology
    adaptation fund, 95

north-south debate, 10, 55, 66, 102–3
  Copenhagen Accord and, 101

most greenhouse gas emissions produced
  in industrialized north, 101

north-south dialogue on nanotechnology, 183

Northwest Atlantic Fisheries Commission
  (NAFO), 112

Norway, 59, 82, 109
  investment in technological development
    for southern states, 189

Norwegian whalers, 109

nuclear accidents, 152, 188

nuclear destruction, 150

nuclear energy, 187–88

nuclear fallout, 153–54

Nuclear Non-Proliferation Treaty (NPT), 154

Nuclear Test Ban Treaty (1963). *See* Limited
  Test Ban Treaty (LTBT)

nuclear waste, 154

nuclear weapons, 152. *See also* atmospheric
  nuclear weapons testing; underground
  nuclear weapons testing

nutrition, 11

Obama, Barack, 132

Obama administration
  on carbon trading, 97
  Kyoto Protocol and, 100

oceans, 4, 132
  acidificaton, 111
  adaptive multi-governance context, 109
  biodiversity, 110
  carbon absorption, 112
  climate change and, 111
  food source for humans, 110
  future of, 124
  on-land sources of pollution, 111
  phytoplankton, 112
  resource extraction, 111
  soft-law framework, 113
  tragedy of the commons, 110
  used as garbage dump, 111

oceans crises, 3, 24, 108, 110–13, 125

OECD Chemical Committee, 183

OECD countries, 131

OECD's International Energy Agency, 187

oil
  dependence on, 189
  intentional oil dumping, 111
  limited oil reserves, 187–88
  pollution from, 46, 118